CONTENTS

III ESTIMATES OF LOUIS XIV DURING THE NINETEENTH CENTURY

IV LOUIS XIV IN TWENTIETH-CENTURY SCHOLARSHIP

INTRODUCTION

If a ruler's greatness is measured by the extent of his personal impact upon his own time, Louis XIV was undoubtedly one of the greatest kings of early modern Europe. Indeed, his reign may easily have been the most momentous in the entire history of the French monarchy. The long, painstaking efforts of earlier French Kings to extend their power he brought to fruition by establishing absolute monarchy in its definitive form. This he accomplished by a program of state-building in the most comprehensive sense. The central institutions of government were strengthened and entered into areas hitherto outside their normal competence. So powerful was the regime that it exerted a variety of controls over every element of the population. A massive effort was made to regulate many areas of the economy according to mercantilist principles, and the resources of the nation were increasingly placed at the disposal of the king's vastly expanded war machine. Louis XIV's desire to enforce religious uniformity among his subjects was dramatically evidenced by his Revocation of the Edict of Nantes, and he even attempted to establish official canons of excellence in the fine arts by means of government-sponsored academies. His foreign policy was his most portentous undertaking in the eyes of his contemporaries, since he utilized his undoubted military preponderance in Europe to engage in a series of wars for personal and dynastic prestige, extension of his frontiers, and military glory. The inevitable reaction by the English, the Dutch and the Imperialists eventually arrested French expansion, but Louis XIV doggedly defended the interests of France and the Bourbon dynasty, as he understood them, until the end of his long reign.

Bernini, *Louis XIV*. This magnificent bronze of Louis XIV is similar to, but not identical with, the famous marble bust that Bernini made during his trip to France in 1665. It catches the spirit of baroque splendor that was so characteristic of the king and his entourage. (*National Gallery of Art, Samuel H. Kress Collection*)

Although Louis XIV enjoyed the services of many able ministers, notably Colbert and Louvois, all factors seemed to conspire to render the king the predominant political personality of his age. With few exceptions, absolutism was the prevailing form of government in continental Europe, and all agreed that Louis XIV was its primary exemplar, since no other sovereign enjoyed power even remotely comparable to his. In France the most recent effort to limit the growth of royal absolutism had merely produced the chaos and miseries of the Fronde, and there was general agreement that the royal government must be sufficiently strong to impose order and discipline upon the turbulent populace. The established administrative system and the doctrine of royal sovereignty placed all political power in the hands of the king. All acts of government were promulgated either by him or by his agents acting in his name, with the result that the sovereign legally held all power, determined all important matters of policy, and assumed all responsibility for the political life of the nation. An elaborate ideological justification of royal absolutism was set forth in the doctrine of divine right of kings which attained its furthest development during this period. In the midst of this extraordinary concurrence of factors favorable to personal government, it is not surprising that Louis XIV viewed himself with great seriousness and consistently strove throughout his long reign to fulfill the enormous responsibilities of his office.

Although Louis XIV was the most important ruler of his age, there was wide disagreement then and later concerning his greatness as king of the most powerful nation of Europe. Opinions concerning his abilities and the historical significance of his rule have shown remarkable divergence from his time to the present, with each succeeding generation of historians providing new perspectives. The matter is complex and involves many interrelated questions. Was Louis XIV an essentially mediocre man upon whom political circumstances and the spirit of his time thrust immense power and responsibilities, or was he a great leader of men and a farsighted statesman? Did Louis largely delegate the work of government and even a large share of policy-making to a series of able subordinates, or was he always the master of his vast administrative machine and in full control over the shaping of policy? Was he an opportunist who met each problem as it arose, or did he consistently pursue a policy that was based upon clearly defined objectives? Did he seek to extend his power primarily for personal glory and the satisfaction of his incredible pride and vanity, or did he consistently place the interests of the state above all else? Was his tendency to confuse his own interests with those of the state justified by political necessity and the well-being of the governed, or was this merely the supreme manifestation of his egocentric absolutism? Should the more important institutional, social, economic, religious, and international developments that occurred during his reign be regarded as his personal contributions to the building of France, or were these developments produced by complex forces within French society and institutions themselves, quite beyond the control of even a Louis XIV?

In the process of assessing the greatness of Louis XIV, the student will necessarily construct an historical judgment. Ideally this should be done by sifting and combining the estimates of the king that were made during his own time with the perspectives that historians have developed during the intervening centuries. In the case of Louis XIV, the views of his contemporaries would seem to have especial significance. Throughout his very long reign, all eyes were upon him; his name was associated with the most momentous events of his age, and the issue of his role and responsibility inevitably presented itself to observers. Furthermore, it may be argued that the only appropriate criteria to apply when judging an historical figure are those that were accepted in his own time and according to which he lived, rather than a different set of values that came to the fore in a later period. Louis XIV's contemporaries not only viewed him from this standpoint but also were aware of a thousand circumstances that have been irretrievably lost to later historians. The judgments of the king's contemporaries are therefore invaluable and have strongly influenced subsequent opinion concerning his exact historical role. From the eighteenth century onward, however, historians have benefited from new information that was not available in Louis XIV's time. With the advantages of hindsight, different perspectives, and improved techniques of investigation, these historians have produced a steady stream of new interpretations of Louis XIV's position in Western history.

Among the selections by Louis XIV's contemporaries, Paul Pellisson's frankly extravagant eulogy expresses the adulation of the monarch that was so widespread during the first generation of the reign. Although the occasion of Pellisson's speech and even his personal interests go far to explain the tenor of this panegyric, it contains the central tenet of absolutism: that the people should willingly submit to the rule of a wise and benevolent monarch who constantly directed, improved, and animated the life of his state. The ideological foundation of this position Bishop Bossuet elaborately set forth in his famous analysis of the divine right of kings, in the next selection. An understanding of this concept, which was upheld by the great majority of Louis' contemporaries, is essential to any evaluation of the reign, since it is clear that the king thoroughly accepted and acted according to this doctrine. With the selection from Leibnitz, we first encounter criticism of the Sun King. Fittingly, this is contained in a non-French source that was directed against Louis' aggressive foreign policy. In this gently ironic but deadly serious pamphlet, Leibnitz argued that Louis XIV had, in effect, set himself above the law and recognized no principles but his interests and grandeur, to the great consternation of the other peoples of Europe. In France, however, the adulation continued. Even so keen an observer as La Bruyère felt justified in detailing Louis XIV's greatness in an otherwise critical work, thereby describing many of the qualities that his admirers attributed to him.

But as the second and more disastrous generation of the reign advanced, criticism of Louis XIV inevitably increased. Our next selection, Fénelon's famous *Letter to Louis XIV,* is one of the most unqualified denunciations of his rule ever penned by one of his subjects. Writing from the standpoint of a Christian moralist, Fénelon found the record of the reign unjustifiable in every essential. He viewed the ruler as a potentially upright but misguided man who preferred fawning sycophants to men of worth. His foreign policy was wrong on all counts, especially legal and moral, and had been the ruination of France. Above all, the spirit of the reign was determined by Louis' monstrous, selfish pride rather than the precepts of Christianity. Fénelon's criticisms, although extreme, express the very significant view that Louis XIV was seeking mere personal glory and was ruining France in the process. Somewhat later, the Duc de Saint-Simon wrote his *Memoirs* which contain his well-known description of Louis XIV. Like Fénelon, Saint-Simon was thoroughly critical of his sovereign, although for entirely different reasons. Briefly, Saint-Simon viewed Louis, whom he knew well, as a promising but unsuccessful ruler who excelled in small things rather than great, who was inferior to his subordinates, and whose passion for glory completely precluded his pursuing any consistent policy for the benefit of the state. While these observations may contain an element of truth, it should be remembered that Saint-Simon had personal reasons for criticizing Louis XIV who consistently excluded the court nobility, including Saint-Simon, from high office.

Leaving the views of Louis XIV's contemporaries and turning to those of historians who wrote in later periods, we immediately encounter new interpretations of the man and the reign, based on new perspectives. During the eighteenth century, the rationalists quickly stripped away the traditional religious sanctions of monarchy and increasingly subjected it to the scrutiny of reason. The first two selections in this section are excellent examples of criticism of Louis XIV from this standpoint. Montesquieu, in his *Persian Letters,* cleverly suggested that the monarchy of Louis XIV was thoroughly anachronistic and was supported chiefly by myths. The Abbé de Saint-Pierre, while similarly rationalistic, criticized Louis XIV for a very different reason—his failure to improve the lot of the people. Taking the position that the only purpose of government is to increase the happiness and prosperity of the governed, Saint-Pierre compared Louis XIV with his illustrious grandfather, Henry IV, very much to the advantage of the latter. Because of the great burdens that Louis XIV had imposed upon his subjects, Saint-Pierre felt justified in denying him the title of "Great." On the other hand, if the eighteenth century produced new rational and utilitarian challenges to monarchy, it also produced Voltaire who thoroughly approved of strong kings. Voltaire was by far the ablest French historian of the century, and his *Age of Louis XIV* is one of the masterpieces of literature on the reign of the Sun King. Essentially, Voltaire believed that France during the reign of Louis XIV experienced one of the greatest ages of Western civilization, and he insisted that this was made possible by the wise and beneficent rule of Louis XIV who to a large extent molded the nation. The excerpt printed in this collection consists chiefly of an extensive recital of the great benefits that Louis, in the eyes of Voltaire, had brought France, and it is clear that Voltaire attributed these to the ruler rather than his subordinates. This interpretation of the reign merits careful consideration not only because it was based on extensive research but also because Voltaire lived in a period when the impact of Louis XIV's reign was still apparent to all observers. Voltaire even regarded Louis' insatiable thirst for glory as a national benefit, since "every king who loves glory loves the public weal." He admitted that custom denied Louis XIV the title of "Great," but insisted that posterity attributed him its substance. Voltaire's basic position is summarized in his statement that "Louis XIV did more for his country than twenty of his predecessors together."

During the nineteenth century, as Louis XIV's reign receded in time, French historians increasingly tended to evaluate its significance in terms of its place in the French national tradition. Among the many works that were written from this standpoint, one of the ablest was Lemontey's *Essay on the Monarchical Establishment of Louis XIV* which appeared in 1818. Rich in interpretations, the book is prejudiced neither for nor against Louis, whose reign is described as "offering at once all the attractions and all the repugnance of absolute power." Lemontey's most important contribution was his analysis of Louis' work as builder of the French state. For the first time in her history, Lemontey maintained, France under Louis XIV acquired a strong, centralized governmental system, and he unhesitatingly described this as the "personal accomplishment of the king." The far-reaching implications of this view of Louis' position in the history of France are evident, yet Lemontey also recognized that absolute monarchy later became atrophied and lost popular support. François Guizot carried this interpretation further by attributing great accomplishments in state-building to Louis XIV, adding that while he may have perfected the French monarchy, he left it absolute, rigid, incapable of adapting to new conditions, and without support from the nation at large. In this fashion, Louis XIV's long-range contributions to the growth of France were significantly qualified. This view was to become fundamental to nineteenth-century French scholarship and was given a much fuller treatment by Michelet. It also appears in Albert Sorel's *Europe and the French Revolution,* with which we come full circle. Sorel regarded the French monarchy as an unprincipled, extralegal despotism which offered protection but suppressed popular liberties and in which the only reality was the will of the king. It was a form of government, he said, in which laws, traditions and ideals meant little and reason of state was the order of the day: in a word, where "men were everything and institutions nothing." Fulfilling their destiny, the kings of France laboriously built the French state by perfecting an absolutism which reached its apogee under Louis XIV, only to find that they had produced an inflexible instrument that was incapable of performing the functions of government and satisfying popular needs. For this reason it was condemned to extinction. Such a view of Louis XIV presents him merely as the terminal link in an abortive chain of historical events and reduces his greatness practically to the vanishing point.

Twentieth century historians have produced many special studies of Louis XIV but relatively few works of synthesis. Among the latter, Ernest Lavisse's elaborate analysis has been one of the most important and successful both because of its comprehensive coverage and the evident abilities of the author. In many ways, Lavisse summarized earlier interpretations of Louis XIV, although he added a number of his own. Lavisse recognized that absolute monarchy was a product of the times and a historical necessity, but he felt that the absolutism of Louis XIV was not quite "French." He found strong Spanish influences in Louis' self-conscious pride and natural arrogance, as well as the extreme etiquette and formalism at Versailles and the bureaucratic tendencies of the reign. Likewise, Louis' willingness to accept imperial honors and to regard himself as a lesser divinity Lavisse regarded as slightly ridiculous. Concerning Louis' personal merit, Lavisse admitted that Louis the king might be called "Great," that is, when he was clothed with the majesty of his office and served as a "functionary of royalty," but he insisted that Louis the man was quite mediocre and lacked the qualities of true greatness. In treating the place of the reign in French history, Lavisse emphasized Louis' massive failure to carry his policies to fruition. More important, Louis may have perfected royal absolutism, but his wars, extravagances, exploitations and personal despotism exhausted the French monarchy and condemned it to death. Thus we find reiterated the view that the work of Louis XIV was partially abortive. In closing, Lavisse admitted that Louis XIV holds a certain fascination for his countrymen, but he clearly felt that this was undeserved.

Somewhat later, Louis Madelin set forth a significant and much simpler view of Louis XIV. For Madelin, the secret of Louis' power, enormous influence and importance in history was merely that he so thoroughly reflected his times. Not only was Louis the product of his age; he also fulfilled its expectations and ideals to the hilt, especially its desire for order and discipline. A taste for authority characterized all phases of life and found its highest expression in divinely sanctioned monarchy. Louis' pride of power, his thirst for glory, even his personal qualities and bearing were all part of his popular and successful absolutism. In sum, Louis XIV was a magnificently appropriate product of his era, drawing his strength from it and doing his best to give it in return all that it expected of him. Madelin had a higher view of Louis' personal abilities and historical stature than did Lavisse, but he essentially viewed Louis as a creature of his times rather than a leader who stood above them.

With the selection by Roland Mousnier we first approach the work of a living historian. Widely known for his publications in a variety of fields, Professor Mousnier returns to the view that Louis XIV was a great constructive statesman, but the interpretation is now broadened to include the social as well as the institutional changes that Louis effected during his reign. Mousnier places great emphasis upon Louis XIV's personal effort to construct a newly efficient and royally controlled administrative system to govern the entire realm. By comparing institutional developments during the ministries of Richelieu and Mazarin with the governmental policies of Louis XIV, Mousnier offers conclusive evidence concerning the importance of the latter, and incidentally denies any Spanish influence. He likewise insists that the most important changes in the upper strata of French society stemmed from Louis' deliberate manipulation of appointments and favors so as to lower the nobles and raise the middle class. The result was a leveling process which rendered all individuals and groups directly subject to the sovereign. In both areas, therefore, Mousnier finds that Louis XIV effected revolutionary changes in that he broke with the old order and prepared the way for the egalitarian society and bureaucratic state of modern times. From this standpoint, Louis XIV was a constructive leader and statesman, since his policies molded and accelerated the most vital evolutionary currents in French society and government.

One measure of a ruler's greatness is surely the legacy that he left at his death. George Peabody Gooch's treatment of this subject brings together a variety of considerations that bear directly upon Louis XIV's stature in history. After reviewing the king's policies in his later years, his personal ideology, and some of the criticisms to which he was subjected, Gooch describes the dreary atmosphere at the royal court in the last years of the reign and examines the king's disastrous legacy to his immediate successors and his people. Gooch's estimate that the population of France had declined by one-fifth is doubtless exaggerated, but his treatment of governmental matters is essentially sound.

Our last selection is from a recent work by Pierre Goubert, one of the outstanding members of the very extensive school of French historians that is currently investigating the economic and social history of early modern France with very sophisticated statistical methods. Unlike the other authors in this collection, Goubert attempts to analyze Louis XIV's historical role within the context of the broader forces that were operative in his time. The result is that Goubert emphasizes the factors that were beyond the king's grasp and the many practical limitations on his power. After sketching the relatively restricted achievements of Louis XIV's ministers and other agents, Goubert notes the persistent opposition of foreign powers, resistance at home, and especially the pressures within the economy and social structure, indicating that many of the major developments of the period were beyond the king's competence to regulate or even to understand. Goubert also suggests that the condition of France in 1715 was not as grievous as was widely believed then and later, although he admits that current research on the subject is far from complete. In sum, Goubert tends to depreciate Louis XIV's personal significance by stressing the limited impact of his policies in the context of prevailing conditions.

In conclusion, certain broader connotations of the problem of Louis XIV's greatness may be mentioned. Fundamentally, any evaluation of the historical role of any "great" ruler is an examination of two perennial issues in human affairs: man's ability to order his world, and the values that he has followed when attempting to do so. Values have varied from age to age, and it would seem appropriate to estimate the greatness of a ruler only from the standpoint of his personal ideology and objectives. Historians have often erred by judging outstanding men of earlier periods according to standards that were unknown in their time. There is also the question whether any man, even the most powerful, is capable of substantially influencing the course of events. Are we all subject to inexorable forces that determine the very shape of our lives, or can we change, ameliorate and ultimately control the world in which we live by using our innate and acquired powers? As every historian knows, the twentieth century has witnessed increasing acceptance of deterministic views that stress the relative helplessness of individuals and groups in the presence of overpowering economic, social and psychological forces, particularly when operative on a mass scale. The contrary view, which is closer to the Western tradition, holds that men may at least partially determine the conditions of their earthly existence by making full use of their many abilities, especially their reason. An investigation of the greatness of Louis XIV should be an instructive inquiry into the extent to which a man of better than average ability, great power, massive popular support, and genuine seriousness of purpose succeeded in leaving his mark upon the growth of the French nation.

Conflict of Opinion

He wished to reign by himself. His jealousy on this point unceasingly became weakness. He reigned, indeed, in little things; the great he could never reach: even in the former, too, he was often governed. The superior ability of his early ministers and his early generals soon wearied him. He liked nobody to be in any way superior to him. . . . This vanity, this unmeasured and unreasonable love of admiration, was his ruin. His ministers, his generals, his mistresses, his courtiers, soon perceived his weakness. They praised him with emulation and spoiled him. . . . This is what gave his ministers so much authority. . . . Suppleness, meanness, an admiring, dependent, cringing manner—above all, an air of nothingness—were the sole means of pleasing him.

SAINT-SIMON

It will be seen by this cursory glance what great changes Louis XIV brought about in the state; and that such changes were useful since they are still in force. His ministers vied with each other in their eagerness to assist him. The details, indeed the whole execution of such schemes was doubtless due to them, but his was the general organization. There can be no shadow of doubt that the magistrates would never have reformed the laws, the finances of the country would not have been put on a sound basis, nor discipline introduced into the army, nor a regular police force instituted throughout the kingdom; there would have been no fleets, no encouragement accorded to the arts; all these things would never have been peacefully and steadily accomplished in such a short period and under so many different ministers, had there not been a ruler to conceive of such great schemes, and with a will strong enough to carry them out. . . . Let the reader picture to himself the condition today, and he will agree that Louis XIV did more good for his country than twenty of his precedessors together; and what he accomplished fell far short of what he might have done.

VOLTAIRE

Louis XIV carried the principle of monarchy to its utmost limit, and abused it in all respects to the point of excess. He left the nation crushed by war, mutilated by banishments, and impatient of the yoke which it felt to be ruinous. Men were worn-out, the treasury empty, all relationships strained by the violence of tension, and in the immense framework of the state there remained no institution except the accidental appearance of genius. Things had reached the point where, if a great king did not appear, there would be a great revolution.

ALBERT SOREL

Regarding this long reign, . . . the general conclusion that incorporates and summarizes all others is indicated by the fact that the monarchy survived Louis XIV only seventy-four years, hardly more than the duration of his reign. Louis XIV exhausted the French monarchy.

ERNEST LAVISSE

The principal legacy of Louis XIV was a powerful and centralized France. Though *Le Roi Soleil* was no superman in the sense that he would have fought his way to the front had he not been of royal descent, he gave his name to the greatest era in French history and his rays penetrated to every corner of Europe. He owed his success to the combination of his personal heritage and his personal qualities . . . but he lived long enough to destroy much of his handiwork. . . . The colossal national debt resulting from many years of war hung like a millstone round the neck of his descendants, and the system of government could only be operated by a ruler of equal capacity. The population had fallen by one-fifth in half a century owing to war casualties, the explusion of the Huguenots, and widespread starvation. Agricultural production had declined in an even more alarming ratio. . . . Direct and indirect taxes, tithes and feudal burdens were a nightmare at a time of bad harvests and dear bread. . . . France, still almost entirely an agricultural country, was sucked nearly dry. . . . The sufferings of the people were far more grievous in 1715 than on the eve of the Revolution in 1789. Such was the price his subjects had to pay for the greater glory of the *Roi Soleil*.

G. P. GOOCH

It is true that Louis XIV, like most men who grew up between 1640 and 1660, was incapable of rising beyond the limits of his education, let alone taking in, at one glance, the whole of the planet on which he lived, to say nothing of infinite space. A king to the depths of his being, and a dedicated king, he had a concept of greatness which was that of his generation: military greatness, dynastic greatness, territorial greatness and political greatness which expressed itself in unity of faith, the illusion of obedience and magnificent surroundings. He left behind him an image of the monarchy, admirable in its way, but already cracking if not outworn at the time of his death. Like most men, and many kings, he had grown stiff and sclerotic with old age. . . . And yet he and his colleagues left behind them a France that was territorially larger, militarily better defended, with a more effective administration and to a large extent pacified. And although he neglected it and often fought against it, there was a time when he built up and maintained what was to be, for a long time to come, the real greatness and glory of France. The Age of Enlightenment was dominated, at least in part, by the language and the culture of France.

PIERRE GOUBERT

I LOUIS XIV AS VIEWED BY HIS CONTEMPORARIES

Paul Pellisson
PANEGYRIC OF LOUIS XIV

Paul Pellisson (1624–1693) was one of the abler men of letters at the court of Louis XIV, although distinctly inferior to the literary giants of the period. He was a member of the French Academy, and was its most important historian during the century. A convert from Calvinism, he was the recipient of many royal favors, accompanied the king on several campaigns, held a number of minor offices in the royal administration, and was appointed royal historiographer. His intimacy with the king is indicated by the fact that he played a major role in the redaction of the Memoirs of Louis XIV. *The following panegyric is typical of the many lyric eulogies that were addressed to Louis during the first half of his reign, and is superior to most.*

Gentlemen. . . . According to our custom, [today] we seek to praise our august founder, Louis XIII, by speaking of his son, the highest and most lasting reward that could possibly have been accorded the earth for his father's wisdom, temperance, justice and piety. . . .

I do not pretend to be complete concerning such a vast subject in a discourse as brief as this, nor to treat equally all elements of the state. . . . I neglect the nobility, either chastened or subjected to the rules of justice, the third estate occupied in useful works unknown earlier, . . . the burdens of the people generally relieved, . . . the laws reformed, and the economy supporting both magnificence and liberality. But neither the great archbishop whom we receive today among ourselves, nor my own sentiments permit me to neglect the Church, recently pacified and flourishing because of the diligence, the care and the piety of the prince. . . . If anyone doubts this, let him merely consider the bloodless victories which the effort, the knowledge and the piety of our prelates and their holy followers continually win over those whom an entirely different era and the misfortune of their fathers separated from the faith. Happy the voluntary captives who joyfully follow the chariot of this triumph! . . .

From Paul Pellisson, *Panégyrique du Roi Louis XIV,* in *Recueil des harangues prononcées par Messieurs de l'Académie françoise,* 2nd ed. (Paris, 1714), vol. 1, pp. 243, 245–257. This speech was delivered on February 3, 1671, before the assembled members of the French Academy on the occasion of receiving into membership Harlay de Champvallon, Archbishop of Rouen and later Archbishop of Paris, in place of Hardouin de Péréfixe. Editor's translation.

It is fitting that in the royal dwellings we admire nature mastered by art, the streams and canals or rather the rivers and seas moving through underground conduits to occupy the place of sterile sands and fallow earth. But who would not admire infinitely more the works of a monarch whose most secret, obscure, and inscrutable methods of government (of which he alone is guide and master) have enabled him to correct, overcome, and improve the customs, propensities and genius of his people?

During the regency of a most pious queen, you have seen impiety callously manifest; today it is either dead or mute at the court.

In the reign of an earlier and most temperate king, you have seen what we no longer observe: the license of the base-born corrupting persons of quality and dishonoring France after the fashion of her neighbors.

The inveterate passion for dueling, prevalent for many centuries, was an incurable illness in our nation; today the remedy is so perfect that we are beginning to forget the malady.

Maritime commerce was impossible to Frenchmen who, it was said, were incapable of winning a profit where one habitually begins with losses, and advances only by good method, perseverance and work. However, this commerce, as well as a thousand other advantages, creates around us today as many jealousies as we have neighbors.

In what part of the world was there formerly more laxity and indiscipline among individuals? In what part of the world today is it more difficult for men to avoid their responsibilities, abuse their authority, secure dispensation from the laws, or neglect their duty?

What histories, peoples, and tongues have not spoken of the insolence of the French soldier and the license of our troops? Now they live in the conquered cities of Flanders even more correctly than the local inhabitants, while the subjects of Spain, trembling, captive and confined within their walls, dare not visit the countryside for fear of their own garrisons.

From whence come, gentlemen, so many remarkable changes all at once? Is there an extraordinary revolution, a conjunction or new constellation in the heavens? Let us excuse ourselves from observing it, leaving the task to those new royal academies, daughters, or sisters of our own, products of the same revolution, or rather, of the same magnificent and powerful hand. For it is certain and unmistakable that our kings are our stars, their glances our influences, their movements and conduct the primary sources on earth of our vices and our virtues.

Perhaps the king of whom we speak has limited his influence to the interior of his state. Ask it, gentlemen, of all the nations of the world, for whom he is and always has been almost as real as he is to us, either because of protection, friendship, fear, or the free and voluntary homage which the most distant so often render to his reputation and his virtue.

I may only touch rapidly, gentlemen, upon the materials of several volumes. . . . An ecclesiastical prince, his ally, is unable to subdue a strong and rebellious city, rendered obstinate by a false love of religion and liberty. The entire Protestant party of the Empire is about to lend its support. However, the city surrenders at the sight of our troops, or rather, at the mere name of our monarch as though its bastions and walls had crumbled; all approve what they could not prevent.

The Turk is very near to Vienna with one hundred thousand men; not a stream stops him. All Germany trembles, almost all Christianity. Six thousand heroic Frenchmen go to deliver Vienna and scatter this terrible army, disregarding their lives in their noble ardor to obey and please their king.

The Dutch, his allies, find themselves hard pressed by a neighboring and vigorous enemy. He generously saves them from extreme peril without considering his future interests, and yet without compromising them. The Dutch are simultaneously engaged in a war with England. He declares for them as he had promised, nevertheless retaining the power and authority of arbitration between the two nations, and magnanimously neglects his own advantage by giving them peace.

The queen is refused the rights that laws and inheritance confer upon her. After seeking a reasonable solution, he marches at the head of his armies, astonishes the oldest and wisest captains by his conduct, and the bravest and most determined soldiers by his valor; he forces, wins and inundates whole provinces like a torrent which even winter accelerates. His glory lacks nothing but that which is always wanting to the glory of heroes: the hesitancy of others to resist him diminishes the opportunities of his arms.

This torrent, it is thought, will drown and ravage both friends and enemies in the same fury. In truth, he surprises friends and enemies, but in a different manner. He retires far behind his rightful boundaries: the conqueror is above his conquests. Neither valuable possessions nor great aspirations persuade him to violate or evade his given promise. Rare example of honor, moderation and equity!

If, in the midst of so many successes and triumphs, it sometimes happens that fortune, or rather, the supreme wisdom above human understanding, may treat him like all other great men and deny success to his plans, this seems merely to humiliate the nation and to increase the worth of the prince. As soon as our best and strongest troops are sent across the seas, away from the eyes of their master and beyond reach of his orders, all is changed. Africa and Crete witness two great, worthy, and pious campaigns against the infidel, well supported by the king but nevertheless ending in failure, as if to bring home to Frenchmen what they already know: that their victories are achieved much less by their valor than by his commands. . . .

From far and near we increasingly discover his true greatness. Never are there anything but the sentiments and utterances of a king. I have thought a thousand times that he was not born but was created our master, superior and more highly endowed than any of his subjects. Another ruler, because of base and wicked views which have only too many examples in history, would be envious of his successor, or would be content merely to have brought into the world a prince whose nature reflected the elements of his own virtues. Instead he chooses for the royal education all that he may discover of the most enlightened, wise, equitable, strong, generous, honest, competent and learned, as if to eliminate the need of his giving it further attention. However, he does consider it further, and as though to forestall assistance by another in this work, with his own hand he puts into writing for his dear son the secrets of royalty and eternal precepts concerning what is to be followed and avoided. Thus he is not only father of the prince and of his people, but of all future kings. . . .

I call to witness the laborious and skillful hands that are occupied day and night in the execution of his great designs, and ask whether anything takes place within or without the realm, in great things or small, which does not pass and repass unceasingly before his eyes; whether it is not through him that negotiations are conducted in all the climes of the globe, that our provinces are peaceful, that Paris daily has more provisions, security and beauty, that industry advances and the liberal arts flourish, that the sciences triumph, that offices are filled and graces granted, that the revenues of the state are dispensed, that the troops are maintained and drilled, that the seas are covered with ships of war and witness the discharge of our cargoes in places where formerly his name was only a rumor, that our fortifications amaze the Flemish, that the multitude, grandeur and pomp of the royal buildings astonish Frenchmen and foreigners alike, that spectacles which surpass the imagination are given the people, not as did the Greeks and Romans in order to acquire dominion, but purely as an act of magnanimity and benevolence; and finally whether it is not true that a single man, in consequence the greatest of men, effects with ease this prodigious number of things which we have difficulty remembering and counting.

Gentlemen, I must contain my admiration within limits. Moved and excited as I am by so many matters, I would forget time and place, and would proceed with bolder and loftier metaphors. I would call into judgment before you the kings of all nations and all centuries. I would interrogate, as if present, the greatest of our own kings who undoubtedly look down from Heaven with pleasure, unenvious of the marvels of their successor. I would ask the very minister who took such pains with his childhood and his state, whether he anticipated this fruit of his counsels and predicted what we now experience, or whether we have surpassed his fondest and greatest hopes. Be consoled, illustrious Cardinal, you who were able to equal or efface all others. It is no shame to be eclipsed by him. It is sufficient to your glory to have had some part in his. But you whose praises we are particularly obliged to celebrate, first Protector and Founder of our society, guardian spirit of these assemblies, famous Cardinal Richelieu, whose memory will be venerated over all the earth as long as this tongue is spoken, as long as there are learned men, and as long as there are ministers, peoples and kings; great, high spirit, eagle whose flight I cannot discern, may you follow with your eyes that of LOUIS XIV and witness what he is accomplishing today without admitting. . . . But where is my zeal carrying me? Let us conclude, gentlemen, and with all your spirit, effort and strength (for they are necessary) let us terminate this panegyric which I have sketched this day in the honor of France and yourselves. And since you are witness of my weakness, observe also my passion, or if you wish, my transport. If it had been possible for me while dazzled by the brilliance of a great king, charmed by his virtues, and imbued with his goodness, I would have done a thousand times more. . . .

Jacques-Bénigne Bossuet

THE DIVINE RIGHT OF KINGS

Jacques-Bénigne Bossuet (1627–1704) is generally regarded as one of the ablest members of the French clergy during his era. Consistently high in royal favor, he was appointed Bishop of Meaux and served as court preacher during much of his career, winning great renown for his eloquence in the pulpit. An outstanding polemicist, he wrote extensively against the Calvinists and sought to demonstrate the providential guidance of human history. His position regarding church-state relations was an uncompromising Gallicanism. His most famous political treatise, the Politique tirée des propres paroles de l'Ecriture sainte, *was written for the education of the dauphin, in order to acquaint him with the true concept of kingship. Although published post-humously, the work is considered to be the classic statement of the theory of the divine right of kings.*

It is God who establishes kings. He caused Saul and David to be anointed by Samuel; He vested royalty in the House of David, and ordered him to cause Solomon, his son, to reign in his place. . . .

*   *   *

Princes thus act as ministers of God and His lieutenants on earth. It is through them that He rules. . . . This is why we have seen that

From Jacques-Bénigne Bossuet, *Politique tirée des propres paroles de l'Ecriture sainte,* in *Œuvres* (Paris, 1828), vol. 16, pp. 59, 82–83, 86–93, 119–120, 125, 157, 235–239, 393–395. Editor's translation.

the royal throne is not the throne of a man, but the throne of God himself. "Jehovah hath chosen Solomon my son to sit upon the throne of the kingdom of Jehovah over Israel" (I Chronicles 28:5). And again: "Then Solomon sat on the throne of Jehovah" (Ibid., 29:33). . . .

It appears from this that the person of kings is sacred, and to move against them is sacrilege. God causes them to be anointed by the prophets with a sacred unction, as He caused the pontiffs and His altars to be anointed.

But even without the external application of this unction, they are sacred in their office, as being the representatives of the divine majesty, sent by His providence for the execution of His designs. . . .

*   *   *

There is something religious in the respect that one renders the prince. Service of God and respect for kings are things united. St. Peter groups these two duties together: "Fear God. Honor the king" (I Peter 2:17).

Thus God has placed in princes something divine. "I have said, Ye are gods; and all of you are children of the most High" (Psalm 82:6). It is God himself who causes David to speak thus. . . .

It is the spirit of Christianity to cause kings to be revered with a type of religion, which Tertullian aptly calls "the religion of the second majesty."

This second majesty is but a token of the first, the divine, which, for the good of things human, has caused a certain part of its lustre to be imparted to kings.

Since their power comes from on high, kings should not believe that they are its masters and may use it as they wish; they should exercise it with fear and restraint as a thing which has come to them from God, and for which God will demand an account. . . . Kings should tremble when using the power that God gives them, and remember how horrible is the sacrilege of using for evil a power that comes from God.

We have seen kings seated on the throne of the Lord, having in hand the sword that God himself placed in their hands. What profanation and audacity of unjust kings to sit in the throne of God in order to publish decrees against His laws and to use the sword that He placed in their hands to do violence and to massacre His children.

Therefore let them respect their power, since it is not theirs but the power of God, and must be used holily and religiously. . . . That is, they should govern as God governs, in a manner at once noble, disinterested, benevolent, in a word, divine. . . .

God, who created all men from the same earth and equally placed His image and likeness in their souls, did not establish distinctions among them so that some might be proud and others slaves and wretches. He made some great only for the protection of the small; He gave His power to kings only to ensure the public welfare and to be the support of the people. . . . Thus princes should understand that their true glory is not for themselves, and that the public good which they procure is a sufficiently worthy recompense on earth, while awaiting the eternal rewards that God has reserved for them. . . .

*   *   *

Princes are gods and participate somehow in divine independence. . . . There is only God who may judge over their judgments and their persons. . . . The prince may correct himself when he knows that he has done evil, but against his authority there is no remedy other than his own authority. . . .

Thus kings like all others are subject to the equity of the laws because they should be just and because they owe to the people the example of preserving justice, but they are not subject to the penalties of the laws. Or, as in theology, they are subject to the laws not as regards their coactive power but only their directive power. . . .

*   *   *

What is there that a wise prince cannot effect? Under him wars are successful, peace is established, justice reigns, the laws govern, religion flourishes, commerce and navigation enrich the land, and the earth itself seems to bring forth fruit more willingly. Such are the effects of wisdom. . . .

*   *   *

I do not call majesty the pomp that surrounds kings, nor the exterior lustre that dazzles the vulgar. This is but the reflection of majesty, not majesty itself.

Majesty is the image of the greatness of God in the prince.

God is infinite; God is all. The prince as prince is not regarded as an individual; he is a public personage. All the state is in him; the will of the entire people is contained in his. As all perfection and virtue are united in God, all the power of individuals is united in the person of the prince. What greatness that a single man contains so much!

The power of God makes itself felt in an instant from one end of the world to the other; royal power acts similarly through all the realm. It keeps the whole realm in order, as God keeps the world.

Let God withdraw His hand, and the world will fall into nothing; let authority cease in the realm, and all will be in confusion.

Consider the king in his council-chamber. From there are sent the orders which unite the efforts of magistrates and captains, citizens and soldiers, provinces and armies on land and sea. It is the image of God, who, seated on His throne in the highest heavens, causes nature to function. . . . We see a small part, but the essence is impenetrable. Thus it is with the secrets of the prince.

The designs of the prince become known only through their execution. Similarly are manifest the counsels of God: to them no man may penetrate except those whom God admits.

As the power of God extends everywhere, magnificence accompanies it. There is no part of the universe in which the unmistakable evidences of His goodness do not appear. Behold the order, the justice and the tranquility in all the realm: it is the natural effect of the authority of the prince. . . .

In a word, gather together the great and glorious things that we have said concerning the royal authority. Behold an immense people united in a single person; behold this sacred, paternal and absolute power; behold the secret intelligence which governs all bodies in the state, contained within a single head: you behold the image of God in kings, and you understand the idea of royal majesty. . . .

Something indescribably divine is attached to the prince and inspires fear in the people. However, let not this cause the king to forget his own nature. . . . You are gods, that is, you have in your authority and you carry on your forehead a divine quality. You are the children of the Most High; it is He who established your power for the good of humanity. But, O gods of flesh and blood, O gods of mud and dust, you will die like men; you will fall like all the great. Greatness divides men but briefly; a common fate finally renders them all equal.

Therefore O kings! Exercise your power boldly, for it is divine and beneficial to humanity, but exercise it with humility. It is given to you from without. Ultimately it leaves you frail; it leaves you mortal; it leaves you sinners and demands from you a greater final reckoning before God. . . .

*   *   *

There is among men a type of government that is called arbitrary, but it is not found among us, nor in properly constituted states.

Four characteristics are associated with this type of government. First, its subjects are born slaves, that is, in true bondage, and among them there are no free persons. Second, nothing is possessed as property since all belongs to the prince, and there is no right of inheritance, even from father to son. Third, the prince has the right to dispose freely not only of his subjects' goods but even of their lives, as would be done with slaves. Finally, there is no law other than his will.

This is what is called arbitrary power. I do not wish to inquire whether it is lawful or unlawful. There are peoples and great empires that are satisfied with it, and it is not for us to disturb them concerning their form of government. It is sufficient for us to say that this type of government is barbarous and odious. These four characteristics are very far removed from our customs, and for this reason arbitrary government does not exist among us.

There is a great difference between a government that is absolute and one that is arbitrary. It is absolute by reason of constraint, there being no power capable of coercing the sovereign who in this sense is independent of all human authority. But it does not follow from this that the government is arbitrary. Because, although anything is permitted to the judgment of God and to a government called arbitrary, it is certain that states have laws against which anything that is done is of no right. And there is always available a means of redress on other occasions and in other times, so that each remains legitimate possessor of his property, no one being able to believe that he may ever possess anything in security contrary to the laws, whose vigilance and action against injustices and violences is immortal. . . . And it is in this that a government called legitimate is opposed by its nature to arbitrary government. . . .

Government is established in order to free all men from every oppression and violence, as has often been stated. And it is this that creates the state of perfect liberty, there being in essence nothing less free than anarchy, which destroys all legitimate rights among men, and knows no law but that of force.

Gottfried Wilhelm Leibnitz
MOST CHRISTIAN MARS

Gottfried Wilhelm Leibnitz (1646–1716) was by far the greatest German philosopher and mathematician of his period, and, indeed, one of the greatest minds of the entire era. The majority of his works dealt with philosophical and mathematical problems, and won him great renown throughout Europe. Although he generally enjoyed good relations with leading French intellectuals, he occasionally indulged in anti-French polemics because of his desire to defend German interests against the persistently aggressive foreign policy of Louis XIV. The following extract illustrates how a philosopher of Leibnitz' stature found little difficulty in criticizing Louis' wars as flagrant violations of international law and morality.

Although the king [Louis XIV] no longer had a preceptor after the death of Cardinal Mazarin, he was governed for a time by the latter's maxims and counsels as though he were still living, especially as M. de Lionne was a product of this school and followed the same principles. At that time they treated the princes of Germany with reasonable civility, subscribed to a semblance of international law, and made a great show of preserving the Peace of Westphalia and German liberty. But after the death of Lionne, M. de Louvois repre-

From Gottfried Wilhelm Leibnitz, *Mars Christianissimus, Autore Germano Gallo-Graeco, ou Apologie des Armes du Roy très-chrestien contre les chrestiens* (Cologne, 1684), pp. 18–23, 55–59, 62–73, 80–81. Editor's translation.

sented to the king that his alliance with the Rhenish princes had
done France more harm than good, that he should no longer be
troubled by the German rulers, that no money was worse employed
than that which had been given to them, that the Empire was a mere
name without substance, and that France might harass it with impunity
and still not lack supporters even in Germany. These counsels being
successful, M. de Pomponne insinuated himself into royal favor with
a new doctrine of his own invention, namely, that the troublesome
Peace of Westphalia had too long placed limits on the progress of
the king, that there was now a new peace of his own making, which
might be cited more plausibly and usefully than that of Münster to
which the Germans wrongfully had recourse since they had violated
it; and that since the Peace of Nimwegen was a pure grace of the
king, he had the sole right to explain its benefits. Now if France is
obligated to M. de Louvois for revealing the weakness of the German
princes, and to M. de Croisi for having freed the king from the con-
straints of the Peace of Münster, I believe that I should deserve no
less than these gentlemen if I were to free the king's council from
all scruples of conscience which some might find embarrassing out
of respect for the rights of peoples and the canons of the Church.
Accordingly, I shall show that although these principles undoubtedly
bind ordinary men, there is a certain law, superior to all others and
yet consonant with sovereign justice, which exempts the king from
observing them. It must be recognized that the just knows no law,
and he who has the authority of extraordinary power is exempt
from universal and humane obligations in virtue of his commission.
Thus it is now my task to show that the king possesses this authority,
and that there lives today no man who has received from heaven or
even from the antipodes greater power in temporal things than
LOUIS XIV. In order to acquit myself the better in proving this, I
must lay the foundations of a new jurisprudence. ... For this purpose,
I advance the principle that all temporal things are subject to the
supreme authority which this great and most powerful king has over
all other creatures in virtue of a certain destiny higher than theirs....
And when I show that the Most Christian King who lives today is the
true and unique vicar of the world in regard to all temporal things,
to this precept I shall add the definition of justice that Plato urges
and explains very well in the person of a certain Thrasymachus whom

he causes to say roundly: *justum est potentiori utile*. All of which accords very well with what we have said concerning the authority of a most powerful monarch over the temporal existence of men. . . .

As the Most Christian King has received from on high full power to do much more than we have thus far seen, it must be admitted that he uses his power with great moderation, since he has the right to carry out anything that enters his mind, provided that it augments his grandeur. . . . Thus the only way that he may falter is through excessive moderation, and all that he may do with the intention of his own aggrandizement is always just. I suppose that the R. P. de La Chaise, Jesuit, ordinary confessor of the king, and whose wisdom and prudence are generally recognized, holds approximately the same opinion; for being a man of conscience, if he were not equipped with such a general remedy for the satisfaction of all scruples, how could he approve many things that are done in the name of the king? There are those who flatter themselves that they are able to justify the aggressions of France with arguments drawn from accepted laws; but they are greatly mistaken, and when they are engaged in disputes, they are soon in desperate straits. From this it results that the wisest of the French avoid all disputes at law, and speak only as politicians, exaggerating with good reason the success and prudence of their monarch who knows so well how to capitalize upon his advantages.

For many do not know and others will not tell what they know regarding the absolute power which heaven has given their king; however, they use it secretly among themselves whenever they wish. Witness the French minister who, when deliberating upon the Peace of the Pyrenees, boldly advised the king to accept all renunciations which might be wrung from the Infanta, to grant them, and to approve them as genuinely as anyone might desire, even by oath, nevertheless, retaining freedom of action when the King of Spain should die. There never will be a good Frenchman (he said) who would wish to advise the king to neglect the advantages of his crown for which he is responsible to the world and to posterity. This is indeed an essential feature of the jurisprudence and morality which we have just established, to wit, that the grandeur of the king and the crown of France are above all other rights and oaths, whatever their nature may be.

Since this is so, it would be wrong to conceal such a great truth that needs to be preached to be believed. It is the more necessary to publish it, since it is impossible to justify the aggressions of France by arguments drawn from ordinary law, as I have remarked. In order to make this better known, at this point I shall frankly set forth some of the accusations that the enemies of France customarily allege against her, in order to show that there is no better means of justifying her actions than by attributing to her king the privilege of doing whatever seems good to him in virtue of his position as temporal vicar of the world. . . .

Surely if there is any means of achieving certainty in the negotiations of men, if the public pledges of kings have any weight, if religion and conscience are not empty words invented to deceive the foolish, the Peace of the Pyrenees should be firm and secure. But since it was broken and trampled under foot at the first opportunity, it must be recognized (they say) that whoever henceforth trusts the word of France is very stupid, and deserves to be deceived. That is why the Dutch, the Spanish, the Emperor and the other allies who negotiated at Nimwegen will sooner or later be punished for their credulity.

If they believed that the French would not encroach upon the Empire and the Low Countries more in the midst of peace than in war, they must have been very blind, or else they preferred fighting together to perishing singly. If we recall the beginning of the recent war, was there anything more outrageous than the manner in which the Duke of Lorraine was despoiled of his state? His sole crime was that he did not wish to be at the mercy of some French governor or intendant, and that he attempted to preserve his security by defensive alliances, the most innocent in the world. The war against the Dutch was so far removed from any appearance of reason (I speak as an enemy of France) that no one was ever able to find a pretext. Yet all the violence which France has perpetrated since then in Germany, in the Low Countries and elsewhere has been excused simply as the necessary sequel to that war. It was for this reason that the French armies traversed Germany (in order to draw away any help that might arrive for the Dutch or serve as a diversion for the French), that they have taken Trier, surprised and dismantled ten cities in Alsace in a manner which hardly resembled good faith, and carried out all sorts of hostilities in the Palatinate of the Rhine, all because of the merest suspicions sanctioned only by the rationale of war, the most unjust war that was ever undertaken. They had the insolence to insist that the Emperor first withdraw his troops from imperial territory, and that the king would do the same only when the Emperor had given his word (with that of other princes as security) that he would never move outside his hereditary estates; that is to say, the King of France had greater authority in the Empire than did the Emperor himself. Everyone should remain quiet and trust the word of the French ministers who were preaching far and wide that their king sought nothing through war but to rebuke some unknown insolence of the Dutch, as though the desire might not come to him to humiliate others in their turn, and as though he had the right to act the part of a schoolmaster with stick in hand, chastising others like little boys. We have seen that his aims went much further than mere bravado, that he made sure of keeping outposts on the lower Rhine by installing strong garrisons in them, that the crime of the Dutch was their having prevented the occupation of the entire Low Countries, and that the ambition of the king was quite egocentric and contemplated as much profit as glory. . . .

They maintain that the capture of Strasbourg was the most violent and the most Turkish act that a Christian prince ever perpetrated, and that it is the height of impudence to attempt to excuse it; that this blow was made in the midst of peace without the slightest shadow of pretext, contrary to the recently sworn agreement which specified that all should remain unchanged after the departure of the king's ambassadors for Frankfort; and that all judicious persons have decided that it would be useless after this to invoke the rules of justice and the laws of honesty.

They maintain that conscience, good faith, and the law of nations are hollow terms and vain illusions, since the French no longer even search for pretexts for doing violence. In earlier times, those who diligently sought to unearth the slightest suggestion of French rights took good care not to bring Strasbourg into question, for fear of appearing as visionaries or Sophists, surprised in flagrant misdemeanor. The terms of the Peace of Münster are so clear and allow so little room for chicanery that it seems that the ministers who framed them foresaw and removed, with prophetic insight, all loopholes which an impudent Sophist might use. But if they were sufficiently skillful to close the mouths of those who retained a residue of shame, they were not able to tie the hands of those who insolently trample reason underfoot. It profited them nothing to have declared in perfectly clear terms that no part of Alsace except that held by the House of Austria should be ceded to France, to have specified the places to be ceded by their exact names, and expressly to have exempted the very principalities and states in the Empire that France now wishes to take. . . .

I have sought to state simply what is said against the pretensions of the king, in order to show that there is no means of justifying them other than the postulate that I have adopted, exempting the king from the necessity of answering arguments of law, no matter what force they may have. But since the vulgar are ignorant of this beautiful invention, one should not be surprised if the recently despoiled among them move heaven and earth with their tragic lamentations, if they point to fields inundated with Christian blood in order to satisfy the ambition of the only nation that disturbs the peace, and if they behold thousands sacrificed by arms, hunger and misery merely to ensure that the name of Louis XIV may be placed on the gates of Paris in letters of gold. Since the peace and happiness of Europe depend on France, they say, what greater crime may be imagined than the assumption of responsibility for all the ills of Christendom: for so much innocent bloodshed, the acts of scoundrels, the prayers of the wretched, the groans of the dying, and the tears of widows and orphans which pierce the heavens and will sooner or later excite God to vengeance—the great God whose judgments are so terrible that the simperings of Tartuffes and the eloquence of Sophists will not deceive Him, since He never distinguishes between a king and a peasant except to augment His punishments in proportion to the greatness of the sinners and the nature and consequences of their crimes. . . .

This is but a part of what is said publicly against France, for the veneration that is owed to great princes has caused me to suppress the sharpest and most violent statements which are rife in books and conversations. . . .

Jean de La Bruyère
THE QUALITY OF GREATNESS

Jean de La Bruyère (1645–1696) was undoubtedly the ablest analyst of French manners and customs during the reign of Louis XIV. In attendance at the royal court but never subservient to it, he witnessed its increasing ostentation and gradual decline during the later years of the century. His most famous work, the Caractères, *was first published in 1688 and presents a series of pithy and often highly critical sketches of various elements of French society and the way of life at the royal court. La Bruyère hesitated to subject the sovereign to such searching criticism, and the following selection, written in praise of Louis XIV, appears to be genuine. However, La Bruyère may well have felt that it was necessary to pay tribute to the king in a work that severely criticized many powerful persons and groups at the court.*

The mastering of the details of business and a diligent application to the smallest necessities of the state are essential to a good administration, though, in truth, too much neglected in these latter times by kings and their ministers; it is a knowledge greatly to be desired in a prince who is ignorant of it, and highly to be valued in him who has acquired it. Indeed, what benefits and what increase of pleasure would accrue to a people by their prince extending the bounds of his empire into the territories of his enemies, by their sovereignties becoming provinces of his kingdom, by his overcoming them in sieges and battles, by neither the plains nor the strongest fortifications affording any security against him, by the neighboring nations asking aid of one another, and entering into leagues to defend themselves and put a stop to his conquests, by their leagues being in vain, by their last hopes being frustrated by the monarch recovering his health, and thus affording him the pleasure of seeing the young princes, his grandchildren, maintain and enhance his glory, beholding them lead an army into the field, take the strongest fortresses, conquer new states, command old and experienced officers rather by their genius and merit than by the privilege of their noble birth, observing them tread in the footsteps of their victorious father and imitate his goodness, his willingness to learn, his justice, vigilance,

From *The "Characters" of Jean de La Bruyère,* translated by Henri Van Laun (London, 1885), pp. 262–270. This is the final portion of the chapter, "Of the Sovereign and the State."

and magnanimity. What signifies it to me, in a word, or to any of my fellow-subjects, that my sovereign be successful and overwhelmed with glory, through his own actions as well as through those of his family and servants; that my country is powerful and dreaded, if, sad and uneasy, I have to live oppressed and poor; if, while I am secured against any inroads of the enemy, I am exposed in the public squares or the streets of our cities to the dagger of the assassin; or if rapine and violence are less to be feared in the darkest nights amidst the densest forests than in our own streets; if security, order, and cleanliness have not rendered the residing in our cities so delightful, and have not introduced there plenty as well as the pleasures of social intercourse; or if, being weak and defenseless, my property is to be encroached upon by some great man in the neighborhood; if there is not a provision made to protect me against his injustice; if I have not within reach so many masters, and excellent masters too, to instruct my children in sciences and arts, which will one day raise their fortunes; if the improvement of trade will not facilitate my providing myself with more decent clothing and wholesome food for my sustenance, at a reasonable rate; if, to conclude, through the care my sovereign takes of me, I am not as satisfied with my lot as his virtues must needs make him with his own?

Eight or ten thousand men are to a prince like money; with their lives he buys a town or a victory; but, if he can obtain either at a cheaper rate, and is sparing of them, he is like a man who is bargaining and knows better than any other the value of money.

All things succeed in a monarchy where the interests of the state are identical with those of the prince.

To call a king the father of his people is not so much to eulogize him as to call him by his name and to define what he is.

There exists a sort of interchange or permutation of duties between a sovereign and his subjects, and between them and him; and I shall not decide which are most obligatory and most difficult. On the one hand, we have to determine what are the bounden duties of reverence, assistance, service, obedience, and dependence, and on the other what are the indispensable obligations of goodness, justice, and protection. To say the prince can dispose of the lives of the people, is to tell us only that through their crimes men have become subjected to the laws and justice which the king administers; to add that he is absolute master of all his subjects' goods without any considerations, without rendering any accounts, or without discussion, is the language of flattery, the opinion of a favorite who will recant on his deathbed.

When on a fine evening a numerous flock of sheep is seen on a hill quietly browsing thyme and wild thyme, or nibbling in a meadow the short and tender grass which has escaped the scythe of the reaper, the careful and diligent shepherd is amongst them; he does not lose sight of them, but follows them, leads them, changes their pasture; if they wander, he calls them together; if a hungry wolf approaches, he sets his dog on to beat him off; he keeps them and defends them; and when the sun rises he is already in the fields, which he leaves at its setting. What an amount of care, watchfulness, and assiduity is needed! Which condition seems to you the most delicious and the most unfettered, that of the sheep or of the shepherd? Was the flock made for the shepherd or the shepherd for the flock? This is an artless representation of a nation and its prince, but then the prince must be good.

A gorgeous and sumptuous monarch is like a shepherd adorned with gold and jewels, with a golden crook in his hands, with a collar of gold about his dog's neck, and a silken and golden string to lead him. What is his flock the better for all this gold, or what avails it against the wolves?

How happy is that station which every instant furnishes opportunities of doing good to thousands of men! How dangerous is that post which every moment exposes its occupant to injure millions!

If men in this world cannot feel a more natural, praiseworthy, and sensible pleasure than to know that they are beloved, and if kings are men, can they purchase the hearts of their people at too high a rate?

There are very few general rules and unvariable regulations for governing well; they depend on times and circumstances, as well as on the prudence and designs of the rulers. A perfect government is, therefore, a masterpiece of the intellect; and perhaps it would be impossible to attain it, if the subjects did not contribute their moiety towards it by their habits of dependence and submission.

Those persons who, under a very great monarch, fill the highest offices, have no very intricate duties to perform, and they do this without any trouble; everything goes on easily; the authority and the genius of the prince smoothes their way, rids them of all difficulties, and makes everything prosper beyond their expectations; their merit consists in being subordinates.

If the care of a single family be so burdensome, if a man has enough to do to answer for himself, what a weight, what a heavy load must be the charge of a whole realm! Is a sovereign rewarded for all his anxieties by the pleasures which absolute power seems to afford and by the prostrations of his courtiers? When I think of the difficult, hazardous, and dangerous paths he sometimes is forced to tread to attain public tranquility; when I think of the extreme but necessary means he often is obliged to employ to compass a good end; when I am aware he is accountable to God for the welfare of his people, that good and evil are in his hands, and that he cannot plead ignorance as an excuse, I cannot forbear asking myself the question if I should like to reign? A man who is tolerably happy as a private individual should not abandon it for a throne, for, even to one who occupies it by hereditary right, it is almost unbearable to be born a monarch.

How many gifts Heaven must bestow on a prince for him to become a good ruler! He must be of royal blood, have an august and commanding air, a presence to satisfy the curiosity of a crowd anxious to see the prince, as well as to command respect from his courtiers. His temper must be always the same; he must be averse to ill-natured raillery, or, at least, be so sensible as to refrain from it; he must never threaten, reproach, nor give way to passion, yet he must be always obeyed; he should be complacent and engaging, so frank and sincere that all may think they plainly see the bottom of his heart, which will tend to gain him friends, partisans, and allies; yet he must be secret, close, and impenetrable in his motives and plans; he must be very grave and serious in public; be brief, precise, and dignified in his answers to ambassadors, as well as in his expressions in council; be careful in choosing fit objects for his favors, and bestow them with that peculiar charm which enhances them; great must be his sagacity to penetrate into the minds, qualifications, and tempers of men, to nominate them to various posts and places, as well as to select his generals and ministers of state. His opinions should be so settled, sound, and decisive in matters of state, as immediately to point out what is the best and most honest thing to do; his mind ought to be so upright and just as sometimes to decide against himself and in favor of his subjects, allies, or enemies; so comprehensive and ready should be his memory as to remember the necessities of his subjects, their faces, names, and petitions. His capacious intelligence should not only exercise itself on foreign affairs, commerce, maxims of state, political designs, extension of the frontiers by conquering new provinces, and ensuring their safety by numerous and inaccessible forts; but also look after the affairs of his own kingdom, and study them in detail; banish from it a false, insidious, and antimonarchical sect, if such a one exists; abolish all barbarous and impious customs, if they are to be found there; reform the abuses of laws and usages, for such may have crept in; render his cities more safe and comfortable by establishing new police regulations, more splendid and magnificent by sumptuous edifices; punish severely scandalous vices; increase the influence of religion and virtue by his authority and example; protect the Church and clergy, their rights and liberties; and govern the nation like a father, always intent on relieving it and making the subsidies as light as those levied in the provinces without impoverishing them. He must have great talents for war, be vigilant, diligent, and unwearied, able to command numerous armies, and be composed in the midst of danger; he ought to be sparing of his own life for the good of the state, and prefer its welfare and glory to that very life; his power must be absolute, to leave no room for indirect influence, intrigues and factions, and sometimes to lessen that vast distance which exists between the great and the common people, so that they may be drawn closer together, and obey that power equally; the knowledge of the prince should be extensive, that he may see everything with his own eyes, act immediately and by himself, so that his generals, though at a distance, are but his lieutenants, and his ministers but his ministers; he should be sagacious enough to know when to declare war, when to conquer and make the best use of a victory, when to make peace, and when to break it; when, sometimes, to compel his enemies to accept it, according to the various interests at stake; to set bounds to his vast ambition, and how far to extend his conquests; he should find leisure for games, festivals, and spectacles; cultivate arts and sciences, and erect magnificent structures, even when surrounded by secret and declared enemies. To conclude, he should possess a superior and commanding genius, which renders him beloved by his subjects and feared by strangers, and makes of his court, and even of his entire realm, as it were, one family, governed by one head, living in perfect unison and harmony with one another, and thus formidable to the rest of the world. All these admirable virtues seem to me comprised in the notion of what a sovereign ought to be. It is true we rarely see them all combined in one man, for too many adventitious qualities, such as intelligence, feelings, outward appearances, and natural disposition, must be found at the same time in him; it therefore appears to me that a prince who unites all these in his single person well deserves the name of Great.

Fénelon

LETTER TO LOUIS XIV

François de Salignac de la Mothe-Fénelon (1651–1715) was one of the ablest members of the French clergy during the second generation of the reign of Louis XIV. Originally in high favor at the court, he was appointed Archbishop of Cambrai and was chosen to be the tutor of the Duke of Burgundy, the grandson of Louis XIV. Later, Fénelon fell from favor and retired to Cambrai, although he maintained contact with many persons at the court. Widely regarded as a brilliant author of great charm and utter sincerity, he became one of Louis' severest critics during the period of French defeats and national decline. His famous Letter to Louis XIV, *probably written in 1694, may be regarded as a sincere outcry of protest by one of the greatest thinkers of the age.*

The person, Sire, who takes the liberty of writing this letter to you, has no interest in this world. He does not write it because of dissatisfaction, ambition, or any desire to take part in great affairs. He loves you without being known to you; he sees God in your person. With all

Because this letter is extremely critical of Louis XIV and certain powerful persons at Versailles, its authenticity was doubted until the original in Fénelon's own handwriting was discovered and published by A. A. Renouard (Paris, 1825). It seems certain that the letter was never read by Louis XIV, although it was probably circulated among a few courtiers. See the edition of *Télémaque* by A. Cahen (Paris, 1920), vol. 1, pp. xxvii–xxviii. The letter was republished in *Fénelon: Ecrits et lettres politiques,* edited by C. Urbain (Paris, 1920), pp. 143–157. Editor's translation.

your power, you are unable to give him any good that he wishes, and there is no evil which he would not willingly suffer in order to bring you to understand the truths that are necessary to your salvation. If he speaks boldly to you, do not be surprised, for the truth is free and strong. You are hardly accustomed to hearing it. Persons inured to flattery may easily sense irritation, bitterness, or intemperance where there is merely pure truth. It is to betray it not to reveal it to you in all its fullness. God is witness that the person who speaks to you does so with his heart full of zeal, respect, fidelity, and emotion for all that concerns your true interests.

You were born, Sire, with an upright and equitable heart; but those who reared you gave you as knowledge of government merely distrust, jealousy, aversion to virtue, fear of all clear merit, a taste for supple and cringing men, arrogance, and concern merely for your own interests.

For thirty years, your principal ministers have shaken and overthrown all the ancient maxims of the state in order to increase your authority beyond all bounds, because it had become theirs since it was in their hands. They no longer spoke of the state or the rules; they spoke merely of the king and his pleasure. They perpetually increased your revenues and your expenses. They exalted you as high as the heavens, in order to efface, they said, the grandeur of all your predecessors together, that is to say, in order to impoverish all France so as to introduce a monstrous and incurable extravagance into the court. They wished to raise you above the ruins of all the social classes in the state, as though you might become great by ruining all your subjects on whom your greatness is founded. It is true that you have been perhaps overly jealous of your authority in foreign affairs, but essentially each minister has been the master throughout his branch of the administration. You believed that you were governing because you regulated the limits between those who governed. They paraded their power before the public, and it was felt only too well. They have been harsh, haughty, unjust, violent and dishonest. They have known no rule of conduct in domestic or foreign affairs but to threaten, crush, and annihilate all that opposed them. They consulted you only in order to remove all your scruples that might cause them embarrassment. They accustomed you to receiving endless, extravagant praises which approached idolatry, and which, for the sake of your honor, you should have rejected with indignation. They rendered your name odious and the French nation unbearable to all our neighbors. They did not retain a single ally, since they only desired slaves. They have caused more than twenty years of bloody wars. For example, Sire, in 1672 they caused Your Majesty to undertake the Dutch War for your glory and the punishment of the Dutch, who had made certain mocking jests in their anger when the rules of commerce established by Cardinal Richelieu were altered. I cite this war in particular because it has been the source of all the others. Its only cause was a desire for glory and vengeance which may never justify a war, and from this it follows that all the frontiers which you extended by this war were unjustly acquired from the first. It is true, Sire, that the subsequent treaties of peace seem to conceal and redress this injustice, since they have given you the conquered places, but an unjust war is not less unjust for being successful. Treaties of peace signed by the vanquished are never signed freely. They sign with a knife at their throats; they sign in spite of themselves in order to prevent greater losses; they sign as if giving their purses to one who demands their money or their lives. Thus it is necessary, Sire, to go back as far as the beginning of the Dutch War to examine all your conquests before God.

It is useless to say that these were necessary to your state: the property of another is never necessary to us. What is truly needful to us is the observation of strict justice. It must not even be pretended that you are within your rights in forever retaining certain places because they insure the security of your frontiers. It is your duty to seek this security by good alliances, by your moderation, and by means of fortifications behind your frontiers; but in any case the need of guarding our security never gives us the right to take the land of our neighbors. Consult with learned and upright men about this; they will tell you that what I set forth is as clear as day.

This is sufficient, Sire, to demonstrate that you have passed your entire life apart from the way of truth and justice, and in consequence apart from that of the Gospel. So many terrible troubles that have ravaged all Europe during more than twenty years, so much blood spilled, so many shameful acts committed, so many provinces pillaged, so many towns and villages reduced to ashes, these are the fatal consequences of the war of 1672, undertaken for your glory and the humiliation of makers of pamphlets and medals in Holland. Consider among upright men and without flattering yourself, whether you should keep all that you possess in consequence of the treaties that you have forced upon your enemies by such a thoroughly unjustified war.

This remains the true source of all the evils from which France is suffering. Since this war, you have always sought to dictate peace and impose conditions, instead of qualifying them with equity and moderation. This is why peace has not endured. Your enemies, ingloriously overwhelmed, have thought only of rising again and reuniting against you. Should this be surprising? You have not even observed the terms of the peace which you dictated with such arrogance. In the midst of peace, you have made war and vast conquests. You established a Chamber of Reunions to be both judge and party; this merely added insult and ridicule to usurpation and violence. You searched for ambiguous terms in the Peace of Westphalia in order to justify seizing Strasbourg. Never during years of negotiation had any of your ministers dared cite these terms to show that you might have the slightest claim to that city. Such conduct has reunited and aroused all Europe against you. Even those who have not openly dared speak their minds eagerly desire at least your humiliation and the diminution of your power, as the only hope of liberty and peace among Christian nations. You, Sire, who might acquire so much solid and peaceful glory by being the father of your subjects and the arbiter among your neighbors, have been rendered the common enemy of your neighbors and have been caused to appear a cruel master in your realm.

The strangest result of these bad counsels is the long duration of the league formed against you. The allies prefer waging a losing war to concluding peace with you, because they are convinced by their own experience that this peace will not be a true one, that you will observe it no more than the others, and that you will merely use it to crush each of your neighbors separately and without difficulty as soon as they are disunited. Thus, the more you are victorious, the more they fear you and cling together in order to avoid the slavery with which they believe themselves threatened. Not being able to conquer you, they hope at least to exhaust you in the course of time. In a word, they no longer hope for security with you except by rendering you powerless to injure them. Put yourself, Sire, in their place for a moment, and observe the fruits of preferring your advantages to justice and good faith.

But your people, whom you should love as your children, and who thus far have been so enamored of you, are dying of hunger. Cultivation of the land is almost abandoned; the cities and the countryside are depopulated; all crafts languish and no longer support the workers. All commerce has been decimated. You have consequently destroyed half the real power within your state, in order to win and defend vain conquests abroad. Instead of squeezing money from the poor people, you should give them alms and nourishment. All France is but a great poorhouse without provisions. The magistrates are degraded and overworked. The nobility, whose entire wealth depends on royal decrees, live only on gifts from the state. You are annoyed by the mob of people who beg and murmur. It is you, Sire, who called down on yourself all these difficulties; for, since the realm is in ruins, you have everything in your hands, and no one can continue to live without your gifts. Such is this great realm, so flourishing under a king who daily is described to us as the delight of the people, and who would truly be this if flattering advice had not corrupted him.

Even the people (one must tell all) who loved you so, and who had every confidence in you, are beginning to lose their affection, their trust, and even their respect for you. Your victories and conquests delight them no longer; they are full of bitterness and despair. Sedition is slowly appearing in all places. They believe that you have no pity for their ills, and that you love only your power and your glory. If the king, they say, felt the tenderness of a father toward his people, would he not rather make use of his glory by giving them bread and letting them breathe again after so many troubles, instead of retaining strongholds on the frontier as a cause of further war? What answer is there to that, Sire? Uprisings of the people, unknown for so long, are becoming frequent. Even Paris, so near to you, is not untouched by them. The magistrates are obliged to tolerate the insolence of the insubordinate, and to pass them money secretly in order to appease them; thus are paid those who should be punished. You are reduced to the shameful and deplorable extremity of either leaving sedition unpunished and thus allowing it to increase, or ordering the inhuman massacre of the very people whom you have reduced to despair by squeezing from them, through taxes for this war, the bread that they try to earn by the sweat of their brows.

But while they lack bread, you yourself lack money and refuse to recognize the extremity to which you are reduced. Because you have always been fortunate, you are unable to imagine that some day you might be otherwise. You fear to open your eyes; you fear being forced to diminish the least part of your glory. This glory, which hardens your heart, is dearer to you than justice, your own tranquility, the preservation of your people who daily perish from maladies caused by famine, and even your own eternal salvation, which is incompatible with such worship of glory.

That, Sire, is the position in which you are. You live as though you have a fatal blindfold over your eyes; you delude yourself with your daily successes which determine nothing. And since you never consider the totality of affairs from the standpoint of general policy, they decline imperceptibly into ruin. While you are assaulting positions and taking the battlefields and cannon of your enemy in fierce combat, you do not dream that you are fighting on ground which is sinking beneath your feet, and that you will fall in spite of your victories.

Everyone sees this, but no one dares bring it to your attention. Perhaps you will see it too late. True courage consists of undeceiving yourself and making firm decisions according to necessity. You willingly lend an ear, Sire, only to those who delude you with vain hopes. The men whom you know to be most trustworthy are those whom you fear and most avoid. Since you are king, you should seek the truth, urge men to tell it to you without alteration, and encourage those who are too timid. On the contrary, you only wish to avoid going to the heart of any matter; but God will eventually be able to lift the veil that covers your eyes, and will reveal to you what you avoid seeing. For long He has held His upraised arms over you, but He is slow to strike you because He pities a prince who has been plagued by flatterers all his life. Moreover, your enemies are also His. But He is fully capable of separating His cause which is just from yours which is not, and will humiliate you in order to convert you, for you may be Christian only in humiliation. You do not love God; you do not even fear Him with the fear of a slave; it is hell and not God that you fear. Your religion consists only of superstitions and petty, superficial practices. You are like the Jews of whom God said: *while they honor me with their lips, their heart is far from me.*[1] You are scrupulous about bagatelles and hardened to terrible wrongs. You love only your glory and your comforts. You view everything in terms of yourself, as though you were God on earth and all others had been created merely to be sacrificed to you. On the contrary, it is you whom God has placed on earth solely for your people. But alas! You understand nothing of these truths. How could you appreciate them? You do not know God; you do not love Him; you do not pray to Him from the heart, and you do nothing to comprehend Him.

You have an archbishop[2] who is corrupt, scandalous, incorrigible, base, wicked, cunning, an enemy of all virtue, and who causes all upright men to grieve. You have accommodated yourself to him because he seeks only to please you with his flattery. For more than twenty years he has enjoyed your confidence while prostituting his honor. You give over upright men to him; you allow him to tyrannize over the Church, and no virtuous prelate is treated as well as he.

As for your confessor,[3] he is not vicious, but he fears solid virtue and cares only for irreverent and loose persons. And he is jealous of his authority which you have raised beyond all bounds. Never before have royal confessors alone made bishops and decided all matters of conscience. You alone in France, Sire, are unaware that he knows nothing, that his mind is limited and vulgar, and that he continually indulges in strategems with grossness of spirit. Even the Jesuits are contemptuous of him, and are indignant to see him so readily reward the ridiculous ambitions of his family. You have made a minister of state of a monk. He is not a good judge of men nor of anything else. He is the dupe of all who flatter him and give him petty gifts. He has no doubts or hesitations concerning any difficult question. An upright and learned man would not dare to decide them alone. But as for him, he only fears having to deliberate with men who know the rules. He proceeds boldly without fearing to lead you astray, and will always incline toward laxity and keeping

---

[1] Forasmuch as this people draw near me with their mouth, and with their lips do honor me, but have removed their heart from me, and their fear toward me is taught by the precept of men" (Isaiah 29:13).

[2] Harlay de Champvallon, Archbishop of Paris, who died in 1695.

[3] Le Père de La Chaise.

you in ignorance. That is to say, he will tend toward decisions in conformity with the rules only when he fears to scandalize you. Thus, it is one blind man leading another, and as Jesus Christ said, *they shall both fall into the ditch.*[4]

Your archbishop and your confessor have caused you difficulties in the affair of the *régale* and your unfortunate relations with Rome. They allowed you to permit the fraud of M. de Louvois against the Order of Saint-Lazare, and would have let you die in this injustice if M. de Louvois had lived longer than you.

It was hoped, Sire, that your council would keep you from going so far astray, but your council has neither the strength nor the vigor to do good. At least Mme. de M . . . and M. le D. de B . . .[5] should avail themselves of your confidence in them in order to undeceive you, but their weakness and timidity dishonor them and disgust everyone. France is in desperate straits; what do they await to speak frankly to you? That all should be lost? Do they fear to displease you? They must not love you, for one must be willing to offend those whom one loves, in preference to flattering them or betraying them with silence. What is their worth, if they do not show you that you should make restitution of the lands which are not yours, prefer the lives of your people to a false glory, redress the wrongs that you have done to the Church, and seek to become a true Christian before you are surprised by death? I know well that to speak with such Christian liberty is to risk the loss of royal favor; but is your favor dearer to them than your salvation? I also know well that one should pity you, console you, comfort you, and speak to you with zeal, kindness, and respect; but after all one must speak the truth. Woe, woe to those who do not speak it, and woe to you if you are not worthy of hearing it! It is scandalous that they have fruitlessly held your confidence for so long. They should withdraw if you are too sensitive and wish only flatterers around you. Perhaps you ask, Sire, what they should say to you. Here it is. They should point out to you that you must humble yourself under the powerful hand of God if you do not wish that He humble you, that you should seek peace and expiate through this humiliation all the glory which you have made your idol, that you should reject the unjust counsels of flattering politicians, and that

---

[4] "If the blind lead the blind, both shall fall into the ditch" (Matthew 15:14).
[5] Madame de Maintenon and M. le Duc de Beauvilliers.

finally, for the sake of the state, you must immediately return to your enemies the conquests which you may not retain without injustice. Are you so happy in your misfortune that God must terminate the successes which have blinded you, and compel you to make the restitutions which are necessary to your salvation, and which you could never bring yourself to make in a state of undisturbed triumph?

The person who tells you these truths, Sire, far from being opposed to your interests, would give his life to see you as God wishes you, and does not cease to pray for you.

Duc de Saint-Simon

DESCRIPTION OF LOUIS XIV

Louis de Rouvroi, Duc de Saint-Simon (1675–1755), was an influential court noble during the latter part of Louis XIV's reign and the subsequent regency. Although he held no important political office prior to the death of Louis XIV, he was thoroughly familiar with the affairs of the royal court and exercised considerable influence through intrigue. Saint-Simon was extremely prejudiced in favor of his social caste, and despised all who stood beneath him socially, especially the powerful royal ministers of bourgeois origin. A very prolific writer, he is chiefly known as the author of his very extensive Memoirs *which were written both during and after the reign of Louis XIV, and embody much contemporary material. The judgments of individuals in Saint-Simon's writings typically combine much court gossip with very penetrating insights into the leading personalities of the period. His description of Louis XIV sets forth the views of a disgruntled but astute observer at the court during the troubled second generation of the reign.*

I shall pass over the stormy period of Louis XIV's minority. At twenty-three years of age he entered the great world as king, under the most favorable auspices. His ministers were the most skillful in all Europe; his generals the best; his court was filled with illustrious and clever

From *The Memoirs of the Duke of Saint-Simon on the Reign of Louis XIV and the Regency*, translated from the French by Bayle St. John (London, 1888), vol. 2, chapter 35.

men, formed during the troubles which had followed the death of
Louis XIII.

Louis XIV was made for a brilliant court. In the midst of other men,
his figure, his courage, his grace, his beauty, his grand mien, even
the tone of his voice and the majestic and natural charm of all his
person distinguished him till his death as the King Bee, and showed
that if he had only been born a simple private gentleman, he would
equally have excelled in fêtes, pleasures, and gallantry, and would
have had the greatest success in love. The intrigues and adventures
which early in life he had been engaged in – when the Comtesse de
Soissons lodged at the Tuileries, as superintendent of the queen's
household, and was the center figure of the court group – had exercised an unfortunate influence upon him: he received those impressions with which he could never after successfully struggle. From
this time, intellect, education, nobility of sentiment, and high principle,
in others, became objects of suspicion to him, and soon of hatred.
The more he advanced in years the more this sentiment was confirmed in him. He wished to reign by himself. His jealousy on this
point unceasingly became weakness. He reigned, indeed, in little
things; the great he could never reach: even in the former, too, he
was often governed. The superior ability of his early ministers and
his early generals soon wearied him. He liked nobody to be in any
way superior to him. Thus he chose his ministers, not for their knowledge, but for their ignorance; not for their capacity, but for their
want of it. He liked to form them, as he said; liked to teach them even
the most trifling things. It was the same with his generals. He took
credit to himself for instructing them; wished it to be thought that
from his cabinet he commanded and directed all his armies. Naturally
fond of trifles, he unceasingly occupied himself with the most petty
details of his troops, his household, his mansions; would even instruct
his cooks, who received, like novices, lessons they had known by
heart for years. This vanity, this unmeasured and unreasonable love
of admiration, was his ruin. His ministers, his generals, his mistresses,
his courtiers, soon perceived his weakness. They praised him with
emulation and spoiled him. Praises, or to say truth, flattery, pleased
him to such an extent, that the coarsest was well received, the vilest
even better relished. It was the sole means by which you could approach him. Those whom he liked owed his affection for them, to

their untiring flatteries. This is what gave his ministers so much authority, and the opportunities they had for adulating him, of attributing everything to him, and of pretending to learn everything from him. Suppleness, meanness, an admiring, dependent, cringing manner – above all, an air of nothingness – were the sole means of pleasing him.

This poison spread. It spread, too, to an incredible extent, in a prince who, although of intellect beneath mediocrity, was not utterly without sense, and who had had some experience. Without voice or musical knowledge, he used to sing, in private, the passages of the opera prologues that were fullest of his praises! He was drowned in vanity; and so deeply, that at his public suppers – all the court present, musicians also – he would hum these self-same praises between his teeth, when the music they were set to was played!

And yet, it must be admitted, he might have done better. Though his intellect, as I have said, was beneath mediocrity, it was capable of being formed. He loved glory, was fond of order and regularity; was by disposition prudent, moderate, discreet, master of his movements and his tongue. Will it be believed? He was also by disposition good and just! God had sufficiently gifted him to enable him to be a good king; perhaps even a *tolerably great king!* All the evil came to him from elsewhere. His early education was so neglected that nobody dared approach his apartment. He has often been heard to speak of those times with bitterness, and even to relate that, one evening he was found in the basin of the Palais Royale garden fountain, into which he had fallen! He was scarcely taught how to read or write, and remained so ignorant, that the most familiar historical and other facts were utterly unknown to him! He fell, accordingly, and sometimes even in public, into the grossest absurdities.

It was his vanity, his desire for glory, that led him, soon after the death of the King of Spain, to make that event the pretext for war; in spite of the renunciations so recently made, so carefully stipulated, in the marriage contract. He marched into Flanders; his conquests there were rapid; the passage of the Rhine was admirable; the triple alliance of England, Sweden, and Holland only animated him. In the midst of winter he took Franche-Comté, by restoring which at the Peace of Aix-la-Chapelle, he preserved his conquests in Flanders. All was flourishing then in the state. Riches everywhere. Colbert had

Nanteuil, *Portrait of Louis XIV,* 1663. This perceptive portrait shows the king as he was during the first years of his personal reign: proud, arrogant, and fully aware of his power. (*Courtesy of the Fogg Art Museum, Harvard University. Gift of Mrs. William Simes*)

placed the finances, the navy, commerce, manufactures, letters even, upon the highest point; and his age, like that of Augustus, produced in abundance illustrious men of all kinds — even those illustrious only in pleasures.

Le Tellier and Louvois, his son, who had the war department, trembled at the success and at the credit of Colbert, and had no difficulty in putting into the head of the king a new war, the success of which caused such fear to all Europe that France never recovered from it, and after having been upon the point of succumbing to this war, for a long time felt the weight and misfortune of it. Such was the real cause of that famous Dutch War, to which the king allowed himself to be pushed, and which his love for Madame de Montespan rendered so unfortunate for his glory and for his kingdom. Everything being conquered, everything taken, and Amsterdam ready to give up her keys, the king yields to his impatience, quits the army, flies to Versailles, and destroys in an instant all the success of arms! He repaired this disgrace by a second conquest, in person, of Franche-Comté, which this time was preserved by France.

In 1676, the king having returned into Flanders, took Condé; whilst Monsieur[1] took Bouchain. The armies of the king and of the Prince of Orange approached each other so suddenly and so closely, that they found themselves front to front near Heurtebise. According even to the admission of the enemy, our forces were so superior to those of the Prince of Orange, that we must have gained the victory if we had attacked. But the king, after listening to the opinions of his generals, some for, and some against giving battle, decided for the latter, turned tail, and the engagement was talked of no more. The army was much discontented. Everybody wished for battle. The fault therefore of the king made much impression upon the troops, and excited cruel railleries against us at home and in the foreign courts. The king stopped but little longer afterwards in the army, although we were only in the month of May. He returned to his mistress.

The following year he returned to Flanders and took Cambrai; and Monsieur besieged Saint Omer. Monsieur got the start of the

---

[1] The younger brother of the king was habitually referred to as "Monsieur." During the reign of Louis XIV, this title was held by Philippe, duc d'Orléans.—Ed.

Prince of Orange, who was about to assist the place, gave him battle near Corsel, obtained a complete victory, immediately took Saint Omer, and then joined the king. This contrast so affected the monarch that never afterwards did he give Monsieur command of an army! External appearances were perfectly kept up, but from that moment the resolution was taken and always well sustained.

The year afterwards the king led in person the siege of Ghent. The peace of Nimwegen ended this year the war with Holland, Spain, etc.; and on the commencement of the following year, that with the Emperor and the Empire. America, Africa, the Archipelago, Sicily, acutely felt the power of France, and in 1684 Luxembourg was the price of the delay of the Spaniards in fulfilling all the conditions of the peace. Genoa, bombarded, was forced to come in the persons of its doge and four of its senators, to sue for peace at the commencement of the following year. From this date, until 1688, the time passed in the cabinet less in fêtes than in devotion and constraint. Here finishes the apogee of this reign, and the fullness of glory and prosperity. The great captains, the great ministers, were no more, but their pupils remained. The second epoch of the reign was very different from the first; but the third was even more sadly dissimilar.

I have related the adventure which led to the wars of this period; how an ill-made window frame was noticed at the Trianon, then building; how Louvois was blamed for it; his alarm lest his disgrace should follow; his determination to engage the king in a war which should turn him from his building fancies. He carried out his resolve: with what result I have already shown. France was ruined at home; and abroad, despite the success of her arms, gained nothing. On the contrary, the withdrawal of the king from Gembloux, when he might have utterly defeated the Prince of Orange, did us infinite harm, as I have shown in its place. The peace which followed this war was disgraceful. The king was obliged to acknowledge the Prince of Orange as King of England, after having so long shown hatred and contempt for him. Our precipitation, too, cost us Luxembourg; and the ignorance of our plenipotentiaries gave our enemies great advantages in forming their frontier. Such was the Peace of Ryswick, concluded in September, 1697.

This peace seemed as though it would allow France some breathing time. The king was sixty years of age, and had, in his own opinion, acquired all sorts of glory. But scarcely were we at peace, without having had time to taste it, than the pride of the king made him wish to astonish all Europe by the display of power that it believed prostrated. And truly he did astonish Europe. But at what a cost! The famous camp of Compiègne – for 'tis to that I allude – was one of the most magnificent spectacles ever seen; but its immense and misplaced prodigality was soon regretted. Twenty years afterwards, some of the regiments who took part in it were still in difficulties from this cause.

Shortly afterwards, by one of the most surprising and unheard-of pieces of good fortune, the crown of Spain fell into the hands of the Duc d'Anjou, grandson of the king. It seemed as though golden days had come back again to France. Only for a little time, however, did it seem so. Nearly all Europe, as it has been seen, banded against France, to dispute the Spanish crown. The king had lost all his good ministers, all his able generals, and had taken good pains they should leave no successors. When war came, then, we were utterly unable to prosecute it with success or honor. We were driven out of Germany, of Italy, of the Low Countries. We could not sustain the war, or resolve to make peace. Every day led us nearer and nearer the brink of the precipice, the terrible depths of which were forever staring us in the face. A misunderstanding amongst our enemies, whereby England became detached from the grand alliance; the undue contempt of Prince Eugène for our generals, out of which arose the battle of Denain; saved us from the gulf. Peace came, and a peace, too, infinitely better than that we should have ardently embraced if our enemies had agreed amongst themselves beforehand. Nevertheless, this peace cost dear to France, and cost Spain half its territory – Spain, of which the king had said not even a windmill would he yield! But this was another piece of folly he soon repented of.

Thus, we see this monarch grand, rich, conquering, the arbiter of Europe; feared and admired as long as the ministers and captains existed who really deserved the name. When they were no more, the machine kept moving some time by impulsion, and from their influence. But soon afterwards we saw beneath the surface; faults and errors were multiplied, and decay came on with giant strides; without, however, opening the eyes of that despotic master, so anxious to do everything and direct everything himself, and who seemed to indemnify himself for disdain abroad by increasing fear and trembling at home.

So much for the reign of this vainglorious monarch.

Let me touch now upon some other incidents in his career, and upon some points in his character.

He early showed a disinclination for Paris. The troubles that had taken place there during the minority made him regard the place as dangerous; he wished, too, to render himself venerable by hiding himself from the eyes of the multitude: all these considerations fixed him at St. Germain soon after the death of the queen, his mother. It was to that place he began to attract the world by fêtes and gallantries, and by making it felt that he wished to be often seen.

His love for Madame de la Vallière, which was at first kept secret, occasioned frequent excursions to Versailles, then a little card castle, which had been built by Louis XIII – annoyed, and his suite still more so, at being frequently obliged to sleep in a wretched inn there, after he had been out hunting in the forest of Saint Leger. That monarch rarely slept at Versailles more than one night, and then from necessity; the king, his son, slept there, so that he might be more in private with his mistress; pleasures unknown to the hero and just man, worthy son of Saint Louis, who built the little chateau.

These excursions of Louis XIV by degrees gave birth to those immense buildings he erected at Versailles; and their convenience for a numerous court, so different from the apartments at St. Germain, led him to take up his abode there entirely shortly after the death of the queen. He built an infinite number of apartments, which were asked for by those who wished to pay their court to him; whereas at St. Germain nearly everybody was obliged to lodge in the town, and the few who found accommodation at the chateau were strangely inconvenienced.

The frequent fêtes, the private promenades at Versailles, the journeys, were means on which the king seized in order to distinguish or mortify the courtiers, and thus render them more assiduous in pleasing him. He felt that of real favors he had not enough to bestow; in order to keep up the spirit of devotion, he therefore unceasingly invented all sorts of ideal ones, little preferences and petty distinctions, which answered his purpose as well.

He was exceedingly jealous of the attention paid him. Not only did he notice the presence of the most distinguished courtiers, but those of inferior degree also. He looked to the right and to the left, not only upon rising but upon going to bed, at his meals, in passing through his apartments, or his gardens of Versailles, where alone the courtiers were allowed to follow him; he saw and noticed everybody; not one escaped him, not even those who hoped to remain unnoticed. He marked well all absentees from the court, found out the reason of their absence, and never lost an opportunity of acting towards them as the occasion might seem to justify. With some of the courtiers (the most distinguished), it was a demerit not to make the court their ordinary abode; with others 'twas a fault to come but rarely; for those who never or scarcely ever came it was certain disgrace. When their names were in any way mentioned, "I do not know them," the king would reply haughtily. Those who presented themselves but seldom were thus characterized: "They are people I never see"; these decrees were irrevocable. He could not bear people who liked Paris.

Louis XIV took great pains to be well informed of all that passed everywhere; in the public places, in the private houses, in society and familiar intercourse. His spies and telltales were infinite. He had them of all species; many who were ignorant that their information reached him; others who knew it; others who wrote to him direct, sending their letters through channels he indicated; and all these letters were seen by him alone, and always before everything else; others who sometimes spoke to him secretly in his cabinet, entering by the back stairs. These unknown means ruined an infinite number of people of all classes, who never could discover the cause; often ruined them very unjustly; for the king, once prejudiced, never altered his opinion, or so rarely, that nothing was more rare. He had, too, another fault, very dangerous for others and often for himself, since it deprived him of good subjects. He had an excellent memory; in this way, that if he saw a man who, twenty years before, perhaps, had in some manner offended him, he did not forget the man, though he might forget the offense. This was enough, however, to exclude the person from all favor. The representations of a minister, of a general, of his confessor even, could not move the king. He would not yield.

The most cruel means by which the king was informed of what was passing – for many years before anybody knew it – was that of opening letters. The promptitude and dexterity with which they were opened passes understanding. He saw extracts from all the letters in which there were passages that the chiefs of the post office, and then the minister who governed it, thought ought to go before him; entire letters, too, were sent to him, when their contents seemed to justify the sending. Thus the chiefs of the post, nay, the principal clerks were in a position to suppose what they pleased and against whom they pleased. A word of contempt against the king or the government, a joke, a detached phrase, was enough. It is incredible how many people, justly or unjustly, were more or less ruined, always without resource, without trial, and without knowing why. The secret was impenetrable; for nothing ever cost the king less than profound silence and dissimulation.

This last talent he pushed almost to falsehood, but never to deceit, pluming himself upon keeping his word – therefore he scarcely ever gave it. The secrets of others he kept as religiously as his own. He was even flattered by certain confessions and certain confidences; and there was no mistress, minister, or favorite, who could have wormed them out, even though the secret regarded themselves.

We know, amongst many others, the famous story of a woman of quality, who, after having been separated a year from her husband, found herself in the family way just as he was on the point of returning from the army, and who, not knowing what else to do, in the most urgent manner begged a private interview of the king. She obtained it, and confided to him her position, as to the worthiest man in his realm, as she said. The king counseled her to profit by her distress, and live more wisely for the future, and immediately promised to retain her husband on the frontier as long as was necessary, and to forbid his return under any pretext, and in fact he gave orders the same day to Louvois, and prohibited the husband not only all leave of absence, but forbade him to quit for a single day the post he was to command all the winter. The officer who was distinguished, and who had neither wished nor asked to be employed all the winter upon the frontier, and Louvois, who had in no way thought of it, were equally surprised and vexed. They were obliged, however, to obey to the letter, and without asking why; and the king never mentioned the circumstances until many years afterwards, when he was quite sure nobody could find out either husband or wife, as in fact they never could, or even obtain the most vague or the most uncertain suspicion.

II THE REPUTATION OF LOUIS XIV DURING THE ENLIGHTENMENT

Montesquieu
LOUIS XIV AND IRRATIONAL MONARCHY

Charles de Secondat, Baron de la Brède et de Montesquieu (1689–1755), the celebrated publicist of the Enlightenment, was the author of many famous and influential works. Among these, the Lettres persanes *(1721) was his first masterpiece and established his literary reputation early in his career. Through the transparent device of fictitious letters which a visiting Persian dignitary wrote for the edification of his compatriots, the work satirized French customs and institutions of the period, even the monarchy of Louis XIV. The following selection purports to ridicule Louis' absolutism from the point of view of an "enlightened" Oriental mind.*

Letter XXIV

We have now been a month at Paris, and all the time constantly moving about. There is much to do before one can get settled, find out the people with whom one has business, and procure the many requisites which are all wanted at the same time. . . .

You must not yet expect from me an exhaustive account of the manners and customs of the Europeans: I have myself but a faint notion of them yet, and have hardly had time to recover from my astonishment.

The King of France[1] is the most powerful of European potentates. He has no mines of gold like his neighbor, the King of Spain; but he is much wealthier than that prince, because his riches are drawn from a more inexhaustible source, the vanity of his subjects. He has undertaken and carried on great wars, without any other supplies than those derived from the sale of titles of honor; and it is by a prodigy of human pride that his troops are paid, his towns fortified and his fleets equipped.

Then again, the king is a great magician, for his dominion extends to the minds of his subjects; he makes them think what he wishes. If he has only a million crowns in his exchequer, and has need of two millions, he has only to persuade them that one crown is worth two,

From Montesquieu, *Persian Letters,* translated by John Davidson (London, 1891).
[1] Louis XIV.

and they believe it.[2] If he has a costly war on hand, and is short of money, he simply suggests to his subjects that a piece of paper is coin of the realm, and they are straightway convinced of it. He has even succeeded in persuading them that his touch is a sovereign cure for all sorts of diseases, so great is the power and influence he has over their minds.

What I have told you of this prince need not astonish you: there is another magician more powerful still, who is master of the king's mind, as absolutely as the king is master of the minds of his subjects. This magician is called the Pope. Sometimes he makes the king believe that three are no more than one; that the bread which he eats is not bread; the wine which he drinks is not wine; and a thousand things of a like nature.

And, to keep him in practice, and prevent him from losing the habit of belief, he gives him, now and again, as an exercise, certain articles of faith. Some two years ago he sent him a large document which he called *Constitution,*[3] and wished to enforce belief in all that it contained upon this prince and his subjects under heavy penalties. He succeeded in the case of the king,[4] who set the example of immediate submission; but some of his subjects revolted, and declared that they would not believe a single word of what was contained in this document. The women are the prime movers in this rebellion, which divides the court, the kingdom, and every family in the land, because the document prohibits them from reading a book which all the Christians assert is of divine origin: it is, indeed, their Koran. The women, enraged at this affront to their sex, exert all their power against the *Constitution;* and they have brought over to their side all the men who are not anxious about their privilege in the matter. And truly, the Mufti does not reason amiss. By the great Hali! he must have been instructed in the principles of our holy religion, because, since women are inferior creatures compared to us, and may not,

[2] The French kings regarded money as a mere symbol, the value of which they could raise or lower at their pleasure. "Kings treat men as they do pieces of money; they give them what value they choose, and people are forced to accept them according to their currency, and not according to their true worth." – La Rochefoucauld.
[3] An anachronism. The date of this letter is 1712, but the Bull *Unigenitus,* which, under the name of the "Constitution," troubled France during the greater part of the eighteenth century, was not issued until 1713.
[4] Louis XIV submitted the more readily because he required the Pope's aid to terminate the theological quarrels which had become insufferable to him.

according to our prophets, enter into Paradise, why should they meddle with a book which is only designed to teach the way thither?

Some things of a miraculous nature have been told me of the king, which I am certain will appear to you hardly credible.

It is said, that, while he was making war against such of his neighbors as had leagued against him, there were in his kingdom an infinite number of invisible foes surrounding him on all sides.[5] They add, that, during a thirty years' search, in spite of the indefatigable exertions of certain dervishes who are in his confidence,[6] not one of these has ever been discovered. They live with him, in his court and in his capital, among his troops, among his legislators; and yet it is believed that he will have the mortification of dying without having discovered them. They exist, as it were, in general, but not in particular: they constitute a body without members. Beyond a doubt, heaven wishes to punish this prince for his severity to the vanquished, in afflicting him with invisible enemies of a spirit and a destiny superior to his own.

I will continue to write you, and acquaint you with matters differing widely from the Persian character and genius. We tread, indeed, the same earth; but it seems incredible, remembering in the presence of the men of this country those of the country in which you are.

Paris, the 4th of the second moon of Rebiab, 1712.

Letter XXVII

The King of France is old.[7] We have no examples in our histories of such a long reign as his. It is said that he possesses in a very high degree the faculty of making himself obeyed: he governs with equal ability his family, his court, and his kingdom: he has often been heard to say, that, of all existing governments, that of the Turks, or that of our august Sultan, pleased him best: such is his high opinion of Oriental statecraft.[8]

---

[5] The Jansenists.
[6] The Jesuits.
[7] Louis XIV was then seventy-five years old, and had reigned for seventy.
[8] When Louis XIV was in his sixteenth year, some courtiers discussed in his presence the absolute power of the Sultans, who dispose as they like of the goods and the lives of their subjects. "That is something like being a king," said the young monarch. Marshall d'Estrées, alarmed at the tendency revealed in that remark, rejoined. "But, Sire, several of these Emperors have been strangled even in my time."

I have studied his character, and I have found certain contradictions which I cannot reconcile. For example, he has a minister who is only eighteen years old,[9] and a mistress who is fourscore;[10] he loves his religion, and yet he cannot abide those who assert that it ought to be strictly observed;[11] although he flies from the noises of cities, and is inclined to be reticent, from morning till night he is engaged in getting himself talked about; he is fond of trophies and victories, but he has as great a dread of seeing a good general at the head of his own troops, as at the head of an army of his enemies. It has never I believe happened to any one but himself, to be burdened with more wealth than even a prince could hope for, and yet at the same time steeped in such poverty as a private person could ill brook.

He delights to reward those who serve him; but he pays as liberally the assiduous indolence of his courtiers, as the labors in the field of his captains; often the man who undresses him, or who hands him his serviette at table, is preferred before him who has taken cities and gained battles; he does not believe that the greatness of a monarch is compatible with restriction in the distribution of favors; and, without examining into the merits of a man, he will heap benefits upon him, believing that his selection makes the recipient worthy; accordingly, he has been known to bestow a small pension upon a man who had run off two leagues from the enemy, and a good government on another who had gone four.

Above all, he is magnificent in his buildings; there are more statues in his palace gardens[12] than there are citizens in a large town. His bodyguard is as strong as that of the prince before whom all the thrones of the earth tremble;[13] his armies are as numerous, his resources as great, and his finances as inexhaustible.

Paris, the 7th of the moon of Maharram, 1713.

---

[9] Barbezieux, son of Louvois, Louis' youngest minister, held office at twenty-three, not eighteen; and he was dead in 1713.
[10] Madame de Maintenon.
[11] The Jansenists.
[12] At Versailles.
[13] The Shah of Persia.

Abbé de Saint-Pierre

CONTRAST BETWEEN HENRY IV AND LOUIS XIV

Charles-Irénée Castel, Abbé de Saint-Pierre (1658–1743), was an important publicist and philosopher of the early Enlightenment. Although he was inferior to the ablest writers of the age, his works evinced a certain originality and idealism, while his most famous book, the Projet de paix perpétuelle, *won a considerable following. In his* Discours sur la Polysynodie, *he implicitly criticized Louis XIV by allowing him the titles of* Le Puissant *and* Le Redoutable, *but not* Le Grand. *This judgment seemed unduly severe in the eyes of certain of his contemporaries, with the result that he was expelled from the French Academy in 1718. In the selection printed here, he reiterates his view of Louis XIV, by comparing him with his illustrious grandfather.*

I recently reread the history of Henry IV by Péréfixe and that of his grandson, Louis XIV, by de Limiers, as well as various historical eulogies by authors who would give the former the name "Great" among the Henrys and the latter the same appellation among our kings who have held the name of Louis. After this reading, it seemed to me useful, either to future kings, their subjects or their neighbors, to consider which of these two rulers had more talent and virtue, which better merited the title of "Great," and which consequently was more deserving of happiness in this life and that to come.

Principles of Decision

When one wishes to compare the merits of two sovereigns, it is not a question of comparing their worth as individuals but merely their merits as rulers and the qualities of their government. I here compare only the latter.

It is not even a question of comparing the greatness of their power. It is rightly only a question of comparing the good or bad use which they made of that power, and consequently of determining through their undertakings and actions the degree to which they were just and beneficient toward their subjects and neighbors, and the extent and

From Charles-Irénée Castel, Abbé de Saint-Pierre, *Annales politiques* (London, 1758) vol. 2, pp. 863–876 (the conclusion of the work). Editor's translation.

greatness of the talents of both for rendering their rule increasingly successful.

Nero was a sovereign fifteen times more powerful than Henry IV. However, Nero, far from being as great and worthy as Henry, was merely a great fool and a despicable scoundrel whom Providence had placed in high office to punish the ungrateful; whereas Henry IV with much less power was a king most worthy, desirable and great, destined by Providence to procure vast benefits for his subjects and other nations.

It is true that Louis XIV was somewhat more powerful than his grandfather. But if Henry IV made much better use of his power, if he was superior in observing justice and practicing benevolence toward his subjects and neighbors, and if his talent for successful government was effectively much greater, he should be regarded as a worthier, more desirable, and a far greater king than Louis XIV.

For after all, men are great only to the degree that they are worthy, and they are worthy and desirable as sovereigns only to the extent that they are capable of utilizing their power to render others less miserable by the observation of justice, and happier by the benefits which they procure for them.

Now let us first examine which of the two kings was the more just toward his subjects and neighbors, second, which was the more beneficent toward them, and third, which had the greater talent and superior breadth of views for successful government of his subjects and other nations.

Justice

Nothing is more just than that the subjects should pay to the king the taxes that are necessary for the maintenance and support of soldiers, sailors, and officers of war on land and sea who protect the state from foreign invasion and restrain the seditious within. It is likewise just that they pay the taxes that are needed for the splendor and support of the king's household, his ministers, the officers of his councils, and the magistrates who render justice to individuals and the public by protecting them from the untoward effects of force and violence through the policing of cities and roads. A beneficent king ought even to erect public buildings when these will bring the people a greater annual profit than that which they receive from personal expenditures, for example, the gain which the subjects derive from ports, roads, canals, bridges, and aid for establishing trading companies and convoying vessels.

Subjects owe the king only *just* taxes, that is, those of value in augmenting their happiness. For to demand taxes that will be used for overly magnificent or useless buildings, or excesses of pure diversion for persons who contribute nothing to the happiness of other subjects, is not to treat the latter justly but to do them injustice.

The king may easily determine whether he is doing injustice to his subjects by such taxes. He has only to ask himself whether he would find the same taxes useful to himself, and whether he would take pleasure in paying them, if he were a tax-paying subject.

For after all, is it not just, according to the rule of natural equity, *that he treat his subjects no worse than he would wish to be treated by a king if he were his subject? Do not do to another that which you would not wish done to you;* is not this law contained in the former, which is a law of nature as well as Revelation? *Therefore all things whatsoever ye would that men should do to you, do ye even so to them* (Matthew 7:12).

First Injustice

Now we know that at the death of Henry IV, the annual taxes of the realm were not a sixth part of those which were taken at the death of Louis XIV, and that Henry IV did not spend on magnificent buildings a sixth of what was spent by Louis.

Second Injustice

The Revocation of the Edict of Nantes was a great mistake, and at the same time an evident injustice quite contrary to the gentle and beneficent character of Henry IV.

It was a mistake in that it is necessary to allow popular maladies of the mind sufficient time to cure themselves little by little, never worsening anything by impatience, violence or persecution.

Because of too great an eagerness for uniformity of opinion, Louis XIV suffered a great loss and strengthened his enemies with twelve or fifteen thousand of his subjects of whom he deprived himself. For the most part these were rich merchants, good officers, sailors, soldiers, and writers who were induced by this persecution to blacken his name throughout Europe.

The injustice was in that his erring subjects were strongly suppressed and punished as rebels, and in that the king did openly against them what he would not have wanted a prejudiced king to do to him under similar circumstances.

Third Injustice

It is an injustice to individuals and the general welfare not to give public offices and employments to subjects who have the greatest patriotic interests in the people. Now both rulers were unjust in establishing and maintaining the system of venality of office, but Henry IV for his part did this only half as much as Louis XIV, who increased venality by more than half, and rendered offices half again more difficult to repurchase because of his augmentation of wages.

Fourth Injustice

Kings owe justice to their neighbors as their neighbors owe it to them. None of Henry IV's neighboring rulers found it necessary to reproach him for any injustice or broken promise, and he never would have undertaken the aggressive war of 1667 against the Spanish contrary to his promise and renunciation of territory, nor the further aggressive war of 1672 against the Dutch who offered reparation for their offending statements. It was these first two wars, so clearly unjust and imprudent, which caused the two recent wars that were so ruinous to Louis and his subjects. His neighbors never would have wished nor dared unite to ruin a powerful, just and neighborly king had they not felt the hatred that he brought upon himself by his first two injustices.

If one compares the criticisms voiced by the neighbors of Louis XIV with those of the neighbors of Henry IV, one will find ten times more against Louis than against his grandfather.

Beneficence

It is true that Louis XIV procured many more benefits for his subjects by his good codes and institutions than did Henry IV, but this was during a reign three times longer than that of Henry. On the other hand, the benefits and conquests of Louis did not compensate the realm for half the additional taxes which were necessary to repay the enormous loans and the greatly augmented wages that he instituted. From the standpoint of beneficence toward his subjects, Louis was in effect less benevolent than Henry who left taxation of his subjects incomparably less burdensome than it was at the death of Louis.

Talent for Good Government

It is apparent that of two kings, he who is worthiest and most to be desired as ruler is he whose talents and policies of government are pre-eminently more effective and appropriate in diminishing the troubles of his subjects, increasing their riches and other benefits, and procuring the good of other sovereigns without diminishing his own.

Whoever will examine the marvelous project of a European congress and the Europe-wide arbitration which the great genius of Henry IV conceived and proposed, and the ease of making such a treaty because of the evident and infinite advantages to all the contracting princes, will readily see that Louis XIV never conceived of anything so advantageous either to his subjects or his neighbors. From this standpoint, Louis had much less genius and talent than Henry IV, not only for successfully governing a great state and assuring it to his posterity but also for living peacefully with his neighbors. Consequently, the grandson had much less ability and was much less desirable to his subjects and his neighbors than was the grandfather.

By means of this permanent arbitration, as Péréfixe, the historian of Henry IV, relates, all the states of Europe would have been spared the horrors of civil and foreign wars; sovereigns and their posterity would always have enjoyed full security in their possessions without any disquiet, and the commerce of Europeans never would have been interrupted or troubled between trading nations. Besides, how greatly would not the laws for increasing happiness within states acquire perfection during such unfailing tranquility?

From these considerations, it follows that no matter how great a king Louis XIV may have been, it would not do him an injustice, but would merely render justice to Henry IV, the grandfather, to regard his as a still greater king than his grandson because Henry was more just and beneficent toward both his subjects and his neighbors, and because he had much greater enlightenment and talent for procuring the happiness of his subjects and other nations of the earth. Let no one ask me which ruler appears to have better merited eternal rewards in the after-life; I can give no answer but that it is he who better observed the precepts of the law and the prophets.

Voltaire
THE AGE OF LOUIS XIV

François Marie Arouet, better known as Voltaire (1694–1778), was not only the most celebrated philosopher of the Enlightenment but also one of the greatest historians of his century. His extensive research and writing in the broader phases of cultural history caused him to become one of the pioneers of historical scholarship. Among his various historical studies, his Siècle de Louis XIV, *first published in Berlin in 1751, is considered to be his masterpiece. Regarding the problems of his own age, he was both critic and idealist, and firmly believed that enlightened despotism offered the most effective means of achieving human betterment. It was from this standpoint that Voltaire wrote the following laudatory analysis of the rule of Louis XIV.*

Every age has produced its heroes and statesmen; every nation has experienced revolutions; every history is the same to one who wishes merely to remember facts. But the thinking man, and what is still rarer, the man of taste, numbers only four ages in the history of the world; four happy ages when the arts were brought to perfection and which, marking an era of the greatness of the human mind, are an example to posterity.

The first of these ages, to which true glory belongs, is that of Philip and Alexander, or rather of Pericles, Demosthenes, Aristotle, Plato, . . .

From *The Age of Louis XIV* by Voltaire, translated by Martyn P. Pollack. Everyman's Library Edition. Published by E. P. Dutton & Co., Inc., and used with their permission.

The second age is that of Caesar and Augustus, distinguished moreover by the names of Lucretius, Cicero, Livy, Virgil, Horace, Ovid, Varro and Vitruvius.

The third is that which followed the taking of Constantinople by Mohamet II. The reader may remember that the spectacle was then witnessed of a family of mere citizens in Italy accomplishing what should have been undertaken by the kings of Europe. The scholars whom the Turks had driven from Greece were summoned by the Medici to Florence; it was the hour of Italy's glory. The fine arts had already taken on new life there; and the Italians honored them with the name of virtue as the early Greeks had characterized them with the name of wisdom. Everything conduced to perfection. . . .

The fourth age is that which we call the age of Louis XIV; and it is perhaps of the four the one which most nearly approaches perfection. Enriched with the discoveries of the other three, it accomplished in certain departments more than the three together. All the arts, it is true, did not progress further than they did under the Medici, under Augustus or under Alexander; but human reason in general was brought to perfection.

Rational philosophy only came to light in this period; and it is true to say that from the last years of Cardinal Richelieu to those which followed the death of Louis XIV, a general revolution took place in our arts, minds and customs, as in our government, which will serve as an eternal token of the true glory of our country. This beneficent influence was not merely confined to France; it passed over into England, and inspired a profitable rivalry in that intellectual and fearless nation; it imported good taste into Germany, and the sciences into Russia; it even revived Italy, who had begun to languish, and Europe has owed both her manners and the social spirit to the court of Louis XIV. . . .

*   *   *

Never were there so many intrigues and expectations in any court as while Cardinal Mazarin lay dying. Women with any pretense of beauty flattered themselves that they would rule a prince of twenty-two, whom love had already so far beguiled as to make him offer his crown to his mistress. Youthful courtiers saw visions of a new reign of favorites. Each minister hoped for the premier place. Not one of them thought that a king brought up in seclusion from affairs of state would dare to take the burden of government upon his own shoulders. Mazarin had prolonged the monarch's childhood so long as he could. It was only quite lately that he had instructed him in public affairs and only because the king had so desired.

It was so little expected that their sovereign would take up the government himself, that of all those who had hitherto worked with the first minister there was not one who asked the king when he would require his services. They all inquired, "To whom shall we address ourselves?" and Louis XIV replied, *"To me."* They were still more surprised to see him persevere in his resolution. He had already tested his forces and secretly examined his talent for ruling; his resolution once taken, he kept it to the last moment of his life. He fixed the limits of the power of each minister, requiring them to render a full account to him at stated times, giving them the confidence necessary to the credit of their office, and keeping a watch on them to prevent their abusing it. . . .

He began by putting his revenues in order, disorganized as they were by prolonged peculation. Discipline was restored among the troops as was order in finance. Magnificence and propriety distinguished his court. Pleasure itself put on splender and grandeur. All the arts were encouraged and all dedicated to the glory of the king and of France.

This is not the place to depict him in his private life nor in the inner working of his government; we shall deal with these matters in their places. It suffices to say that his people, who had not known a real king since the death of Henri-Quatre, and who detested the rule of a first minister, were filled with admiration and hope when they saw Louis XIV accomplish at twenty-two years of age what Henry had done at fifty. Had Henry IV had a first minister, he would have been lost, because hatred of one particular man would have stirred up twenty factions too powerful to be suppressed. Had Louis XIII not had one, his mind, enervated by a poor and feeble body, would have sunk under the burden of government. Louis XIV took no risk either in retaining or discarding a first minister. Not the least trace remained of the old factions; there was now but a master and his subjects in France. From the first he showed that he aspired to every kind of glory and that he wished to be as respected abroad as he was absolute at home. . . .

Whilst upholding his dignity he did not forget to increase his power (27 October, 1662). The state of his finances wisely administered by Colbert enabled him to buy Dunkirk and Mardick from the King of England for five million livres, at twenty-six livres ten sous to the mark. . . .

Louis set thirty thousand men to work on the fortifying of Dunkirk, both by land and sea. Between the town and fortress he constructed a harbor large enough to contain thirty ships of war, so that the English had scarcely sold this town than it became a source of dread to them. . . .

Louis extended his territories even in time of peace and held himself always in readiness for war, fortifying his frontiers, keeping his troops well-disciplined, adding to their number, and holding frequent reviews.

The Turks were at this time very formidable to Europe; they were attacking both the Emperor of Germany and the Venetians. Since the time of Francis I the policy of France has always been to ally herself with the Turkish Sultans, not only for the benefits of trade but to prevent the House of Austria from becoming too powerful. Nevertheless, a Christian king could not refuse help to the Emperor in real danger; and it was to the interest of France that the Turks should harass Hungary, but not that they should invade her: in a word, her treaties with the Empire made it her duty to take this honorable step. Louis therefore sent six thousand men into Hungary under the command of the Count of Coligni, the sole survivor of that house of Coligni so famous in our civil wars, and who deserves perhaps for his courage and honesty as great a fame as that of the admiral. Friendship had attached him to the great Condé and not all the offers of Cardinal Mazarin had been able to persuade him to betray his friend. He had under him the flower of the French nobility, among them La Feuillade, young, enterprising and eager for glory and fortune (1664). These French troops went to serve under General Montecuculi in Hungary, who was then engaged against the grand vizier Kiuperli or Kouprogli, and who later, when fighting against France, equalled the reputation of Turenne. A great battle was fought between the

Turks and the Emperor's army at Saint-Gothard on the banks of the Raab. The French performed prodigies of valor; even the Germans, who were by no means friendly towards them, were compelled to do them this justice; but it is unjust to the Germans to say, as may be read in many books, that the French alone had the honor of this victory.

While openly throwing his weight on the side of the Emperor and adding luster to the French arms, the king directed his policy towards supporting Portugal secretly against Spain. By the Treaty of the Pyrenees Mazarin had formally deserted the Portuguese; but Spain had broken several of the smaller provisions of the peace. France now broke out boldly and decisively; Marshal de Schomberg, a foreigner and a Huguenot, marched into Portugal with four thousand French soldiers, whom he paid with money from Louis XIV, but pretended to do so in the name of the King of Portugal. These four thousand French soldiers joined with the Portuguese troops, and obtained a complete victory at Villa-Viciosa (17 June, 1665) which established the House of Braganza on the throne. Louis XIV was thus already regarded as a warlike and diplomatic prince, and Europe feared him even before he had yet made war.

It was by his diplomacy that he evaded his promise to unite the few vessels he then possessed to the Dutch fleet. He had allied himself with Holland in 1662. About that time, that republic renewed the war with England on the absurd and idle pretext of respecting the national flag, the real issue being the question of trade in the Indies. Louis was delighted to see these two maritime powers launch year by year fleets of more than a hundred vessels, which mutually destroyed one another in some of the most stubborn fights that have ever taken place, the net result of which was the weakening of both powers. One fight lasted three whole days (11, 12 and 13 June, 1666). It was in these engagements that the Dutchman, Ruyter, gained the reputation of being the greatest seaman that had ever lived. It was he who burnt the finest English ships within harbor, but four leagues from London. He made Holland supreme on the seas, the sovereignty of which had hitherto been held by the English, and in which Louis XIV had as yet no part. For many years the supremacy of the sea had been divided between these two nations. The art of building ships and of utilizing them for trade and war was properly understood by them alone. During the ministry of Richelieu, France thought herself to be powerful at sea, because out of about sixty men-of-war lying in her ports, nearly thirty were seaworthy and one carried seventy cannon. Under Mazarin, the few vessels she possessed were bought from Holland. Sailors, officers and materials for their construction and equipment were alike lacking. With incredible activity Louis set about reestablishing the navy and providing France with everything she lacked; but in 1664 and 1665, whilst the English and the Dutch were overrunning the seas with nearly three hundred large ships of war, he had as yet but fifteen or sixteen vessels of the poorest class, which the Duke of Beaufort was employing against the Barbary pirates; and when the Netherland States urged Louis XIV to join his fleet to theirs, only a single fireship could be found in the port of Brest, which he was ashamed to send, but it was necessary to do this at their repeated requests. With all speed Louis XIV hastened to remove this ignominy.

He rendered more material and creditable aid to the Netherlands with his land forces, sending six thousand French to defend them against Christopher Bernard Van Galen, Bishop of Münster, a warrior prelate and their implacable enemy, who had been bribed by England to lay waste Holland; but he made them pay dearly for this help and treated them like a powerful man who sells his protection to wealthy merchants. Colbert charged them not only with the soldiers' pay, but even with the expenses of sending an ambassador to England to conclude peace with Charles II. Never was help given with so bad a grace nor received with so little gratitude. Having thus accustomed his troops to war and made fresh officers on the fields of Hungary, Holland and Portugal, the king, respected and revenged in Rome, found himself with not a single ruler to fear. With England ravaged by the plague, and London reduced to ashes by a conflagration unjustly attributed to the Catholics, with the perpetual extravagance and poverty of Charles II, as perilous to the state as plague and fire, France had no cause of fear so far as England was concerned. The Emperor was hardly yet recovered from the exhaustion of a war against the Turks. The King of Spain, Philip IV, whose kingdom was as feeble as himself, lay dying and Louis XIV remained the sole powerful and formidable monarch. He was young, rich, well-served, blindly obeyed, and eager to distinguish himself by foreign conquest. . . .

*   *   *

[However, after the cutting of the dikes during the Dutch War], the toils of the king, the genius of Vauban, the stern vigilance of Louvois, the experience and matchless skill of Turenne, the intrepid courage and activity of the Prince de Condé, all could not repair the error that had been made in garrisoning too many towns, in thus weakening the army, and in failing to take Amsterdam.

The Prince de Condé desired in vain to penetrate into the heart of flooded Holland. Turenne could neither hinder Montecuculi from joining forces with the Prince of Orange nor prevent the Prince of Orange from taking Bonn. The Bishop of Münster, who had sworn to destroy the States-General, was himself attacked by the Dutch. The English parliament forced its king to enter genuinely upon negotiations for peace, and to cease to be the mercenary tool of French aggrandizement. It had now become necessary to evacuate the three Dutch provinces as rapidly as they had been conquered. This was not done without exacting ransoms; the commissary, Robert, collected in one year from the province of Utrecht alone 668,000 florins. They were in such haste to evacuate a country which had been so quickly conquered that 28,000 Dutch prisoners were liberated at a crown a head. The triumphal arch at the gateway of Saint-Denys and the other monuments of the conquest were scarcely finished when the conquest was already being abandoned. In the course of this invasion the Dutch could boast of having disputed the empire of the sea and of having skillfully transferred the theatre of war outside their own country. In Europe Louis XIV was regarded as having rejoiced too soon and too loudly over a short-lived triumph. The expedition resulted in his being engaged in a desperate war against the united forces of Spain, the Empire and Holland, in being deserted by England, later by Münster and even Cologne, and in leaving more hatred than admiration for this name in the countries he had invaded and abandoned.

The king stood alone against all the enemies that he had made. The foresight of his government and the resources of the state appeared to but greater advantage when he had to defend himself against a number of allied powers and their famous generals, than when he had taken in his stride French Flanders, Franche-Comté and half Holland, from enemies who were off their guard.

Especially noteworthy was the advantage that an absolute king possesses over other monarchs, provided his finances are in good order. At one and the same time he furnished Turenne with an army of about 23,000 men to oppose the Imperial forces, and Condé with 40,000 to oppose the Prince of Orange; another regiment was on the frontier of Rousillon; a fleet laden with soldiers was sent as far as Messina to make war on Spain, and he himself marched on Franche-Comté to make himself master of that country for the second time. He defended himself and attacked in every part at the same time.

At first, in his new expedition upon Franche-Comté, the superiority of his government appeared to be unquestionable. It was important to gain to his side, or at any rate to allay the suspicions of, the Swiss, a nation valiant but poor, always in arms, jealous to excess of their liberty, and invincible on their frontiers, but already murmuring, and disturbed at seeing Louis XIV a second time in their neighborhood. The Emperor and Spain appealed to the thirteen cantons to allow at least a free passage to their troops, so as to send aid to Franche-Comté, which was left defenseless through the negligence of the Spanish government. On his side the king urged the Swiss to refuse such a passage; the Emperor and Spain were prodigal of nothing but reasons and entreaties; the king persuaded the Swiss to do what he desired by means of hard cash, and the passage was refused.

Accompanied by his brother and the son of the great Condé, Louis besieged Besançon. He took great delight in siege warfare and might well consider that he understood the art as well as Condé and Turenne; but jealous as he was of his own glory, he confessed that those two great men knew more about open warfare than himself. Moreover he never besieged a town without being certain of taking it. Louvois made such complete preparations, the troops were so well provided for, Vauban, who conducted nearly all the sieges, was such a past master in the art of taking towns, that the king's glory was assured. Vauban directed the attacks on Besançon, which was taken in nine days (15 May, 1674), and in six weeks the whole of Franche-

Comté had surrendered to the king. It still belongs to France and seems destined to be a monument of the weakness of the Austrian-Spanish government and of the strength of that of Louis XIV. . . .

*   *   *

[At the Peace of Nimwegen], the king was at this time at the height of his greatness. Victorious since he had begun to reign, having besieged no place which he had not taken, superior in every way to his united enemies, for six years the terror of Europe and at last her arbitrator and peacemaker, he now added Franche-Comté, Dunkirk and half Flanders to his possessions; moreover, and he might well count this the greatest of his advantages, he was the king of a nation happy in itself and the model of all others.

Some time afterwards, in 1680, the Council of Paris conferred the title of "Great" upon him with due solemnity and decreed that henceforth the title alone should be used in all public records. Since 1673 a few medals had been struck bearing his cognomen. Europe, though jealous, made no protest against such honors. Nevertheless the name of *Louis-Quatorze* has prevailed in the public mind over that of *the Great.* Custom is all-powerful: Henry, justly surnamed *the Great* after his death, is commonly known as Henri-Quatre, and the name speaks loudly enough. The Prince de Condé is always called *the great Condé,* not merely on account of his heroic deeds, but because it is easier to distinguish him by that surname from the other princes of the same name. Had he been called *Condé the Great,* the title would not have clung to him. We speak of *the great Corneille* to distinguish him from his brother. We do not say *the great* Virgil, nor *the great* Homer, nor *the great* Tasso. *Alexander the Great* has come to be known as Alexander, and Caesar is never called *the Great.* Charles V, whose career was more brilliant than that of Louis XIV, has never had the title of *great,* and the title survives in Charlemagne only as a proper name. Posterity has no use for titles; the name of a man who has done great deeds inspires more reverence than any epithet. . . .

*   *   *

One owes this much justice to public men who have benefited their own age, to consider the point from which they started in order to perceive more clearly the changes they wrought in their country.

Posterity owes them eternal gratitude for the examples they gave, even though such examples have been surpassed. Such lawful glory is their only reward. It is certain that the love of such glory inspired Louis XIV, at the time of his taking the government into his own hands, in his desire to improve his kingdom, beautify his court and perfect the arts.

Not only did he impose upon himself the duty of regularly transacting affairs with each of his ministers, but any well-known man could obtain a private audience with him and any citizen was free to present petitions and projects to him. The petitions were first received by a master of requests who wrote his recommendations in the margin; and they were then dispatched to the ministerial offices. Projects were examined in council if they were thought worthy of such attention, and their authors were on more than one occasion admitted to discuss their proposals with the ministers in the king's presence. There was thus a channel between the throne and the nation which existed notwithstanding the absolute power of the monarch.

Louis XIV trained and inured himself to work; work which was the more arduous to him as he was new to it and the allurement of pleasures might easily distract him. He wrote the first dispatches to his ambassadors. The more important letters were often revised by his own hand, and he made it a habit to read every document which bore his name.

Colbert had scarcely restored the finances of the country after the fall of Fouquet, when the king rescinded all the taxes owing for the years 1647 to 1658—in particular, three millions of poll taxes. Certain burdensome duties were removed by payment of five hundred thousand crowns a year. The Abbé de Choisi seemed thus much misinformed or very prejudiced when he said that the receipts had not decreased. They were undoubtedly decreased by such abatements and increased as a result of better methods of collection.

It was due to the efforts of the first president of Bellièvre, assisted by the benefactions of the Duchess d'Aiguillon and a few citizens, that the general hospital was founded. The king enlarged it and had others built in all the principal towns of the kingdom.

The great highways hitherto impassable were no longer neglected and became gradually what they are today under Louis XV—the admiration of foreigners. Leaving Paris in any direction one may now travel from fifty to sixty miles to various places near at hand on well-paved roads bordered by trees. The roads constructed by the ancient Romans were more lasting, but not so wide and beautiful.

Colbert's genius was chiefly directed to commerce, which was as yet undeveloped and whose fundamental principles were as yet unknown. The English, and to a still greater extent the Dutch, carried nearly all the trade of France in their ships. The Dutch especially loaded up in our ports with French produce and distributed it throughout Europe. In 1662 the king took steps to exempt his subjects from a tax known as *freight duty,* which was payable by all foreign ships; and allowed the French every facility for transporting their own goods themselves at lower charges. It was then that maritime trade sprang up. The council of commerce which is still in existence was established, and the king presided over it every fortnight. Dunkirk and Marseilles were declared free ports, a privilege which soon attracted the trade of the Levant to Marseilles and that of the north to Dunkirk.

A West India Company was formed in 1664 and an East India Company was established in the same year. Previous to this the luxury of France had been entirely dependent upon the industry of Holland. The supporters of the old system of economy, timid, ignorant and narrow-minded, vainly declaimed against a system of commerce by which money, which is imperishable, was continually being exchanged for perishable goods. They did not reflect that these wares from the Indies, which had become indispensable, would have been much dearer if bought from a foreign country. It is true that more money is sent to the East Indies than is received from them, and that Europe is thus impoverished. But the bullion itself comes from Peru and Mexico, being the price paid for our wares at Cadiz, and more of this money remains in France than is absorbed by the East Indies.

The king gave more than six millions of present-day money to the company; and urged wealthy people to interest themselves in it. The queens, princes and all the court provided two millions in the currency of the time, and the higher courts furnished twelve hundred thousand livres; financiers, two millions; the company of merchants, six hundred and fifty thousand livres. Thus the whole nation supported their ruler. . . .

In 1669 the king also formed a Northern Company; he contributed to its funds as to the Indian company. It was then clearly shown that there is nothing derogatory in trade, since the most influential houses took an interest in such establishments, following the example of their monarch.

The West India Company was no less encouraged than the others, the king supplying a tenth part of the total funds.

He gave thirty francs for every ton exported and forty for every ton imported. All who built ships in national ports received five livres for every ton of carrying capacity.

One cannot be too much astonished that the Abbé de Choisi should have condemned these institutions in his *Memoirs,* which must not be relied upon. We perceive today all that Colbert in his capacity as minister did for the good of the nation, but it was not perceived at the time; he worked for ungrateful people. . . .

Nevertheless, there is little that was not either reestablished or created in his time. In 1665, visible proof of a liberal circulation was forthcoming when the interest on the loans of the king and private individuals was reduced to five per cent. He wanted to enrich France and increase her population. People in the country were encouraged to marry by exempting those who had done so by the age of twenty from paying poll tax for a period of five years; and every head of a family of ten children was exempt for the remainder of his life, since he gave more to the state by the product of his children's work than he would have done by paying taxes. Such a law should never have been repealed.

Each year of this ministry, from 1663 to 1672, was marked by the establishment of some manufacture. Fine stuffs, which had hitherto come from England and Holland, were now manufactured at Abbeville. The king advanced to the manufacturer two thousand livres for each loom at work, in addition to considerable grants. In the year 1669 there were 44,200 wool looms at work in the kingdom. Fine silk manufactures produced more than fifty millions in the currency of the time, and not only were the profits much greater than the outlay on the necessary silk, but the growing of mulberry trees enabled the manufacturers to dispense with foreign silk for the weaving of their material.

In 1666 glass began to be made as fine as that of Venice, which had hitherto supplied the whole of Europe, and soon French glass attained a splendor and beauty which have never been surpassed elsewhere. The carpets of Turkey and Persia were excelled at La Savonnerie. The tapestries of Flanders yielded to those of Les Gobelins. At that time more than eight hundred workmen were employed in the vast Gobelin works, and three hundred of them were actually lodged there; the finest painters directed the work, which was executed either from their designs or copied from those of the old Italian masters. It was in the precincts of the Gobelins that inlaid work was also produced – a delightful kind of mosaic work – and the art of marquetry was brought to perfection.

Besides the fine tapestry factory at Les Gobelins another was established at Beauvais. The first manufacturer in the town employed six hundred workmen, and the king made him a present of sixty thousand livres. Sixteen hundred girls were employed in making lace; thirty of the best operatives in Venice were engaged, and two hundred from Flanders; and they were presented with thirty-six thousand livres to encourage them.

The manufactures of Sedan cloth and of Aubusson tapestry, which had deteriorated and dwindled, were again set going. Rich stuffs, in which silk was interwoven with gold and silver, were made at Lyons and Tours, with a fresh outburst of industry.

It is well known that the ministry bought from England the secret of that ingenious machine by which stockings can be made ten times more quickly than with the needle. Tin, steel, fine crockery ware, morocco leather, which had always been brought from foreign countries, were now worked in France. But certain Calvinists, who possessed secrets of tin and steel smelting, carried them away with them in 1686, and shared them and many others with foreign nations.

Every year the king bought about eight hundred thousand livres' worth of works of art, manufactured in his kingdom, and gave them away as presents.

The city of Paris was very far from being what it is today. The streets were unlighted, unsafe and dirty. It was necessary to find money for the constant cleaning of the streets, for lighting them every night with five thousand lamps, completely paving the whole city, building two new gates and repairing the old ones, keeping the permanent guard, both foot and mounted, to ensure the safety of the citizens. The king charged himself with everything, drawing upon

funds for such necessary expenses. In 1667 he appointed a magistrate whose sole duty was to superintend the police. Most of the large
cities of Europe have imitated these examples long afterwards, but
none has equalled them. There is no city paved like Paris, and Rome
is not even illuminated.

In every sphere matters tended to become so perfect that the
second-lieutenant of police in Paris earned a reputation in the per-
formance of his duties which placed him on a level with those who
did honor to their age; he was a man capable of anything. He was
afterwards in the ministry, and would have made a good general in
the army. The position of second-lieutenant of police was beneath his
birth and capabilities; yet in filling that post he earned a much greater
reputation than when occupying an uneasy and transient office in the
ministry towards the end of his life.

It should be here pointed out that M. d'Argenson was not by any
means the only member of ancient chivalry who performed the office
of a magistrate. France is almost the only country in Europe where the
old nobility has so often donned the robe. Nearly all other countries,
swayed by the relic of Gothic barbarism, are unaware of the greatness of this profession.

From 1661 the king was ceaseless in his building at the Louvre,
Saint-Germain and Versailles. Following his example private individuals erected thousands of dwellings in Paris as magnificent as they
were comfortable. Their number increased to such an extent that in
the environs of the Palais-Royal and St. Sulpice two new towns sprang
up in Paris, both vastly superior to the old. It was about this time that
those magnificent spring carriages with mirrors were invented, so that
a citizen of Paris could ride through the streets of that great city in
greater luxury than the first Roman triumvirs along the road to the
Capitol. Inaugurated in Paris, the custom soon spread throughout the
whole of Europe, and, became general, it is no longer a luxury.

Louis XIV took delight in architecture, gardens, and sculpture, his
delight being for all that was grand and imposing. From 1664 the
Comptroller-General Colbert, who was in charge of buildings, a duty
properly belonging to the ministry of arts, devoted himself to the
carrying out of his master's plans. The Louvre must first be finished,
and François Mansard, one of the greatest French architects of all
time, was chosen to construct the immense buildings that had been

projected. He declined to proceed, unless he were allowed to alter certain parts already built which appeared to him defective. These doubts he cast on the scheme, to alter which would have entailed too great an expense, were the cause of his services being dispensed with. The cavalier Bernini was summoned from Rome, famous already for the colonnade surrounding the parvis of St. Peter's, the equestrian statue of Constantine, and the Navonna fountain. An equipage was provided for his journey. He was brought to Paris as a man come to do honor to France. He received, in addition to the five louis a day for the eight months he remained, a present of fifty thousand crowns and a pension of two thousand, and five hundred for his son. This generosity of Louis XIV towards Bernini was yet greater than the munificence accorded to Raphael by Francis I. In gratitude Bernini afterwards cast at home the equestrian statue of the king which now stands at Versailles. But once arrived in Paris with so much pomp as the only man worthy to work for Louis XIV, he was not a little astonished to see the design of the facade of the Louvre on the Saint-Germain-l'Auxerrois side, which when finished shortly afterwards became one of the most imposing architectural monuments to be found in the world. Claude Perrault was the draftsman, and it was executed by Louis Levau and Dorbay. He invented machines for conveying the stone blocks, fifty-two feet long, which form the pediment of this majestic building.

Men sometimes seek very far afield for what they have at home. Not a Roman palace has an entrance comparable to that of the Louvre, for which we are indebted to that Perrault upon whom Boileau dared to try to pour ridicule. In the opinion of travellers, those famous vineyards are not comparable to the Château de Maisons, which was built at such small cost by François Mansard. Bernini was magnificently remunerated, but did not deserve his rewards: he merely drew up plans which were never executed.

After building the Louvre, the completion of which is greatly to be desired, founding a town at Versailles close to the palace which cost so many millions, building Trianon, Marli, and beautifying so many other buildings, the king had completed building the Observatory, begun in 1666, at the time that he founded the Academy of Sciences. But the work glorious for its utility, its vastness and the difficulties of its construction, was the Languedoc Canal, which connected the two seas, and finds an outlet in the port of Cette, built for that purpose. All these undertakings were begun after 1664 and were continued uninterrupted until 1681. The founding of the Invalides and its chapel, the finest in Paris, the building of Saint-Cyr, the last of the edifices to be erected by that monarch, would alone suffice to hallow his memory. Four thousand soldiers and a large number of officers, who find consolation in their old age and relief for their wounds and needs in the former of those great institutions; two hundred and fifty girls of noble birth who receive in the latter an education worthy of their high position, are so many witnesses to the glory of Louis XIV.

The institution of Saint-Cyr will be surpassed by the one which Louis XV is about to found for the education of five hundred noblemen, but so far from causing Saint-Cyr to be forgotten it will remind one of it; the art of doing good is thus brought to perfection.

Louis XIV resolved at the same time to do greater things, of more general utility as they were more difficult of accomplishment, and one of these was the remodelling of the laws. He instructed the chancellor Séguier, Lamoignon, Talon, Bignon and, above all, the state councillor, Pussort, to set to work. He was sometimes present at their meetings. The year 1667 marked the epoch of his earliest statutes as it did his earliest conquests. The civil code appeared first to be followed by the law of rivers and forests, and later statutes concerning every kind of manufacture; the criminal code, the laws of commerce and the marine laws were passed in annual succession. A new kind of justice was even introduced in favor of the Negroes in French colonies, a people who had not hitherto possessed the rights of mankind.

A sovereign need not possess a profound knowledge of jurisprudence; but the king was well versed in the principal laws; he entered into their spirit, and knew when either to enforce or modify them as occasion demanded. He often passed judgment on his subjects' lawsuits, not only in the council of the state secretaries, but in that one bearing the name of the council of the parties. Two judgments of his have become famous, in which he decided against himself.

The first case, which was tried in 1680, was an action between himself and certain private individuals in Paris who had erected buildings on his land. He gave judgment that the houses should remain to them with the land belonging to him, which he made over to them.

The other one concerned a Persian, named Roupli, whose merchandise had been seized by the clerks of his farms in 1687. His decision was that all should be returned to him, and he added a present of three thousands crowns. Roupli carried back to his own country his admiration and gratitude. When the Persian ambassador, Mehemet Rixabeg, came afterwards to Paris, it was discovered that he had long known of that action by the fame which it had spread abroad.

The suppression of dueling was one of the greatest services rendered to the country. Formerly such duels had been sanctioned by kings, even by parliament and by the Church, and though forbidden since the days of Henry IV, the pernicious practice was more prevalent than ever. The famous combat of the La Frettes in 1663, when eight combatants were engaged, determined Louis XIV to pardon such duels no longer. His well-timed severity gradually reformed the nation and even neighboring nations, who conformed to our wise customs after having copied our bad ones. At the present day the number of duels in Europe is a hundred times less than in the time of Louis XIII.

Legislator of his people, he was no less so of his armies. It is astonishing that before his time the troops had no uniform dress. It was he who in the first year of his administration decreed that each regiment should be distinguished by the color of their uniform, or by different badges – a regulation which was soon adopted by all other nations. It was he who organized the brigadiers and gave the king's household troops the status they hold at the present day. He formed a company of musketeers from Cardinal Mazarin's guards and fixed the number of men for the two companies at five hundred, whom he furnished with the uniform they still wear today.

During this reign the post of High Constable was abolished, and after the death of the Duke of Épernon there were no more colonels general of infantry; they were too much the master; he resolved to be the only master, and deserved to be so. Marshal Grammont, a mere colonel in the French guards under the Duke of Épernon, and taking his orders from this brigadier general, now only took them from the king, and was the first to bear the title of colonel of the guards; Louis himself appointed these colonels to the head of their regiments, presenting them with his own hand a gold gorget with a pike, and afterwards a spontoon, when the use of pikes was abolished. In the king's regiment, which is of his creation, he founded the grenadiers, at first to the number of four to each company; afterwards he formed a company of grenadiers in each infantry regiment, and provided the French guards with two of them; at the present day there is one in every infantry battalion in the army. He greatly enlarged the corps of dragoons and gave them a brigadier general. Nor must be forgotten the institution of breeding-studs in 1667. Heretofore, they had been absolutely neglected, and they were of great assistance in providing mounts for the cavalry; an important resource which has since been too much neglected.

The use of the bayonet attached to the end of the musket originated with him. Before his time they were sometimes employed, but only a few of the regiments fought with this weapon. There was no regular practice and no drill, all being left to the will of the general. Pikes were considered to be the most formidable weapon. The Fusiliers, founded in 1671, were the first regiment to employ bayonets and to be drilled in the use of that weapon.

The use to which artillery is put at the present day is entirely due to him. He established schools at Douai, and later at Metz and at Strasbourg, and the artillery regiment found itself at last provided with officers who were nearly all capable of efficiently conducting a siege. All the magazines in the country were well stocked and eight thousand hundredweights of powder were distributed amongst them every year. He formed a regiment of bombardiers and hussars; before his time hussars were only to be found among the enemy.

In 1688 he established thirty militia regiments, furnished and equipped by the communes. These regiments were trained for war, but they did not neglect the tilling of the land.

Companies of cadets were maintained at most of the frontier towns; they were taught mathematics, drawing, and all manner of drill, and carried out the duties of soldiers. This system was pursued for ten years. At length the difficulties in the way of training insubordinate youths proved too great; but the corps of engineers, formed by the king and for which he drew up regulations which still obtain, will last for ever. Under Louis XIV the art of fortifying towns was brought to perfection by Marshal Vauban and his pupils, whose works surpassed those of Count Pagan. He constructed or rebuilt one hundred and fifty fortresses.

For the maintenance of military discipline, he created inspectors general, and afterwards superintendents, who reported on the condition of the troops, and their reports showed whether the commissaries had carried out their duties.

He founded the Order of Saint Louis, and this honorable distinction was often more sought after than wealth itself. The Hôtel des Invalides crowned the efforts he made to be worthy of the faithful service of his subjects.

It was by such efforts that, from the year 1672, he possessed one hundred and eighty thousand regular troops, and increasing his forces proportionately to the increase in the number and power of his enemies he had at length as many as four hundred and fifty thousand men under arms, including the marines.

Before that time no such powerful armies had been seen. His enemies were able to put in the field armies almost as large, but to do so their forces were compelled to be united. He showed what France could do unaided and had always, if not great success, at any rate great resources.

He was the first to give displays of war maneuvers and mimic warfare in times of peace. In 1698 seventy thousand troops were mustered at Compiègne. They performed all the operations of a campaign, the display being intended for the benefit of his three grandsons. The luxurious accompaniments of this military school made of it a sumptuous fête.

He was as assiduous in his efforts to secure the sovereignty of the seas as he had been to form numerous and well-trained armies upon land, even before war was declared. He began by repairing the few ships that Cardinal Mazarin had left to rot in the ports. Others were bought from Holland and Sweden, and in the third year of his government he dispatched his maritime forces in an attempt to take Jijeli on the coast of Africa. In 1665 the Duke of Beaufort began to clear the seas of pirates, and two years later France had sixty warships in her ports. This was only a beginning, but while in the midst of making new regulations and fresh efforts, he was already conscious of his strength, and would not allow his ships to dip their flag to the English. It was in vain that King Charles II's council insisted on this right, which the English had acquired long since by reason of their power and labors. Louis XIV wrote to his ambassador, Count d'Estrades, in these terms: "The King of England and his Chancellor may see what forces I possess, but they cannot see my heart. I care for nothing apart from my honor."

He only said what he was determined to uphold, and in fact the English surrendered their claims and submitted to a natural right and Louis XIV's firmness. Equal conditions obtained between the two nations on the seas. But while insisting upon equality with England, Louis maintained his superiority over Spain. By reason of the formal precedence conceded in 1662, he compelled the Spanish admirals to dip their flag to his ships.

Meanwhile the work of establishing a navy capable of upholding such arrogant sentiments progressed everywhere. The town and port of Rochefort were built at the mouth of the Charente. Seamen of all classes were enrolled, some of whom were placed on merchant vessels and others distributed among the royal fleets. In a short time sixty thousand were enrolled.

Building commissions were set up in the ports so that ships might be constructed on the best possible lines. Five naval arsenals were built at Brest, Rochefort, Toulon, Dunkirk and Havre-de-Grâce. In 1672, there were 60 ships of the line and 40 frigates. In 1681, there were 198 ships of war, counting the auxiliaries and 30 galleys in the port of Toulon, either armed or about to be so; 11,000 of the regular troops served on the ships and 3000 on the galleys; 166,000 men of all classes were enrolled for the various services of the navy. During the succeeding years, there were a thousand noblemen or young gentlemen in this service, carrying out the duties of soldiers on board ship, and learning everything in harbor to do with the art of navigation and tactics; they were the marine guards, having the same rank at sea as the cadets on land. They had been formed in 1672, but in small numbers; they have since proved themselves a school which has produced the finest ships' officers in the navy.

As yet no officer in the marine corps had been made a Marshal of France, a proof that this vital part of France's forces had been neglected. Jean d'Estrées was made the first marshal in 1681. It seems that one of Louis XIV's great objects was to stir up rivalry for this honor in all classes, without which there is no initiative.

The French fleets held the advantage in every naval battle fought until the engagement of La Hogue in 1692, when Count de Tourville, obeying the orders of the court, attacked with forty ships a fleet of ninety English and Dutch ships; he was forced to yield to superior numbers and lost fourteen ships of the first class, which ran aground and were burnt in order to prevent them falling into the enemy's hands. In spite of this setback the naval forces still held their own; but they deteriorated during the war of the succession. Subsequently Cardinal Fleury neglected to repair their losses during the leisure of a prosperous peace – the very time in which to reestablish them.

The naval forces greatly assisted in protecting trade. The colonies of Martinique, San Domingo and Canada, hitherto languishing, now flourished, and with unhoped-for success; for from 1635 to 1665 these settlements had been a burden upon the nation.

In 1664, the king established a colony at Cayenne and soon afterwards another in Madagascar. He sought by every means to redress the folly and misfortunes which France had brought upon herself by ignoring the sea, while her neighbors were founding empires at the ends of the world.

It will be seen by this cursory glance what great changes Louis XIV brought about in the state; and that such changes were useful since they are still in force. His ministers vied with each other in their eagerness to assist him. The details, indeed the whole execution of such schemes was doubtless due to them, but his was the general organization. There can be no shadow of doubt that the magistrates would never have reformed the laws, the finances of the country would not have been put on a sound basis, nor discipline introduced into the army, nor a regular police force instituted throughout the kingdom; there would have been no fleets, no encouragement accorded to the arts; all these things would never have been peacefully and steadily accomplished in such a short period and under so many different ministers, had there not been a ruler to conceive of such great schemes, and with a will strong enough to carry them out.

His own glory was indissolubly connected with the welfare of France, and never did he look upon his kingdom as a noble regards his land, from which he extracts as much as he can that he may live in luxury. Every king who loves glory loves the public weal; he had no longer a Colbert nor a Louvois, when about 1698 he commanded each comptroller to present a detailed description of his province for the instruction of the Duke of Burgundy. By this means it was possible to have an exact record of the whole kingdom and a correct census of the population. The work was of the greatest utility, although not every comptroller had the ability and industry of M. de Lamoignon of Basville. Had the comptroller of every province carried out the king's intent so well as the magistrate of Languedoc with regard to the numbering of the population, this collection of records would have been one of the finest achievements of the age. Some of them are well done, but a general scheme was lacking since the same orders were not issued to each comptroller. It is to be wished that each one had given in separate columns a statement of the number of inhabitants of each estate, such as nobles, citizens, laborers, artisans, workmen, cattle of all kinds, fertile, mediocre, and poor land, all clergy, both orthodox and secular, their revenues, and those of the towns and communes.

In most of the records submitted all these details are confused; the matter is not well thought out and inexact; one must search, often with great difficulty, for the needed information such as a minister should have ready to hand and be able to take in at a glance so as to ascertain with ease the forces, needs, and resources at his disposal. The scheme was excellent, and had it been methodically carried out would have been of the greatest utility.

The foregoing is a general account of what Louis XIV did or attempted to do in order to make his country more flourishing. It seems to me that one can hardly view all his works and efforts without some sense of gratitude, nor without being stirred by the love for the public weal which inspired them. Let the reader picture to himself the condition today, and he will agree that Louis XIV did more good for his country than twenty of his predecessors together; and what he accomplished fell far short of what he might have done. The war which ended with the Peace of Ryswick began the ruin of that flourishing trade established by his minister Colbert, and the war of the succession completed it.

Had he devoted the immense sums which were spent on the aque-

ducts and works at Maintenon for conveying water to Versailles –
works which were interrupted and rendered useless – to beautifying
Paris and completing the Louvre; had he expended on Paris a fifth
part of the money spent in transforming nature at Versailles, Paris
would be in its entire length and breadth as beautiful as the quarter
embracing the Tuileries and the Pont-Royal; it would have become
the most magnificent city in the world.

It is a great thing to have reformed the laws, but justice has not
been powerful enough to suppress knavery entirely. It was thought to
make the administration of justice uniform; it is so in criminal cases,
in commercial cases and in judicial procedure; it might also be so
in the laws which govern the fortunes of private citizens.

It is in the highest degree undesirable that the same tribunal
should have to give decisions on more than a hundred different customs. Territorial rights, doubtful, burdensome or merely troublesome
to the community, still survive as relics of a feudal government which
no longer exists; they are the rubbish from the ruins of a Gothic
edifice.

We do not claim that the different classes of the nation should all
be subject to the same law. It is obvious that the customs of the
nobility, clergy, magistrates and husbandmen must all be different,
but it is surely desirable that each class should be subject to the
same law throughout the kingdom; that what is just or right in
Champagne should not be deemed unjust or wrong in Normandy.
Uniformity in every branch of administration is a virtue; but the difficulties that beset its achievement are enough to frighten the boldest
statesman. It is to be regretted that Louis XIV did not dispense more
readily with the dangerous expedient of employing tax-farmers, an
expedient to which he was driven by the continual advance drawings
he made on his revenues, as will be seen in the chapter on finance.

Had he not thought that his mere wish would suffice to compel a
million men to change their religion, France would not have lost so
many citizens. Nevertheless, this country, in spite of the shocks and
losses she has sustained, is still one of the most flourishing in the
world, since all the good that Louis XIV did for her still bears fruit,
and the mischief which it was difficult not to do in stormy times has
been remedied. Posterity, which passes judgment on kings, and
whose judgment they should continually have before them, will ac-

knowledge, weighing the greatness and defects of that monarch, that though too highly praised during his lifetime, he will deserve to be so for ever, and that he was worthy of the statue raised to him at Montpellier, bearing a Latin inscription whose meaning is *To Louis the Great after his death.* A statesman, Don Ustariz, who is the author of works on finance and trade of Spain, called Louis XIV *a marvel of a man.* . . .

The age of Louis XIV has been compared with that of Augustus. It is not that their power and individual events are comparable; Rome and Augustus were ten times more considered in the world than Louis XIV and Paris, but it must be remembered that Athens was the equal of the Roman Empire in all things whose value is not dependent upon might and power.

We must also bear in mind that there is nothing in the world today to compare with ancient Rome and Augustus, yet Europe taken as a whole is vastly superior to the whole of the Roman Empire. In the time of Augustus there was but a single nation, while at the present day there are several nations, all civilized, warlike, and enlightened, who cultivate arts unknown to the Greeks and Romans; and of these nations, there is none that has shone more brilliantly in every sphere for nearly a century, than the nation molded to a great extent by Louis XIV.

III ESTIMATES OF LOUIS XIV DURING THE NINETEENTH CENTURY

Pierre-Edouard Lemontey

LOUIS XIV, THE ADMINISTRATOR

Pierre-Edouard Lemontey (1762–1826) was alternately a jurist, administrator, and historian during the various French regimes of the late eighteenth and early nineteenth centuries, and achieved his greatest success in the latter field. Thoroughly imbued with the ideas of the Enlightenment, Lemontey hated the abuses of the Old Regime and supported the Revolution by serving in the Legislative Assembly. His moderate opinions, however, caused him to go into exile during the violent period of the Revolution. He later returned to France and received minor offices and favors under Napoleon and during the Restoration. He was elected to the French Academy in 1819. Although he published a large number of works on various subjects, it is now recognized that the volume excerpted below contains his most important contributions to historical knowledge. Based on research in hitherto unused materials, it sets forth a number of new interpretations which have gained recognition and are widely accepted today, especially among historians whose interests lie in institutional history.

The experience of centuries and the nature of their inclinations had sufficiently demonstrated to the turbulent French that hereditary monarchy was not only indispensable to their external security and domestic peace, but was the *sine quâ non* of their very existence. Such was the honored and revered principle which occasioned the work of Louis XIV. Negligently reared by a Spanish mother and an Italian Cardinal, this prince had only one true tutor: civil war. In it he steeped his soul and ripened his mind; from it he acquired the strength that amazed Europe at the death of Mazarin. From these childhood impressions, he derived inclinations that were not always masked by his policies. Although he was undoubtedly born with an instinct for domination, the recent troubles during his minority strengthened his love of absolute power, and to this extent may excuse its rigor. It was necessary that an active arm reunite all that discord had scattered. The ancients aptly compared this policy with the painful splints which encase the broken limb, in order to restore it to life.

The French monarchy was founded by the clergy upon the Holy

From Pierre-Edouard Lemontey, *Essai sur l'établissement monarchique de Louis XIV* (Paris, 1818), pp. 323–334, 381–382, 449–452. Editor's translation.

Scriptures, by the magistrates upon Roman Law, and by the nobility upon ancient custom. Louis XIV scorned all these foundations, either because his limited education did not permit him to understand them, or because none of the three suited him. . . . Thus, in all the documents dictated, written, or reviewed by Louis XIV, never did he cite an authority of any nature from the past. Although he constructed his system slowly and seemed to retain elements left by his father and grandfather, he deprived these of influence and withdrew their support. Earlier monarchy survived as a hollow trunk, sustained only by its bark. Everything in the new monarchy testified that the king was an innovator, or rather I might say a revolutionary, without the unduly specific connotation which the word has acquired in our time.

This monarchy was pure and absolute. It was centered entirely in royalty, and royalty was entirely in the king. The king mirrored the Divinity, and had similar right to blind obedience. He was the soul of the state, and held his rights only from God and his sword. He became the source of all grace, of all power, of all justice, and all glory reverted to him. His will became law without limitation, and he regarded as infamous those aristocratic or popular mixtures which are designated rather than defined by the name, tempered monarchy. Like the Caliphs, he enjoyed the rights and the disposition of all property, and whatever he permitted to the people, even the clergy, was merely a benefit of his moderation. If he was sparing with the blood of his subjects, this was neither from duty nor pity, but because of his proprietary interest. The sanction of this doctrine was his own will, and he took care that the souls of his heirs were thoroughly impregnated with this view from childhood. The Koran of France was contained in these words, which Louis XIV uttered one day: "I am the state."

It was a bold fiction to reduce France to a single man and to deny political and patriotic life to the descendants of the Franks and the Gauls. Fear and admiration were the foundations of the new system. The first was maintained by force, and the second by never-ending brilliance. It was the preservation of these twin foundations that determined the policies of the king. The army, as the principal element of force, had to be given new life. It was reformed, and the veterans who had been infected by the license of civil discord were sent to perish in Crete, in Africa, or Hungary. . . . A new army of

adolescent soldiers was created and submitted easily to severe training in the new military art which had recently been developed by
Gustavus Adolphus during the Thirty Years' War. All branches of the
service, particularly the corps of engineers, the artillery, as well as
the supply and armament of the infantry, were perfected and regu-
larized. The art of conquest was enriched by Puységur and Vauban
with new principles, and by Condé, Turenne and Luxembourg with
new examples. Uniforms, which were introduced merely as means of
discipline, had the profound effect of completing the divorce between
soldier and citizen. . . . Finally, the presence of the king, the genius
of the greatest generals, the spectacle of the development of forces
heretofore unknown, and a common glory won by numerous triumphs
brought the enthusiasm and devotion of the army to the highest pitch.
An admirable but unnecessary precaution assured it retreat behind
a triple line of fortified strongpoints. This fortress of twenty million
men felt complete security and won substantial respect from abroad.

The enemy was not alone in feeling the strength of this skillfully
disposed army. Royal power made of it an ordinary, prompt, and
willing instrument to be used without hesitation to support all branches
of the administration. Troops were sent to the provinces in order to
protect the constant extension of the authority of the intendants. They
manned citadels from which fire rained upon insubordinate cities.
In difficult times and places, they brought terror to hasten the collection of taxes. They were finally assigned the extraordinary task of
returning wayward consciences to the unity of the faith. . . . It was
easier to issue than to enforce orders which regulated the relations
between soldiers and citizens during the march and in their homes; . . .
military power was used so widely that it was impossible not to suffer
from the power of the soldiery.

The civil administration shared the vigor of the army. The depotism
of the ministers and their independence of the rare deliberations of
the councils preserved the chain of royal command. Thus a prompt
and uniform obedience demonstrated that a single power was present
everywhere. Louis XIV taxed persons and properties without restraint;
casuists reassured him concerning the legitimacy of this prerogative.
Mézeray lost his pension because he recalled contrary principles,
while Bossuet and Fénelon, the tutors of the two dauphins, had the
weakness to hide from their pupils the very existence of this forth-

right historian. The Parlements bowed their heads before the new dogma, and the people brought their tribute with respect. In conquered areas, the king carefully effaced all democratic customs, even in the government of the Church. In the ancient provinces that were sufficiently distant from the border to render momentary resistance innocuous, he destroyed the governmental authority of the estates which were inspired by a now useless liberty. Codes of law, admirable for the period, regulated various branches of the public economy, and were welcomed by the French as benefits and by the foreigner as models. Public revenue, formerly in disorder in the hands of superintendents, was placed under the thumb of an inflexible minister who disciplined the finances as Peter the Great policed the Russians. The institution of the intendants, revoked earlier by the influence of the Parlements, was restored throughout France with increased strength and competence. These representatives of an authority without limits supported its active and harsh policies, for their power was so great that they feared neither the obstruction of subordinates nor the flood of critical writings which later overwhelmed the administration.

Without pronouncing judgment concerning the merits of this system, I must stress how much its creation was the personal accomplishment of the king. Until that time, public affairs had been a confused arena in which violence, ruse, and chance fought pell-mell. Sully was buffeted by it. Villeroy and President Jeannin vainly attempted to disentangle certain parts. Richelieu disdained this task and preferred to rule without method. Louis XIV's regime brought order out of the chaos. The government of peoples which had had, so to speak, only a rude and fortuitious existence, received from him its ways and its life. This prince combined with rare harmony the talent, the aptitude, the power, and the occasion for accomplishing his objective, while he found the means of its fulfillment in his love of detail and his indefatigable application, in the long duration of his reign, and in his consistent support of staunch and laborious ministers. Among the four hundred medals which justice or flattery lavished upon him, that which would have crowned his effigy with this simple legend, LOUIS THE ADMINISTRATOR, would have been both the most glorious and the most truthful. For surpassed as he has been in all other duties of sovereignty, he has remained without equal in that which this tribute would have indicated. His century and his country were not alone in profiting from the consistent operation that he imparted to public functions. Today Europe is still governed by the synthesis which it borrowed from him, and whose influence is manifest in two diverse ways. On the one hand, he taught kings and peoples to do without charters of liberties, and to be content with the empirical maxim that the best administered state is also the best constituted. On the other hand, he rendered less frequent those great crimes which are called *coups d'état*, and which are in reality merely the convulsions of power seeking to regain the dimensions that its incompetence has caused it to lose.

A new instrument was developed for this new machine. The king equally distrusted military power which seemed strong because it was harsh, and judicial power which seemed benevolent because it was slow. At the expense of both, he developed the institution of the police which had the activity of the former and certain elements of the latter. His real aim was hidden under apparent benefits. The institution seemed to spring from the very progress of civilization; it protected the peace of cities, the pleasures of the rich, and the well-being of the poor. Minds that had been the most indignant at temporary delegation of power now became accustomed to this permanent commission. The police became the eyes of the throne and the cement of monarchy. The less it was in evidence, the more it was respected. D'Argenson, who devised its operations, introduced certain methods that he had studied when ambassador to Venice, the home of the powerful despots of the Adriatic. Through this mechanism, the operations of power acquired an extreme efficiency. Louis XIV had said, "I am the state." If Louvois did not say, "I am the king," his actions seemed indicative of this attitude, while certain intendants of the character of M. de Basville might well have said, "I am the minister." Thus royal power was extended without diminution to the furthest extremities of the social organism. Everywhere, the administration's efficiency substituted the action of the magistrate for the zeal of the citizen, killed public spirit in its slightest manifestations, and exhibited a body politic skillfully impregnated with despotism. . . .

The monarchy whose elements and progress we have considered might be defined thus: an absolute and extravagant royalty, harsh toward the people, hostile toward the foreigner, based upon the army, the police and the glory of the king, and tempered by the justice of the monarch, by the wisdom of the counsel which was solicited from various orders in the state, and by the need of conserving the lives and goods of the subjects for purposes of war and taxation. . . .

But why did this vaunted monument, this beacon which had been erected to guide the kings of Europe, survive its creator only seventy-four years? I have studied the weaknesses of this colossus, and have indicated its incoherent and contradictory elements, its baseless foundations and the germs of its destruction. . . . I have similarly rendered homage to its healthy and vigorous branches, the discipline of the army, the dignity of public order, the vigilance of power, the creation of the first administrative system, and the habit of obedience firmly rooted in the people. However, it required less than a century to break this badly balanced machine in which authority without counterpoise was lost in the midst of useless mechanisms and deceptive apparatus. Dissimilar measures had only this perilous end in common. Men of false wisdom, who abounded in courts, exhausted the chicanery of pedants in seeking to strengthen servitude to the state; instead they merely fomented revolution. It was they who placed royalty in an isolated castle, forgetting that famine might one day force it to descend, and that everything would dissolve when, through an inconceivable oddity, one found despotism everywhere in France but the despot nowhere. . . .

It is far from my thoughts to tarnish the lustre of this reign which the French have called an age, without Europe daring to deny it. We bought it so dearly that we might well yield to its attraction. It is its stability rather than its grandeur that I have attempted to judge in this essay. Louis XIV has always appeared to me as the dominant figure on this vast stage. If the title of majesty had not already belonged to crowned heads, the respect of men would have invented it for him. I am convinced that the extravagance which produced his aberrations was the fault of an unduly elevated nature and a purity of intention that would have done honor to a man of lesser rank. Surely the spirit of the times, the necessity of circumstances, and the traditions of his councils had their part in his errors. . . . But there are favors that time reserves for glorious careers. Whether useful or ostentatious, their monuments remain standing after them, while the groans of the generations that were sacrificed to them are soon stilled in the tomb. The memory of Louis XIV is perpetuated by imposing edifices which obliterate many sorrows. Quick to forget evils that they no longer felt, within a few years the French revived the glory of a prince whose passing they had not regretted.[1] But admiration revived when fear had disappeared, even as fear had arisen during his declining years when admiration had ceased – a singular division which, after 1680, separated and weakened the two columns that he had joined together as the foundations of monarchy. But whatever the event, his renown was henceforth within an orbit that no human hand could touch. The successive stages of brilliance and decline, which the House of Austria had experienced through four generations from Charles V to Philip IV, were accomplished by Louis XIV during a single lifetime. This unique period has the merit of presenting something instructive and complete. Posterity will involuntarily pause in contemplation before this great reign, astride the paths of history like a two-faced Hermes, offering at once all the attractions and all the repugnance of absolute power.

[1] Voltaire has made the greatest contribution toward refurbishing the laurels of Louis XIV. The account which he has given of the reign of this monarch is a masterpiece of grace and reason, rendered popular by an inimitable talent. It would be perfect if it were complete. The author finds much to praise, and always with judgment and moderation, but one readily perceives that certain parts of the picture are deceptive and others are undeveloped. Voltaire was too impressed by literary achievement to be entirely accurate. He described the king who had founded academies in the same manner that monks formerly described princes who endowed churches. In passing from the Cenobites to the Academicians, the pen of history merely changed its bias. This partiality, or, preferably, this gratitude of men of letters is even more remarkable in their judgment of Francis I, whose reign was full of violence, corruption, and merited disasters; and, although slightly less odious, was much more calamitous than the tyranny of Louis XI.

François Guizot

LOUIS XIV, BUILDER OF FRANCE

The activity of François-Pierre-Guillaume Guizot (1787–1874) as historian and statesman extended well over half a century. In addition to the political career for which he is chiefly remembered, he was a highly successful professor of history at the Sorbonne, where his lectures won great acclaim. The work excerpted below was a product of his teaching during the years 1828–1830. During his lifetime, Guizot's historical writing was praised because of the depth of his views and his ability to present a coherent picture of the evolution of civilizations and nations. In treating national growth, he invariably stressed institutional developments, as in the present selection.

When we occupy ourselves with the government of Louis XIV, when we endeavor to appreciate the causes of his power and influence in Europe, we scarcely think of anything but his renown, his conquests, his magnificence and the literary glory of his time. It is to external causes that we apply ourselves and attribute the European preponderance of the French government. But I conceive that this preponderance had deeper and more serious foundations. We must not believe that it was simply by means of victories, fêtes, or even masterworks of genius, that Louis XIV and his government, at this epoch, played the part which it is impossible to deny them.

Many of you may remember, and all of you have heard speak of the effect which the consular government produced in France twenty-nine years ago, and of the condition in which it found our country. Without was impending foreign invasion, and continual disasters were occurring in our armies; within was an almost complete dissolution of power and of the people; there were no revenues, no public order; in a word, society was prostrate, humiliated and disorganized: such was France on the advent of the consular government. Who does not recall the prodigious and felicitous activity of this government, that activity which in a little time, secured the independence of the land, revived national honor, reorganized the administration, remodeled the legislation and, after a manner, regenerated society under the hand of power.

From François-Pierre-Guillaume Guizot, *History of Civilization in Europe,* translated by William Hazlitt (New York, 1900), pp. 208–216.

Well, the government of Louis XIV when it commenced, did something analogous to this for France; with great differences of times, proceedings and forms, it pursued and attained nearly the same results.

Recall to your memory the state into which France was fallen after the government of Cardinal Richelieu, and during the minority of Louis XIV: the Spanish armies always on the frontiers, sometimes in the interior; continual danger of an invasion; internal dissensions urged to extremity, civil war, the government weak and discredited at home and abroad. Society was perhaps in a less violent, but still sufficiently analogous state to ours, prior to the eighteenth *Brumaire*. It was from this state that the government of Louis XIV extricated France. His first victories had the effect of the victory of Marengo: they secured the country, and retrieved the national honor. I am about to consider this government under its principal aspects – in its wars, in its external relations, in its administration, and in its legislation; and you will see, I imagine, that the comparison of which I speak, and to which I attach no puerile importance (for I think very little of the value of historical parallels), you will see, I say, that this comparison has a real foundation, and that I have a right to employ it.

First of all let us speak of the wars of Louis XIV. The wars of Europe have originated, as you know, and as I have often taken occasion to remind you, in great popular movements. Urged by necessity, caprice, or any other cause, entire populations, sometimes numerous, sometimes in simple bands, have transported themselves from one territory to another. This was the general character of European wars until after the Crusades, at the end of the thirteenth century.

At that time began a species of wars scarcely less different from modern wars than the above. These were the distant wars, undertaken no longer by the people but by governments, which went at the head of their armies to seek states and adventures afar off. They quitted their countries, abandoned their own territories, and plunged, some into Germany, others into Italy, and others into Africa, with no other motives than personal caprice. Almost all the wars of the fifteenth and even a part of the sixteenth century were of this description. What interest – I speak not of legitimate interest – but what possible motive had France that Charles VIII should possess the kingdom of

Naples? This evidently was a war dictated by no political consideration: the king conceived that he had a personal right to the kingdom
of Naples, and with a personal aim and to satisfy his personal desire,
he undertook the conquest of a distant country, which was in no way
adapted for annexation to his kingdom; which, on the contrary, did
nothing but compromise his power externally, and internally his
repose. It was the same with the expedition of Charles V to Africa.
The latest war of this kind was the expedition of Charles XII against
Russia. The wars of Louis XIV had no such character; they were the
wars of a regular government, fixed in the center of its states, and
laboring to make conquests around it, to extend or consolidate its
territory; in a word, they were political wars.

They may have been just or unjust; they may have cost France too
dearly; there are a thousand reasons which might be adduced against
their morality and their excess; but they bear a character incomparably more rational than the antecedent wars: they were no
longer undertaken for whim or adventure; they were dictated by some
serious motive; it was some natural limit that it seemed desirable to
attain; some population speaking the same language that they aimed
at annexing; some point of defense against a neighboring power,
which it was thought necessary to acquire. No doubt personal ambition had a share in these wars; but examine one after another of the
wars of Louis XIV, particularly those of the first part of his reign, and
you will find that they had truly political motives; and that they were
conceived for the interest of France, for obtaining power, and for the
country's safety.

The results are proofs of the fact. France of the present day is
still, in many respects, what the wars of Louis XIV have made it.
The provinces which he conquered, Franche-Comté, Flanders and
Alsace, remain yet incorporated with France. There are sensible as
well as senseless conquests: those of Louis XIV were of the former
species; his enterprises have not the unreasonable and capricious
character which, up to this time, was so general; a skillful, if not
always just and wise policy, presided over them.

Leaving the wars of Louis XIV, and passing to the consideration
of his relations with foreign states, of his diplomacy, properly so
called, I find an analogous result. I have insisted upon the occurrence
of the birth of diplomacy in Europe at the end of the fifteenth century.

I have endeavored to show how the relations of governments and states between themselves, up to that time accidental, rare and transitory, became at this period more regular and enduring, how they took a character of great public interest; how, in a word, at the end of the fifteenth, and during the first half of the sixteenth century, diplomacy came to play an immense part in events. Nevertheless, up to the seventeenth century, it had not been, truly speaking, systematic; it had not led to long alliances, or to great, and, above all, durable combinations, directed, according to fixed principles, toward a constant aim, with that spirit of continuity which is the true character of established governments. During the course of the religious revolution, the external relations of states were almost completely under the power of the religious interest; the Protestant and Catholic leagues divided Europe. It was in the seventeenth century, after the Treaty of Westphalia, and under the influence of the government of Louis XIV, that diplomacy changed its character. It then escaped from the exclusive influences of the religious principle; alliances and political combinations were formed upon other considerations. At the same time it became much more systematic, regular, and constantly directed toward a certain aim, according to permanent principles. The regular origin of this system of balance in Europe belongs to this period. It was under the government of Louis XIV that the system, together with all the considerations attached to it, truly took possession of European policy. When we investigate what was the general idea in regard to this subject, what was the predominating principle of the policy of Louis XIV, I believe that the following is what we discover:

I have spoken of the great struggle between the pure monarchy of Louis XIV, aspiring to become universal monarchy, and civil and religious liberty, and the independence of states, under the direction of the Prince of Orange, William III. You have seen that the great fact of this period was the division of the powers under these two banners. But this fact was not then estimated as we estimate it now; it was hidden and unknown even to those who accomplished it; the suppression of the system of pure monarchy and the consecration of civil and religious liberty were, at bottom, the necessary result of the resistance of Holland and its allies to Louis XIV, but the question was not thus openly enunciated between absolute power and liberty.

It has been often said that the propagation of absolute power was the predominant principle of the diplomacy of Louis XIV; but I do not believe it. This consideration played no very great part in his policy, until latterly, in his old age. The power of France, its preponderance in Europe, the humbling of rival powers, in a word, the political interest and strength of the state, was the aim which Louis XIV constantly pursued, whether in fighting against Spain, the Emperor of Germany, or England; he acted far less with a view to the propagation of absolute power than from a desire for the power and aggrandizement of France and of its government. Among many proofs, I will adduce one which emanates from Louis XIV himself. In his *Memoirs,* under the year 1666, if I remember right, we find a note nearly in these words:

"I have had, this morning, a conversation with Mr. Sidney, an English gentleman, who maintained to me the possibility of reanimating the republican party in England. Mr. Sidney demanded from me, for that purpose, 400,000 livres. I told him that I could give no more than 200,000. He induced me to summon from Switzerland another English gentleman named Ludlow, and to converse with him of the same design."

And, accordingly, we find among the *Memoirs* of Ludlow, about the same date, a paragraph to this effect:

"I have received from the French government an invitation to go to Paris, in order to speak of the affairs of my country; but I am distrustful of that government."

And Ludlow remained in Switzerland.

You see that the diminution of the royal power in England was, at this time, the aim of Louis XIV. He fomented internal dissensions, and labored to resuscitate the republican party, to prevent Charles II from becoming too powerful in his country. During the embassy of Barillon in England the same fact constantly reappears. Whenever the authority of Charles seemed to obtain the advantage and the national party seemed on the point of being crushed, the French ambassador directed his influence to this side, gave money to the chiefs of the opposition, and fought, in a word, against absolute power, when that became a means of weakening a rival power to France. Whenever you attentively consider the conduct of external relations under Louis XIV, it is with this fact that you will be the most struck.

You will also be struck with the capacity and skill of French diplomacy at this period. The names of MM. de Torcy, d'Avaux, de Bon-repos, are known to all well-informed persons. When we compare the dispatches, the memoirs, the skill and conduct of these counsellors of Louis XIV with those of Spanish, Portuguese, and German negotiators, we must be struck with the superiority of the French ministers; not only as regards their earnest activity and the application to affairs, but also as regards their liberty of spirit. These courtiers of an absolute king judged of external events, of parties, of the requirements of liberty, and of popular revolutions, much better even than the majority of the English ministers themselves at this period. There was no diplomacy in Europe in the seventeenth century which appears equal to the French, except the Dutch. The ministers of John de Witt and of William of Orange, those illustrious chiefs of the party of civil and religious liberty, were the only ministers who seemed in condition to wrestle with the servants of the great and absolute king.

You see, then, that whether we consider the wars of Louis XIV, or his diplomatic relations, we arrive at the same results. We can easily conceive that a government, which conducted its wars and negotiations in this manner, should have assumed a high standing in Europe, and presented itself therein, not only as dreadworthy, but as skillful and imposing.

Let us now consider the interior of France, the administration and legislation of Louis XIV; we shall there discern new explanations of the power and splendor of his government.

It is difficult to determine with any degree of precision what we ought to understand by *administration* in the government of a state. Nevertheless, when we endeavor to investigate this fact, we discover, I believe, that, under the most general point of view, administration consists in an aggregate of means destined to propel, as promptly and certainly as possible, the will of the central power through all parts of society, and to make the force of society, whether consisting of men or money, return again, under the same conditions, to the central power. This, if I mistake not, is the true aim, the predominant characteristic of administration. Accordingly we find that in times when it is above all things needful to establish unity and order in society, administration is the chief means of attaining this end, of bringing together, of cementing, and of uniting incoherent and scattered elements. Such, in fact, was the work of the administration of

Louis XIV. Up to this time, there had been nothing so difficult, in France as in the rest of Europe, as to effect the penetration of the action of the central power into all parts of society, and to gather into the bosom of the central power the means of force existing in society. To this end Louis XIV labored, and succeeded, up to a certain point; incomparably better, at least, than preceding governments had done. I cannot enter into details; just run over, in thought, all kinds of public services, taxes, roads, industry, military administration, all the establishments which belong to whatsoever branch of administration; there is scarcely one of which you do not find either the origin, development, or great amelioration under Louis XIV. It was as administrators that the greatest men of his time, Colbert and Louvois, displayed their genius and exercised their ministry. It was by the excellence of its administration that his government acquired a generality, decision, and consistency which were wanting to all the European governments around him.

Under the legislative point of view this reign presents to you the same fact. I return to the comparison which I have already made use of, to the legislative activity of the consular government, to its prodigious work of revising and generally recasting the laws. A work of the same nature took place under Louis XIV. The great ordinances which he promulgated, the criminal ordinances, the ordinances of procedure, commerce, the marine, waters, and woods, are true codes, which were constructed in the same manner as our codes, discussed in the council of state, some of them under the presidency of Lamoignon. There are men whose glory consists in having taken part in this labor and this discussion, M. Pussort, for instance. If we were to consider it in itself, we should have much to say against the legislation of Louis XIV; it was full of vices, which now fully declare themselves, and which no one can deny; it was not conceived in the interest of true justice and of liberty, but in the interest of public order, and for giving more regularity and firmness to the laws. But even that was a great progress; and we cannot doubt but that the ordinances of Louis XIV, so very superior to anything preceding them, powerfully contributed to advance French society in the career of civilization.

You see that under whatever point of view we regard this government, we very soon discover the source of its power and influence.

It was the first government that presented itself to the eyes of Europe as a power sure of its position, which had not to dispute its existence with internal enemies – tranquil as to its dominions and the people, and intent only on governing. Up to that time all European governments had been unceasingly thrown into wars, which deprived them of security as well as leisure, or had been so beset with parties and internal enemies that they were compelled to spend their time in fighting for their lives. The government of Louis XIV appeared as the first which applied itself solely to the conduct of affairs, as a power at once definitive and progressive; which was not afraid of innovating, because it could count upon the future. There have, in fact, existed very few governments of such an innovating spirit. Compare it with a government of the same nature, with the pure monarchy of Philip II in Spain; it was more absolute than that of Louis XIV, and yet far less regular and less tranquil. But how did Philip II succeed in establishing absolute power in Spain? By stifling the activity of the country, by refusing to it every species of amelioration, by rendering the condition of Spain completely stationary. The government of Louis XIV, on the contrary, showed itself active in all kinds of innovations, favorable to the progress of letters, of arts, of riches, and, in a word, of civilization. These are the true causes of its preponderance in Europe; a preponderance such that it became upon the continent, during the whole of the seventeenth century, the type of government, not only for sovereigns, but even for nations.

And now we inquire – and it is impossible to help doing so – how it happened that a power, thus brilliant, and, judging from the facts which I have placed before you, thus well established, so rapidly fell into decline? How, after having played such a part in Europe, it became, in the next century, so inconsistent, weak, and inconsiderable? The fact is incontestable. In the seventeenth century the French government was at the head of European civilization; in the eighteenth century it disappeared; and it was French society, separated from its government, often even opposed to it, that now preceded and guided the European world in its progress.

It is here that we discover the incorrigible evil and the infallible effect of absolute power. I will not go into any detail concerning the faults of the government of Louis XIV; he committed many; I will speak neither of the War of the Spanish Succession, nor of the Revocation of the Edict of Nantes, nor of excessive expenses, nor of many other of the fatal measures that compromised his fortunes. I will take the merits of the government as I have described them. I will agree that perhaps there has never existed an absolute power more fully recognized by its age and nation, nor one which has rendered more real services to the civilization of its country and of Europe in general. But, by the very fact that this government had no other principle than absolute power, and reposed upon no other base than this, its decline became sudden and well merited. What France, under Louis XIV, essentially wanted, was political institutions and forces, independent, subsisting of themselves, and, in a word, capable of spontaneous action and resistance. The ancient French institutions, if they merited that name, no longer existed: Louis XIV completed their ruin. He took no care to endeavor to replace them by new institutions; they would have cramped him, and he did not choose to be cramped. All that appeared conspicuous at that period was will, and the action of central power. The government of Louis XIV was a great fact, a fact powerful and splendid, but without roots.

Free institutions are a guarantee, not only of the wisdom of governments, but also of their duration. No system can endure except by means of institutions. When absolute power has endured, it has been supported by true institutions, sometimes by the division of society into strongly distinct castes, sometimes by a system of religious institutions. Under the reign of Louis XIV institutions were wanting to power as well as to liberty. In France, at this period, nothing guaranteed either the country against the illegitimate actions of the government, or the government itself against the inevitable action of time. Thus we see the government helping in its own decay. It was not Louis XIV alone who was becoming aged and weak at the end of his reign: it was the whole absolute power. Pure monarchy was as much worn out in 1712 as was the monarch himself: and the evil was so much the more grave, as Louis XIV had abolished political morals as well as political institutions. There are no political morals without independence. He alone who feels that he has a strength of his own is always capable either of serving or opposing power. Energetic characters disappear with independent situations, and dignity of soul alone gives birth to security of rights.

This, then, is the state in which Louis XIV left France and power: a society in full development of riches, power and all kinds of intellectual activity; and side by side with this progressive society, a government essentially stationary, having no means of renewing itself, of adapting itself to the movement of its people; devoted, after half a century of the greatest splendor, to immobility and weakness, and already, during the life of its founder, fallen into a decline which seemed like dissolution. Such was the condition of France at the conclusion of the seventeenth century, a condition which impressed the epoch that followed with a direction and a character so different.

Albert Sorel

LOUIS XIV, ARBITRARY DESPOT

Albert Sorel (1842–1906) has been called the last of the great French historians of the nineteenth century. A professor of diplomatic history at the Ecole libre des sciences politiques, he was the author of a large number of works, but the one here excerpted is considered to be his masterpiece. Fundamentally, Sorel viewed the French Revolution as stemming from the inherent characteristics of the Old Regime, and regarded these as forces which caused French history to unfold with inexorable logic. In the following selection, he describes the French monarchy as an unlimited, arbitrary, extra-legal despotism in which individual rulers supplied the necessary motivation but were caught in a network of forces more powerful than themselves.

It has been widely debated whether France possessed a constitution during the Old Regime. Actually, the most secret archives of the realm might have been searched without discovering its text. The kings did not believe in it, and their jurists denied its existence.

"We should return to the fundamental laws" was the cry in all places whenever the state was troubled and power faltered, but these laws were nowhere to be found. All appealed to them, but no one knew them. . . . It was necessary that the principle of power remain a mystery, and if there was somewhere a fundamental law, it rested

From Albert Sorel, *L'Europe et la révolution française,* 3rd ed. (Paris, 1893), vol. 1, pp. 187–191, 195–199. Editor's translation.

upon this maxim which eliminated the necessity of establishing others: "The rights of peoples and those of kings never concur better than in silence."[1]

However, a powerful monarchy such as that of France did not prevail against so many foreign enemies and internal revolutions during eight consecutive centuries, and did not continue to develop in strength and brilliance, without this noble idea of fundamental law having a justification and producing certain rules which were derived from it. From accumulated precedents, one may draw a custom, and from custom one may abstract certain principles of public law. But this is only a theory. All its authority rests upon the history of the past, its entire sanction upon the history of the future. It does not concern the present, and men of practical politics pay no attention to it. Montesquieu composed certain chapters of his admirable work from this viewpoint, but all his genius could not cause the *Spirit of the Laws* to take the place of a writ of habeas corpus for a French subject or protect him against a *lettre de cachet,* an order of confiscation, or the arbitrary collection of a tax. If the custom of the old monarchy is to be reduced to its elements, one quickly reaches this formula which summarizes the whole spirit of its policy, as the preceding one epitomized the spirit of its public law: a wise monarch served by intelligent ministers. "The fickleness and inconstancy of the French," said Richelieu, "may be overcome only by the presence of their master. They are capable of anything, provided that those who command them are competent to indicate precisely what they must practice. I dare urge your majesty that if you will find leaders worthy of command, you will not lack subjects ready to obey. It is certain that the opinion which has spread throughout the world that the French are unfit for rule and discipline has no other foundation than the incompetence of their leaders who are unable to choose the necessary means to the ends which they envisage."[2] Such, in truth, was the entire foundation of the old monarchical establishment, and one might add, the true source of the greatness and the decline of French royalty.

---

[1] Retz, *Mémoires,* edited by A. Feillet (Paris, 1870), vol. I, p. 294.
[2] This seems to be composed of several quotations taken from the *Testament politique,* as found on pages 270, 388, and 389 in the edition by Louis André (Paris, 1947).—Ed.

It was necessary to have great kings with good ministers, or at least prudent kings with great ministers. Henry IV and Sully, Louis XIII and Richelieu were the perfect models of this earlier government in which men were everything and institutions nothing. If superior men were lacking, there was a void, for there was no law which enabled the nation to do without them or even to anticipate them, and one sees brilliant and fruitful reigns succeeded by long periods of trouble and sterility.

It was not the caprice of a few despots or the accidental accession to power of certain ambitious men that determined its course; rather, it was the general conditions of development of the nation and the state, even the force of circumstances. From the fourteenth century onward, says a historian, it was already decided, for the misfortune of royalty as well as the people, that the monarchy would be absolute and that old France would not know liberty.[3] The causes of this go back to the origins of monarchy and were derived as it were from its very reason for existence. In France, the nation and the state were formed together and grew in unison. Feudalism had fragmented the state and the fatherland; when the nation sought to reunite, the monarchy brought it together. The first condition of success in this endeavor was the destruction of the feudal system. Royalty might increase its power and the nation might be consolidated only at the expense of the nobles. The king regarded them as rivals or rebels, the bourgeois and peasants as oppressors. The bourgeois and the peasants appealed from them to the king. This horror of the French for feudalism provided all the strength of the king in his struggles against the nobles. It formed the basis of national history, and established its unity from the Middle Ages to the Revolution. Parallel impulses, which induced royalty to concentrate its power and the nation to gather around the king, availed themselves of the same instrument: the jurists, who sprang from the bourgeoisie, became the king's ministers and caused the principle of royal omnipotence to prevail in government.

There are no national histories which differ more in this respect than those of France and England. The great contrast which is mani-

---

[3] Ernest Lavisse, "Du pouvoir royal en France sous le règne de Charles V," *Revue politique et littéraire* (April 24, 1880), pp. 1009–1018, and "Etude sur le pouvoir royal au temps de Charles V," *Revue historique* 26 (1884): 233–280.

fest in the course of their histories is evident from their very beginning. In France, all effort toward growth was directed against the
feudal system; the primary element of the nation, the third estate,
worked for the king against the nobles. In England, all effort was
directed against royalty; the primary element of the nation was the
gentry, that is, the lesser country nobility allied with the bourgeoisie
against the king. Everything in France contributed to the unification
of power, in England toward its division. The national expression of
old England was a strong Parliament, that of old France a great king.
Furthermore, the English did not have to reckon with foreign inva-
sions; in the struggles which they undertook against royal supremacy,
and in the civil wars which ensued, they did not have to worry about
enemy intervention. On the contrary, this was a concern which dominated all the preoccupations of the French in their domestic upheavals. The threat of conquest continually weighed upon them, and
the danger of servitude to a foreign power left them very little
occasion for discord. It was in periods of disorder and anarchy that
the English set forth great demands against royalty; the French in
similar cases had neither the freedom nor the opportunity for this.
They might attempt to profit from their troubles by fettering their
king, but the foreigner would already have taken advantage of their
difficulties by fettering them. They had to attend to the most pressing
matters first, and the principle of national independence triumphed
over the desire for public liberty. . . .

It would be a misunderstanding of our national character to believe
it indifferent to affairs of state at that time and merely capable of
subservience. In sacrificing liberty to public safety, France had by no
means lost her desire for the former. In her history there is a constant
tradition of independence. Demands for rights were periodic, and
the French never allowed much time to pass without interrupting the
growth of despotism. The spirit of democratic liberty never showed
itself more markedly than in the communes; the *cahiers* of the Estates-
General, from the fourteenth century to the seventeenth, contain in
essence all the great demands of 1789. If the Estates failed in their
attempts to take over the government, this was because they were
called only in time of trouble, under the shadow of disaster and in the
midst of tumult. They had neither the experience nor the strength
necessary to govern; they could only formulate requests. Royalty put

these into effect. It executed with precision what the Estates had attempted with confusion, by deducing practical reforms from their *cahiers*. By assuring the people of the most important benefits which they expected from liberty, it caused them to forget the principle for a time. . . .

With Louis XIV, royalty reached its zenith. The apotheosis of the king was decreed, and statues were erected to him; he was a Roman Emperor placed in the ranks of the gods. "Then there was," says Michelet, "the most complete triumph of royalty, the most perfect union of a people and a man that will ever be found."[4] But toward the middle of the reign and during the final years of the century, the current which until then had sustained monarchy lessened imperceptibly, and the waters gathered as though thrown back on themselves. The promulgation of the Edict of Nantes by Henry IV had demonstrated the maturity of the monarchy; the revocation of this edict by his grandson marked its decline. Until then it had had coherence but no system; now it sought to create for itself a system and to deduce from this a dogma. It had lived by transactions; now it became exclusive. Its moderation had been its strength; now it began to languish through excess. It ruled no longer for the nation or the state; it ruled for itself and itself alone. It was its own purpose, its objective and its god. It was swallowed up in this cult and disappeared in it. It had grown like a great oak which gathers all the moisture of the neighboring fields into its sap, and gives them in return the coolness of its shadow and the salubriousness of the air, purified by the mysterious work of its foliage. At the time when it seemed most majestic in the splendor of its most beautiful summer, the sap ceased to flow in its branches; they fell little by little as though struck by paralysis. Its trunk became desiccated and silently wasted away. Its rotten roots no longer held the soil, and its stripped branches no longer cleansed the air; the rains beat its summit and parasites sapped its base. Formerly it offered shelter from hurricanes; now it no longer resisted. The first that arose broke and toppled it.

In order that royalty might maintain and renew itself, it was necessary that it accomplish reforms and continue its work of national emancipation, govern with brilliance and moderation at the same time,

---

[4] J. Michelet, *Précis de l'histoire moderne,* 9th edition (Paris, 1876), pp. 338–39.

Drevet, *Portrait of Louis XIV* (after Rigaud). Rigaud's full-length portrait is probably the most famous representation ever made of Louis XIV. It shows the king with his symbols of office, the sword, crown and scepter, in a setting of truly regal magnificence and splendor. It also shows the high heels that he wore to increase his stature and the calf of his leg of which he was inordinately proud. (*Courtesy of the Fogg Art Museum, Harvard University. Gray Collection*)

RKX.   LUDOVICUS.   LUDOVICUS REX.

This cartoon by William Makepeace Thackeray is from his *Paris Sketch Book* (1839) and is obviously a satire on Rigaud's portrait of Louis XIV. Thackeray's comments: "A king is not every inch a king, for all the poet may say; and it is curious to see how much precise majesty there is in that majestic figure of Ludovicus Rex. In the plate [above], we have endeavored to make the exact calculation. The idea of kingly dignity is equally strong in the two outer figures; and you see, at once, that majesty is made out of the wig, the high-heeled shoes, and cloak, all *fleurs-de-lis* bespangled. As for the little lean, shrivelled, paunchy old man, of five feet two, in a jacket and breeches, there is no majesty in *him* at any rate; and yet he has just stepped out of that very suit of clothes. Put the wig and shoes on him and he is six feet high;—the other fripperies, and he stands before you majestic, imperial, and heroic! Thus do barbers and cobblers make the gods that we worship; for do we not all worship him? Yes; though we all know him to be stupid, heartless, short, of doubtful personal courage, worship and admire him we must; and have set up, in our hearts, a grand image of him, endowed with wit, magnanimity, valor, and enormous heroic stature."

keep the state prosperous and the people satisfied, refrain from excesses and correct abuses, suppress the now useless rights of the
nobles as it had earlier destroyed their powers in government, free
the land and complete the emancipation of men. It was expected to
be tolerant in the sixteenth century, powerful in the seventeenth, and
enlightened in the eighteenth. When it demurred and avoided its
tasks, the people regained sufficient consciousness of themselves
and their rights to demand what they desired; and the king found
before him, leading the campaign, those same jurists who for five
centuries had fought for him against the nobles. After having won
power for him, they sought to exercise it with him; but when he
resisted, they used it against him.

Royalty disarmed itself in their hands; it dismantled all its fortresses and gave over their approaches; resistance was forbidden
to it when this meant resisting the nation. Everyone merged into the
people before him, said Saint-Simon in speaking of Louis XIV. This
colossus of state was isolated in the midst of the mob, and nothing
protected it. Louis XI had subdued the collateral dynasties, Henry IV
the religious factions, Richelieu the political parties, Louis XIV the
Parlements; as for the nobility, for four centuries royalty had sought
to deprive them of all influence, organization, and political power.
The edifice of the state enjoyed incomparable brilliance and splendor,
but it resembled a Gothic cathedral in which the height of the nave
and the arches had been pushed upward beyond all reason, weakening the walls as they were raised ever higher. This done, in order to
disengage the monument and give it greater distinction, all at once
they destroyed the wings and the buttresses which supported its
sides. It was seen to totter on its foundation, and at the slightest blow
of a battering ram against its walls, it collapsed under the thrust of
its vaults and the crushing weight of its towers.

Louis XIV carried the principle of monarchy to its utmost limit, and
abused it in all respects to the point of excess. He left the nation
crushed by war, mutilated by banishments, and impatient of the yoke
which it felt to be ruinous. Men were worn-out, the treasury empty,
all relationships strained by the violence of tension, and in the immense framework of the state there remained no institution except
the accidental appearance of genius. Things had reached the point
where, if a great king did not appear, there would be a great
revolution.

IV LOUIS XIV IN TWENTIETH-CENTURY SCHOLARSHIP

Ernest Lavisse

LOUIS XIV, PERFECTER AND DESTROYER OF MONARCHY

Ernest Lavisse (1842–1922) is considered by many to have been the out-standing French historian of his generation. Professor at the University of Paris, member of the French Academy and recipient of many honors, he published a number of exceptional works and had considerable influence upon the writing of history and its place in the French educational system. As editor of the Histoire de France depuis les Origines jusqu'à la Révolution, *he planned and carried to completion one of the most successful collabora-tive projects of modern historical scholarship. The excerpt given below is of especial interest in that it was written by Lavisse himself. It may be regarded as the classic exposition of the strengths and weaknesses of the French monarchy according to the liberal tradition.*

Louis XIV – and this was evident as early as his first words and actions – simply made himself the aim and end of things. He was probably familiar in general with the long, learned theories of the ecclesiastics and jurists concerning the excellence of the royal power, but he did not know what to make of this erudition. He believed in himself as an act of faith. If he ever pronounced the words, "I am the state," he merely meant, "It is I, Louis, who speaks to you."

This ego, which dominated an entire era and gave it its character, was the product of a long history. In Louis XIV, the line of the Cape-tians and the line of the Hapsburgs, noble, ancient and tired, gave forth a final flowering, haughty and grave. He was the grandson of Henry IV but also of Philip II, the great-grandson of Antoine de Bour-bon, but also of Charles V.[1] He was of France, but also, even more, of Spain. He did not resemble his father, a thin, slight French gentle-man; like his mother, he was stout, sedate, and grave. The unceasing gravity was not typically French, nor the natural arrogance, nor the sacerdotal order imposed on the court whose confusion and over-

From Ernest Lavisse, *Histoire de France depuis les Origines jusqu'à la Révolution,* Librairie Hachette, Paris, 1911, vol. 7[1], pp. 131–138; vol. 8[1], pp. 476–480. Reprinted by permission of Librairie Hachette. Editor's translation.

[1] This is erroneous. Anne of Austria, Louis XIV's mother, was the daughter of Philip III, not Philip II. Thus, there was an additional generation on the Hapsburg side of Louis' ancestry.—Ed.

familiarity Anne of Austria found lamentable, nor the distance between the king and all other men, nor the mingling of lewdness and
devotion, nor the government by inner chamber and bureaux, nor
the ambition to appear to dominate Europe, nor the policy of inter-
fering in all matters, nor the total confusion of the state and religion
which seemed to preserve the memory of the autos-da-fé of Aragon
and Castile, nor Versailles which, like the Escorial, became the
abode of a majesty which isolated itself from ordinary life in order
to live merely with itself. Without doubt, one may not claim to weigh
exactly the effects of undeniable but obscure hereditary influences,
yet it should not be forgotten that kings also are sons of their
mothers. The sons of Catherine de Medicis were obviously Italians
on the throne of France. Actually, when examining the matter closely,
it is evident that few kings of France were true Frenchmen.

It was from Spain and Austria, it seems, much more than from
France, that Louis XIV received his enormous, incredible Pharaoh-like
pride; but historical circumstances in France awakened and stimulated an atavistic attitude in him.

His first precise recollection went back to Saint-Germain, to the
moment when his mother left the deathbed of Louis XIII, came to his
room, and knelt before him "to hail her son and her king."[2] Two days
later, it was the trip to Paris under the escort of the superb corps of
the royal household and the mounted nobility in all their finery, the
advance body of Parisian carriages as far as Nanterre, the adoration
by the kneeling city magistrates at the Porte Saint-Honoré, the people
swarming in the streets or perched on the roof tops, the immense
acclamation, "Long live the king," and the cry of the women, "How
handsome he is!" Two days later, the little child, carried in the arms
of the captain of the guard and preceded by heralds at arms, entered
the Parlement. He was placed on the throne; an empty space ac-
centuated the distance between himself and his mother; before him
ushers knelt. The queen raised him from the throne, and he assured
"his" Parlement of "his good-will." The Chancellor, dressed in purple
and holding in his hand the cap of state "filled with gold," knelt before him and received his orders.[3] At the age when most children

[2] Madame de Motteville, *Mémoires,* Michaud et Poujoulat. 2ᵉ série, vol. 10 (Paris, 1838), p. 44.—Ed.
[3] Ibid., pp. 46–47. Cf. Mathieu Molé, *Mémoires,* vol. 3 (Paris, 1856), pp. 56–65.—Ed.

watch puppets, it was for Louis XIV the raising of the curtain on life. He has been criticized for being always a king and never a man, but he could not distinguish the king from the man within himself, he who had always known himself as king. Royalty was essential to him; it was his very nature.

The first writing that we have from his own hand is a copy of an exercise in penmanship: "Homage is owed to kings; they do all that is pleasing to them."[4] During the period of his education, he heard nothing else. He experienced the ordeal of the Fronde, but the rebels cried "Long live the king alone!" He was not aware of the insults of any writers. Whenever he appeared, it was a triumph. When the court traveled to Normandy early in 1650 in order to check the intrigues of the party of the princes, "the appearance of the king" settled all matters. "It was said that if the queen wished to conquer all the realms of the universe, she had only to cause the king to travel through them long enough to show himself."[5]

After the Fronde, confusion remained in men's minds. Faith in monarchy was obscured by vivid recollections and the bad government of the Cardinal, but it awaited only an opportune moment to reappear in all its splendor.

Destiny was fulfilled. The earlier government of France had left behind only decayed ruins, and the recent revolt had been wretched; in it had perished the idea of monarchy limited by magistrates and tempered by resistance. There remained to the nation no means of respecting and admiring itself other than respecting and admiring itself in the king, by whom it was represented. It desired that he become greater than the greatest kings, a more powerful potentate than the potentates ruling over all others. Since the pride of our ancestors made a virtue and glory of necessity, the perfection of monarchical authority seemed to them a privilege of France. They boasted that their king was "truly Emperor within his realm, for there he recognized no law but his own ordinances," and that, alone among monarchs, he gave no reason for his decisions other than this: "For such is our good pleasure."[6]

---

[4] G. Lacour-Gayet, *L'Education politique de Louis XIV,* 2nd ed. (Paris, 1923), p. 97. —Ed.
[5] P. H. Chérot, *La Première Jeunesse de Louis XIV* (Lille, 1892), pp. 71–72.—Ed.
[6] Cf. Lacour-Gayet, op. cit., Book II, chapter 7.—Ed.

Incessant emphasis upon the idea of God almost resulted in confounding divine monarchy with human, since royalty was the divinity visibly projected among men. Indeed, it was constantly re-iterated by highly divergent voices, Huguenot as well as Catholic, that the king was the image of God. One might even wonder whether, on the contrary, it might not be God who modeled Himself after the king: "The God of the seventeenth century was a species of Louis XIV who was the image and suzerain of the other. The same inversion transformed heaven and the state. The local, independent saints of the Middle Ages were effaced and subordinated, as were the free and feudal lords, in order to form a corps of worshipers. . . . Superstitions declined. Purified and pompous religion offered the most correct and the noblest of spectacles."[7] The two cults, that of the king and that of God, were united in a profound intimacy, and gave to their devotees a very simple rule for all life: to live submissively under the power of the God who was God, and the king who was His image. The king, as God, did whatever was pleasing to him. His greatest faults and the greatest miseries of his subjects no more undermined faith in the monarchy than storms and pestilence troubled faith in God. This state of conscience well suited an era in which it was impossible to resist the church and royalty that had emerged together from the peril of revolt. Religious sentiment and loyalty to the crown gave a beautiful adornment to this renunciation of intelligence and will.

Actually, man in all eras has sought to invent superhuman beings, as a means of rising above all his weaknesses. The ancients had their demigods; the philosophers of today dream of a superman who will enslave humanity but in whom it will be exalted. Old France had its superman, who was the king.

It wished the king to be glorious. A certain sentiment of glory had returned to us from pagan antiquity. The men of the Middle Ages admired the valiance of heroes who downed an adversary; they loved and sung of great deeds of the sword; but they erected no columns or arches of triumph, carved no trophies or medals to perpetuate individual countenances, and engraved no lists of honors in stone or bronze. They erected no effigies in public squares; statues of kings

---

[7] H. Taine, *La Fontaine et ses fables* (Paris, 1861), pp. 217–218.

and the great lay humbly upon squat tombs awaiting the day when the trumpet of the angel would announce the resurrection and last judgment. All the life to come was in God, and glory was reserved for God, the Virgin, and the saints. The Renaissance revived for us arches of triumph on which modern heroes were either nude or costumed like the ancients, bas-reliefs where the bent backs of the vanquished filed past, trophies of captured arms, medals with laudatory inscriptions, statues upon high pedestals, heroes who tossed crowns about and hurled extravagant eulogies with their trumpets, and the pagan pride of living in the memory of great men by acquiring glory. In the middle of the seventeenth century, the love of glory impassioned all France, that is to say, three or four hundred thousand persons, clerics, nobles and jurists who had been educated by the Jesuits and the colleges in the universities. It was celebrated in French and Latin verse; it inspired the theatre, the novel, and the pomp of decorative festivals in which the king was costumed as the sun and the princes as heroes.

A great reign was awaited and predicted. From the pulpit, it was proclaimed that "something great and illustrious was stirring for His Majesty."[8] Writers sought to find greatness in their master. The servants of the king, Colbert, Louvois and Lionne, wished to act grandly. Thus there was enthusiasm and adoration from the moment that they perceived in Louis XIV the possibility of a Louis the Great. He was imagined to be much more handsome than he actually was; the eyes of contemporaries surveyed his build and were dazzled by his majesty even when they saw him in his dressing gown or playing billiards. There seemed to be a universal conspiracy to view him as a man of genius. The great power and authority of Louis XIV were derived from the conformity of his person with the spirit of his times.

He was a lover of glory. He declared this love on every occasion: "The love of glory assuredly takes precedence over all others in my soul." In his *Memoirs*, he compared it with true love:

> . . . The impetuosity of my youth and the great desire that I had to augment my reputation gave me a very strong passion for action, but from this moment I realized that the love of glory has the same tenderness,

---

[8] Bossuet, "Sermon on the Duties of Kings," April 2, 1662, quoted in Lacour-Gayet, op. cit., p. 207.—Ed.

and, if I dare say it, the same timidities as the most tender passions. For
the greater my ardor to distinguish myself, the greater was my apprehen-
sion of failure, and regarding the shame that follows the smallest faults
as a great misfortune, I sought to take all possible precautions in my
conduct. . . . I found myself impeded and pressed forward almost equally
by this unique desire for glory.[9]

In his lust for glory which was as strong in him as that of the flesh,
he wished to be glorious like Augustus, the protector of letters; like
Constantine and Theodosius, the defenders of the Church, and like
Justinian, the legislator. It was necessary, he thought, to have "variety
in glory." But while still young, he had "a secret predilection for
arms,"[10] which he deeply regretted in his final confession: "I have
been too fond of war."[11]

For himself as well as for his contemporaries, glory in arms was
more admirable and more royal than any other: "the role of conqueror
was deemed the noblest and highest of titles." A king made war as a
duty, because of his destiny one might say. Whenever he made peace,
Louis XIV boasted that his "paternal love" for his subjects had prevailed over his "own glory"; his subjects praised him for this as a
meritorious sacrifice and benefit, while he in order to demonstrate
that war was strictly his own doing, thanked them for their "assistance." Everyone admired and celebrated the glory of his arms, the
Te Deums of the churches, the odes of poets, the art of the painters,
architects and sculptors. The king posed before the painters, sculptors, and poets who awaited his feats. Exhausted from praising, they
begged him to cease the pose for a moment:

Great king, cease to conquer or I cease to write. . . .[12]

One force alone might have restrained this fatal pride and passion
for glory; this was religion. But religion as Louis XIV understood it
merely increased his pride.

---

[9] Louis XIV, *Mémoires,* edited by Charles Dreyss (Paris, 1860), vol. 2, pp. 397, 374.
—Ed.
[10] Ibid., vol. 1, p. 251.—Ed.
[11] This is found in the version of Louis' last words to the Dauphin as printed in
Voltaire, *Siècle de Louis XIV,* chapter 28 (page 160 in the edition of Paris, 1819).
However, a more accurate text of Louis' words is given by A. de Boislisle in his
edition of Saint-Simon, *Mémoires* (Paris, 1915), vol. 27, p. 275. This version does not
include the phrase in the form given by Lavisse.—Ed.
[12] Boileau, Epitre VIII, *Au Roi,* line 1, in *Œuvres* (Paris, 1868), p. 160.—Ed.

The young king was not yet "devout" in 1661. It did not even seem that he might become so. He was entirely wrapped up in his glory, work, love, and festivals. He traveled from Paris to Saint-Germain, to Chambord, Fontainebleau and Versailles, increasingly abandoning Paris, which the Fronde had dishonored, until he might quit and disown it altogether. The first summer that he passed at Fontainebleau after the death of the Cardinal was delightful. Madame de La Fayette has described those days when the youthful court journeyed through the forest to bathe in the river, and then returned to the chateau. The ladies on horseback, gallantly clad and with a thousand feathers on their heads, were accompanied by the king and by the spirit of youth. After supper, they mounted the carriages and went driving for part of the night around the canal, to the sound of languorous violins. During these nocturnal outings, the king "placed himself near the carriage of La Vallière, whose door curtain was down, and in the obscurity of the night he spoke to her with great ease."[13] For La Vallière, the first of the publicly recognized mistresses, the king gave at Versailles, then a small chateau in a little park, the "Pleasures of the Enchanted Isle," which lasted nine days during the spring of the year 1664, and was brilliant and wondrous. Molière was its principal figure; mounted in an allegorical chariot, he represented the god Pan, the most pagan of the gods. In the *Princess d'Elide*, he celebrated the right to love at random:

> *At the age when one is lovable,*
> *Nothing is so beautiful as to love. . .*[14]

Finally, on Tuesday, May 12, he gave the first three acts of *Tartuffe,* that sacrilegious comedy which the Company of the Holy Sacrament sought to have condemned. Was the King of France about to be led astray in the company of libertines?

He did not believe it for a moment. Undoubtedly, he did not like to be crossed in his love affairs, and he was not instructed in religion and would never instruct himself in it; but his mother and his con-

---

13 Madame de La Fayette, *Histoire de Madame Henriette d'Angleterre,* Michaud et Poujoulat, 3e série, vol. 8 (Paris, 1839), p. 185. See the entire passage, pp. 183–185.—Ed.
14 Molière, *La Princesse d'Elide,* Prologue, scene 1.—Ed.

fessors had given him pious habits. He recited his prayers in the morning and evening, told his beads, heard mass every day, listened attentively to long and numerous sermons, and already demanded good behavior and an appearance of devotion from the young courtiers when in chapel. Besides, he had personal reasons for loving religion, reasons which guide individuals without noise or debate, unperceived in their consciences. His birth had been a miracle which King Louis XIII and Queen Anne had won by vows and prayers after long, sterile years. They called him Heaven-sent. In gratitude for his coming, Queen Anne had dedicated the Church, *Val de Grâce,* "To the Infant Jesus and the Virgin Mother." They told him all this, as likewise that he was the Most Christian King and the eldest son of the Church. These were agreeable things to hear, and he believed them. He did not doubt that he was blessed among all men and the nearest to God.

The proximity of God did not trouble Louis XIV. The priests told him that he was a man and mere dust, but he did not believe them. Did they believe it themselves? He also heard them say that he was the image of God: "O kings! ye are as gods!"[15] He set forth his duties toward God in such curious maxims as this: "God is infinitely jealous of His glory. He perhaps made us so great merely to ensure that our deference would honor Him the more."[16] Thus, without embarrassment and with evident sincerity, he established a reciprocal relationship between himself and God. He even believed that God needed him to a certain extent. After recounting his initial successes, he added that he felt obliged to thank Him. He enumerated a long series of evidences of his gratitude: a rule adopted to restrict the "adherents of the pretended reformed religion" to the precise terms of the Edict of Nantes, prohibition of Huguenot assemblies, alms given to the poor of Dunkirk in order to bring them back to Catholicism, negotiations with the Dutch in favor of the Catholics of Guelders, and dispersion of "communities where the Jansenist spirit of innovation was fostered."[17] This was, on the one hand, a poor idea of God whom the king assumed to be troubled by passion for glory like any wretched

[15] Bossuet, *Politique tirée de l'Ecriture sainte,* edition cited, pp. 86, 239, 389, etc. —Ed.
[16] Louis XIV, *Mémoires,* vol. 2, p. 423.—Ed.
[17] Ibid., vol. 2, pp. 418–419.—Ed.

mortal, and, on the other, a very high idea of himself. The two views, in combination, inspired a formidable program of action that would be followed during the entire reign. But Louis XIV nevertheless desired it to be known that on the occasion of the Jubilee, "he followed a procession on foot, accompanied by his servants."[18] He seemed to believe that God, in the highest heaven, inclined His white head and with a certain pleasure of pride, beheld the King of France taking the trouble to make this journey on foot.

Handsomeness, vigor, grace, a nature far from wicked, a just and upright intelligence, love of his profession, a high-minded view of professional duty and application to that duty; but a spiritual training that was almost nil, an insufficient and unprincipled political education, and above all this religion, this passion for glory, this pride, these legacies of the past weighing upon a man who after all was quite ordinary and did not have it in him to counterbalance this powerful and oppressive fate; this man in peril of being perverted: the peril that egotism might become adoration of self, that his just and upright intelligence might be blinded, that his love of his profession and application to duty would be diverted from great and serious ends to the satisfactions of pure pride, that his prudence might be restricted to occupying himself with precautions and artifices in order to prepare and rectify rash actions; peril of a conduct and a policy guided by extravagant eulogies and arches of triumph – thus appeared, charming and yet disquieting, the man whom they would call the Great King. He must be permitted to retain this appellation, but it is remarkable that no one has ever said that Louis XIV was a great man. He was great as king, as a functionary of royalty, The glory of his ancestors, and the wealth, fortune and beauty of France, clothed him with a splendor which he wore as a garment that was natural to him. He was the high priest of the cult whose idol he was, believing with an undisturbed faith, and impeccably performing its rites. It was not in vain that he sought to demonstrate as he said, "that there is still a king in the world." Not only in his own time, when kings imitated his palace, his court, his personal qualities, his deeds, and his entire way, but for all time to come, he was the type of personage who would be called king. He was an exemplification and a brilliant

---

[18] Ibid., vol. 2, p. 421.—Ed.

witness in the history of monarchical power, likewise demonstrating the astonishing aptitude of men for admiration and obedience. But, divested of royalty, he was an "honest gentleman," of whom there were many at the court and in the cities at that time. Neither La Bruyère nor Saint-Simon recognized him as such.

*   *   *

Regarding this long reign, . . . the general conclusion that incorporates and summarizes all others is indicated by the fact that the monarchy survived Louis XIV only seventy-four years, hardly more than the duration of his reign. Louis XIV exhausted the French monarchy.

The ceaseless warfare, the mad, enormous expenditures for luxuries, the errors of an exaggerated Colbertism into which Colbert himself would not have fallen, the aggravated defects of a fiscal system best fitted to discourage work, the Revocation of the Edict of Nantes and the consequent wastage of strength reduced this industrious land, capable of admirable effort and endurance in the worst adversity, to great miseries which were attested by much certain and lamentable evidence. As for the management of state finances, it was the history of an individual who was born rich but annually spent beyond his means, maintained himself by ruinous expedients, lost all credit with his suppliers, regarded it as meritorious to sell his plate and to offer to his intendant to pawn his jewels, and who finally resorted to swindling and ended in bankruptcy.

Louis XIV regarded his religious policy as the most important element of his rule; he did not succeed in it. He wished to render his reign an "enlightened pontificate"; but he thereby entered into rivalry with the Pope, the ecumenical pontiff who was unwilling to be dispossessed by this provincial pontiff. After great deeds and haughty, insulting words, he was finally forced to stoop to the prayers of a humble penitent who asked that secrecy surround the admission of his sins. Louis XIV was no more successful in his effort to restore his subjects to the unity of the faith. He said, "there was nothing that he would not sacrifice for the preservation of the faith in his realm." His sacrifices, which were enormous, remained unavailing; toward the end of his reign he witnessed a strange revival of Protestantism and Jansenism. Protestants and Jansenists would remain the enemies of this persecuting regime, since resentments and hatreds for the cause of religion endure as long as religions themselves. In the struggle that was about to begin against absolute monarchy, the persecuted would again be found. Already politics were mingled with religious affairs; Gallicanism, almost abandoned by the king, found a refuge in the muzzled Parlement which was fuming in silence and would speak again on the very day after the death of Louis XIV.

The clearest success of Louis XIV was to secure political obedience. But this was not without difficulty. Each year brought revolts, some of them very serious. It is necessary to construct the exact history of these insurrections, the motives invoked, the insults and the menaces uttered, if we wish to understand clearly the prodromes of the Revolution. But these were only short and isolated rumbles of thunder; the general storm was foreseen only by a few who doubtless did not entirely believe their premonitions. Besides, the rebels were usually found only among the most wretched "individuals"; their fate was quickly settled by the firing squad, hangings, or sentences to the galleys. The only thing that mattered was the obedience of the "corporate bodies," the Parlements, nobles and clergy.

Did Louis XIV ever ask himself whether they might serve the state other than with obedience? This was asked very near to him. Fénelon thought that it was necessary "to recall again the true form of the realm and to temper despotism, the cause of all our ills," as well as to persuade "all bodies in the nation that they must sustain the monarchy which is on the brink of ruin."[19] But if Louis XIV "recalled" any ancient form of the realm, this was to despise it, and he certainly did not believe that "monarchy was on the brink of ruin." He said that Fénelon was a "beautiful visionary spirit." All aims of reformers seemed vain imaginings to him; he knew no reality but himself. More and more he made himself the master; he became the autocrat who gave orders directly into the ears of those who would execute them. The ministers, each in his department, imitated him; bureaucracy was perfected. Through the acts of the intendants, it penetrated everywhere, even into the smallest communities and workshops, heaping regulation upon regulation until the statutes of the merchants and artisans equaled "in volume the entire body of

---

[19] Fénelon, *Lettre au duc de Chevreuse,* pp. 181, 178 in the edition by Charles Urbain.—Ed.

Roman law." In this great realm, there was no longer anyone who could breathe freely.

Louis XIV was not the "enlightened" despot that Colbert wished him to be. He allowed everything to survive that would not inconvenience him, the king, but likewise all that so thoroughly handicapped Colbert, the diversity among the provinces, differences of customs, weights and measures, quotas and kinds of taxes, a sort of anarchy under the beautiful appearance of monarchical order. In the same manner he maintained the privileges of the now subordinated church and nobility, and preserved the Parlements after having taken away "their authority and almost their honor." The era that would soon be called the Old Regime, that compound of useless and fatal remnants, settings in shreds, rights that lacked duties and were becoming abuses, those ruins of a long past above which towered a solitary despot who refused to prepare for the future – it would be unjust to attribute all this to Louis XIV alone, but he brought it to the highest degree of imperfection and stamped it with death.

He extended the frontiers of the realm. It is not to him that we should attribute the acquisition of Roussillon, Artois and Alsace; this was accomplished by Louis XIII and the two Cardinals; but he conquered and retained the Franche-Comté, a part of Flanders, a part of Hainaut, the Cambrésis and Strasbourg. With an admirable ring of fortresses, he made his realm a solidly "entrenched camp of twenty million men."[20] But however considerable these gains may have been in the history of our national territory, the great power of France in the year 1661 and the equally great weakness of Europe warranted the hope of much more. . . .

Without doubt, the annexation of the Low Countries and the establishment of great maritime strength would have met with very considerable resistance, and it has been shown that France has always experienced difficulty in fulfilling her two-fold destiny to be amphibious. But one may with good reason think that Louis XIV, given the exceptional circumstances that were presented to him, might have turned them to much better account if he had not followed a policy of divergent and contradictory intentions based upon the fixed idea of winning glory for himself by humiliating others; a mixture of pru-

---

[20] Lemontey, op. cit., p. 330.—Ed.

dence, trickery, and arrogant acts that destroyed in an instant many an elaborate stratagem; methods whereby everyone was browbeaten, insulted or duped so that hostile coalitions continually expanded and finally included all Europe; a policy of perpetual wars, conducted by a man who had the abilities of a good "staff officer" but neither the mind of a general nor the heart of a soldier.

For long, France loved her king and almost adored him, admiring his personal greatness and glory in his words and deeds. When she suffered cruelly from the many errors that he committed, anger and curses burst forth. It seemed that the glory of Louis XIV was quite dead, but it would soon come to life again. Early in the following reign, Frenchmen endeavored to live and to act in a manner unlike anything that they had ever known, but they could not. Louis XIV had given old France its final political form, despotism. No one after him was able to guide this regime, and they fell into the incredible position of "finding despotism everywhere but the despot nowhere."[21] Internal government and foreign policy suffered from weakness and incoherence, and France declined; then Voltaire once more called attention to the greatness of Louis XIV whose faults had been forgotten. In later periods, although the great king has been scrutinized by severe critics and accurate historians, he has retained his great renown. Reason, which exposes the "destructive foundations" of this reign, is resisted by the imagination, captivated by the "brilliant exterior." It is pleased by the memory of this man who was not in the least wicked, who had good qualities and even virtues, beauty, grace, and the gift of able speech; who, at the moment when France was resplendent, represented her brilliantly, and refused to admit defeat when she was overwhelmed; who sustained his great role from the lifting of the splendid curtain to the dismal scenes in the last act, in a fairy-like setting, the palaces built in unknown places and on barren soil, the fountains that sprang from an earth without water, the trees brought from Fontainebleau or Compiègne, the retinue of similarly uprooted men and women who were transplanted there in order to participate in the chorus of a tragedy which is so remote from our eyes, unaccustomed to such spectacles and ways, that it partakes of some of the charm and greatness of an antiquity.

21 Ibid., p. 450.—Ed.

Louis Madelin

LOUIS XIV, EPITOME OF HIS TIME

Louis Madelin (1871–1956) is regarded as ranking high among twentieth cen-
tury French historians. His works are generally characterized by extensive
research, considerable literary skill, and, most important, an ability to rep-
resent the diverse elements of a given period as forming a genuine synthesis,
an organic whole. Repeatedly in his writings, he stressed that the govern-
ment of France during the period of absolute monarchy (and later) was not
usurpation, even when most despotic, but mirrored the French nation and was
conceived in its likeness. Such is his fundamental view of the strength and
historical significance of Louis XIV, as set forth in the following selection.

On March 7th, 1661, while Cardinal Mazarin was breathing his last,
the young king made his wishes known. "We beheld," said a witness,
"the living replace the dying."[1] He would keep the ministers, Lionne,
Le Tellier, Fouquet and the others because this was "useful"; however, "they were destined not to govern but to serve the king."[2] The
secretaries of state received an order "to sign nothing more without
speaking of it to the king"; the Superintendent was directed "to do
nothing further concerning finances without its being enregistered in
a book that should remain with him."[3] When the president of the
Assembly of the Clergy came to him to ask to whom he should address himself henceforth, now that the Cardinal was dead, Louis
answered, "To me, my Lord Archbishop."[4] It was the moment which
he had awaited with a certain anguish: "that which I had hoped for
and feared simultaneously for so long."[5] From these words, one
senses the solemnity that his appearance on the scene had in his
eyes. In any case, with a firm hand, "he alone," said the surprised
Gramont, "grasped the helm of state."[6]

From Louis Madelin, *Histoire de la nation française*, edited by G. Hanotaux (Paris:
Librairie Plon, 1924), vol. 4, pp. 285–297. Reprinted by permission of Librairie Plon.
Editor's translation.

[1] Madame de Motteville, *Mémoires*, Michaud et Poujoulat, eds. (Paris, 1838), p. 505.
—Ed.
[2] Louis XIV, *Mémoires*, edited by Charles Dreyss (Paris, 1860), vol. 2, p. 269.—Ed.
[3] Ibid., vol. 2, pp. 429–430.—Ed.
[4] Abbé de Choisy, *Mémoires*, Michaud et Poujoulat, eds. (Paris, 1839), p. 577.—Ed.
[5] Louis XIV, *Mémoires*, vol. 2, p. 375.—Ed.
[6] Maréchal de Gramont, *Mémoires*, Michaud et Poujoulat, eds. (Paris, 1839), p. 328.
—Ed.

His land and his century were awaiting him. Before he had done anything, his subjects said that a great king was about to appear. The century would long continue to accord him this widespread support, for the land and the times were reflected in him, since he was born of the century and of France.

"Heaven itself seemed to promise me its aid by arranging everything according to the very design that it inspired in me," he wrote. "Everywhere, all was calm. . . ."[7]

"All was calm," but earlier, all had been violently agitated: political and personal passions had been unloosed; the ruins that they had created had not been rebuilt. In his *Memoirs,* the king himself has described without vehemence, and with a certain proud satisfaction, the troubles from which everyone had barely emerged, and the great calm that followed.

The France that still remembered the League detested the Fronde. It hated its brief folly; indeed, it hardly understood the Fronde, which seemed an inconceivable aberration in this century of reason. We know in what terms the populace came to curse it at the feet of the restored ruler.

This was the century that in its youth had acclaimed Corneille and adopted Descartes. When studying Richelieu, I showed how this statesman had brought his times to fruition. After this short-lived crisis, the times returned to reason.

The generation of Richelieu was dead – the generation which had learned from its fathers to hate the great disorders that had almost been the death of France. At the sight of the unloosing of all manner of passions after the death of the great Cardinal, for an instant one might have thought that the generation born during his "reign" was about to abandon the teachings of its elders. This was a false impression. At the end of the sixteenth century, disruption had been so deep-rooted that the reaction toward order could not be limited to a single generation. Its successor imbibed from infancy the taste for discipline that the other had learned from the lessons of life. It was reared in the school of Richelieu, Descartes, and Corneille, when the most independent minds submitted to controls or were at least obliged to acknowledge them. In the final analysis, all bowed down

[7] Louis XIV, *Mémoires,* vol. 2, p. 379.—Ed.

before a discipline. Later another generation, less vigorous and less individual, would come, now exaggerating its submission and now evading it, doubly preparing itself for the reactions of freethinking under a great and aging king. But for the moment, it was the rule of the "wise." As a whole, the century remained wise. It had a taste for authority, for all the authorities: God, the king, tradition – the "rules."

Education nurtured this taste. The Jesuits were its masters. Dupont-Ferrier has recently shown how the College of Clermont molded men's minds, and this single college which, in 1630, counted 1800 pupils, increased to 2000 in 1650 and boasted of 3000 in 1675, while in the single province of Paris, 13,000 pupils annually were ruled by the rod, however gentle, of this celebrated society.[8] What did it teach? If it concerned the soul, an imperturbable religion; and, if it concerned the mind, Greek and Latin antiquity, especially the Latin, but an antiquity which also taught discipline.

In this way, there were two primary sources of discipline: the Christian and the ancient. From this education, the century emerged grave, viewing life and death with great seriousness. When Louis XIV so deliberately took power, the freethinking that had appeared for an instant during the "indulgent regency" had already gone underground. There it survived hidden, revealing its secret existence from time to time. But in the main, the century adhered to great formulas. The Marquise de Sévigné, who was far from ascetic, counselled only austere remedies for human sufferings: "reflection, devotion and philosophy." An age that was passionately fond of the *Augustinus* was ripe for the rigorous eloquence of Bourdaloue.

It was grave, but possessed serenity. Indeed, this gravity was far from being harsh, barren, or melancholy. Contemporaries said that Bossuet was "gay," and indeed, one senses a trace of a smile in that full Burgundian face, preserved for us by Rigaud. The correspondence of Madame de Sévigné is full of good humor. Although the age was serious, it was not dreary. It experienced an intense life, and although it had its passions, to these it opposed the "reflection, devotion and philosophy" so dear to the marquise, in a word, reason

[8] G. Dupont-Ferrier, *Du Collège de Clermont au lycée Louis-le-Grand (1563–1920)*, vol. I: *Le Collège sous les Jésuites (1563–1762); Le Collège et la Révolution (1763–1799)* (Paris, 1920).—Ed.

based upon firm foundations. In reality, this serene gravity arose from mastery of the passions.

It loved morality, and this explains the success of the great preachers whose eloquence resounded through the century. These physicians of the soul were the favorites of society.

Furthermore, the age was religious. "Hypocrisy," its critics have cried, and they would set its weaknesses, vices, debauchery and crimes against its great expressions of piety. Man is man; there always have been and always will be foolish passions, base souls, and corrupt hearts. Later I shall describe the gangrenous portion of the nation. It is probable that many libertines belatedly adopted the mask of religion in order to conform to opinion and to please the king; it is certain that among those who edified the century, many knew sin and practiced it. Also many avowed it and repented it; the century was one of great conversions. Turenne said to Retz: "Following your example, I shall avail myself of some time between life and death,"[9] a saying which reveals the spirit of a world that continually asked itself the question of Madame de Sévigné: "How shall I be with God?"[10] In reality, that which so many souls sought in religion was a rule of life, a discipline; that which all society craved from a Bossuet, a Bourdaloue, a Flechier and later a Massillon was again and again a law.

It was likewise a law that the age sought from the monarchy. For all, the monarchy was supreme order, and the age sought to re-establish order through discipline. It was strongly stamped with the seal of the two restorers, Henry IV and Richelieu. The spirit of the great king and the great minister who had ordered all things persisted. Balzac supplied the formula of this ideal order, and the century admired it. It was profoundly Cartesian: Madame de Grignan, a true daughter of the century, called philosophy "her father." Emile Krantz has searched for the esthetic of Descartes in the writers and artists of the age; we shall see how Colbert, in final analysis, personified what one might call the politics of Descartes. Malebranche and the whole Congregation of the Oratory caused his doctrine to triumph, even against the powerful influence of the Society of Jesus. Now,

---

9 Madame de Sévigné, *Lettres,* August 2, 1675.—Ed.
10 Ibid., March 16, 1672.—Ed.

how was this doctrine formulated by the pen of the celebrated Oratorian? Essentially as the triumph of absolute order. "It is true that the visible world would be more perfect if the lands and seas had more exact form, . . . if the rains were more regular and the earth more fruitful; in a word, if there were not so many aberrations and disorders." It was a lament: nature was not susceptible of complete correction by reason. But Descartes himself had sought to create a *tabula rasa* upon which to build an ordered construction. Denying the validity of any work that had not sprung from a single mind, he cited, with evident disgust, the example of ancient cities with irregular streets "so badly proportioned in comparison with the geometrical, fortified towns that an engineer traces at will on a plain."[11] Like Balzac, the philosopher dreamed of a geometrical city such as new countries have brought into being in our time. As we shall see, this was the same spirit that inspired Colbert who dreamed of rebuilding France and even Paris with order and symmetry; it was the aspiration of the age toward a perfect order regulated by reason. Reason, which Pascal opposed to the imagination, "mistress of error," was the recourse of this entire period; it was preached by Boileau in the realm of letters, and the pious Bourdaloue addressed himself to it in the realm of the soul. It was expected that reason be essentially disciplinary.

Such a love of order was evident in a majority of the great minds. For a Boileau was possible only because he wrote in the name of opinion; the *Art poétique,* which established a sort of literary absolutism in the name of order, has been called the credo of this entire generation. Thirty years earlier, the Academy had legislated concerning language, and had acquired an authority which indicates much concerning submission to rules during the century, as well as its passion for order in all things. Such a frame of mind encouraged the production of many dictionaries, grammars, manuals of rhetoric and poetics. France continued to "speak Vaugelas" in all fields. For this age, order was the sole source of grandeur. The taste for grandeur was everywhere, but magnificence was found by all in the well ordered and the strongly ordered.

Now, nothing might embody more grandeur than the throne

---

[11] Descartes, *Discours de la méthode,* p. 11, in *Œuvres* (Paris, 1902).—Ed.

elevated above the subjects; the final expression of a great order was organized monarchy. From the recent troubles, as we have seen, there resulted an intense movement in favor of political as well as moral order, coincident with the return of the king. No one recalled the sedition of the Fronde without horror, and no one dreamed of beginning it anew. In this nation that had always gloried in its "beautiful and honorable servitude to its sovereigns," never had a king known such "violent" love. Great evils were necessary before resentment would be directed toward the king during the final years of the century. "If only the king knew!" the malcontents continued to say. Love remained among the masses; only the elite would one day tire of loving – and more!

The king, for all as for himself, was the state. But there was more: the king was God. Until recently this theory had been formulated only with caution. For long, divine right had not been a stated condition of royal absolutism. Against the Emperor who habitually called himself "half god," and against the Pope who pretended to dispose of crowns in the name of God, it was now claimed that the King of France received his crown from God alone. It was the hour when Bossuet proclaimed this without contradiction. "Princes are gods, according to the witness of Holy Scripture, and participate somehow in divine independence. . . ; the royal throne is not the throne of a man, but the throne of God Himself. . . ."[12] Again and again, the great orator formulated this thought: the royal authority is sacred because of its divine origin. And because the king holds his power from God alone, he is answerable for it only to God. The monarch has great duties, but, when defaulting in these, God alone is the judge and no other. "In order to establish this power which represents his own, God places on the forehead of sovereigns and on their visage a mark of divinity."[13] But forty years earlier, in his *Institutes coutumières,* Loyseau had written: "The king holds only from God and his sword"; "Emperor in his realm," he recognizes only God above himself. And Loyseau was accepted as an authority.[14] Originally intended to combat

---

[12] Bossuet, *Politique tirée de l'Ecriture sainte,* edition cited, pp. 119–120, 182.—Ed.
[13] Bossuet, sermon preached before Louis XIV, April 2, 1662, on the text, *Per me reges regnant.* Lacour-Gayet, op. cit., p. 297.—Ed.
[14] This seems an error. The *Institutes coutumières* was the work of Antoine Loisel, not Charles Loyseau, and was first published in 1607. The first quotation is from Loisel's second maxim. The work does not contain the statement that the king is

the pretensions of the Emperor who claimed to hold from Rome an ancient right to regard kings as his vassals, and later designed to preserve the independence of crowns against the claims of Rome herself, the doctrine was essentially national. But in its extreme form, it resulted in making the king master of all. "All the state is in him; the will of the people is contained in his."[15] Again it is Bossuet who is speaking. But as early as 1649, it had been written: "God is the absolute Lord of all creation, and kings are the absolute lords of all that breathe the air throughout the entire area of their realms."[16] The king has the right of disposal, if not proprietary right, relative to the goods of his subjects, asserted Lebret in a treatise written under Richelieu and reprinted six times during the reign of Louis.[17] Besides, he is above the law since he makes the law. *A Deo rex, a rege lex.* It is God who dictates laws through the sovereign. How may the laws bind the monarch any more than God? Legislative sovereignty was "no more divisible than a geometrical point," wrote this same Lebret. It belongs only to the king.[18]

Divine right: in effect, kings were not merely born of God and inspired by God; they were God himself. "Their person," proclaimed Talon, "enjoys a certain divinity, for their prescience participates in the privileges of the prophets and the certainty of oracles."[19] The ancestors of Louis XIV would have been surprised to find themselves attributed such a privilege; it had been accorded only to the Roman Emperor, the deified Caesar. But the fact is that now we had reached the apogee of this imperial doctrine which the jurists for so many centuries had sought to render triumphant in Capetian France. Boileau said: "I admire Colbert who is unable to appreciate Suetonius, because Suetonius revealed the depravity of the Emperors." This son of shopkeepers was an imperialist; likewise Louvois, but with a differ-

---

Emperor within his realm, although this is found in much of the legal literature of the period. Cf. Lacour-Gayet, op. cit., p. 247.—Ed.

[15] Bossuet, *Politique* . . . , p. 236.—Ed.

[16] Lacour-Gayet, op. cit., p. 298.—Ed.

[17] Cardin Lebret, *De la Souveraineté du Roy,* in *Œuvres* (Paris, 1689) (first published in 1632). In Book III, chapter 7, Lebret attributed to the king the right to levy taxes from his subjects without their consent. But in Book IV, chapter 10, he specifically maintained the distinction between the property of the crown and that of the subjects, adding that the latter was normally inviolate and might be seized by the king only in a national emergency.—Ed.

[18] Lebret, loc. cit., Book II, chapter 9. The quotation is on page 19.—Ed.

[19] Omer Talon, *Mémoires,* Michaud et Poujoulat, eds. (Paris, 1839), p. 87.—Ed.

Nanteuil (?), *Louis XIV on the Battlefield.* Although Louis XIV was not expert in military affairs, it was *de rigueur* that he be represented as a warrior. Here he is shown as a Roman Emperor commanding operations in the field. His grandson holds a chart of an emplacement to be besieged. (*Courtesy of the Fogg Art Museum, Harvard University. Bequest of Arnold Knapp*)

ent temperament, and Pontchartrain after them, and all the ministers of the reign. For them, Louis XIV was less the successor of Hugh Capet than of Augustus, to whom Louis commended himself in his *Memoirs.* And the theorists now pronounced the word: in 1652, a Doctor of Theology called the sovereign Caesar: *"Nam res est publica Caesar."*[20] With the aid of the cult of ancient Rome, the King of France would soon be visualized by many artists as dressed in the costume of the Roman Emperors. "My Caesar is king," exclaimed Louise of Savoy at the accession of Francis I,[21] and this king aspired more than any other to be Caesar. Louis XIV was now proclaimed Caesar, whose crown of laurels was adorned only with the lilies of France. France consented, because, against all others and with the grandeur that she loved, Caesar assured the order to which this wise age aspired.

*   *   *

Louis the king reflected his times. This was his strength. Like his era, he was grave with serenity and yet had certain flashes of gaity; like it, he valued the serious side of things, enjoyed a universal but practical intelligence, was reasonable and logical, moderate and balanced, polished and circumspect, and if, like his century, he had his moments of licentiousness, he preserved, even in his sins, his respect for decorum and honor. Like his times, he loved order: order in things and in minds, order in consciences and actions, order in the realm of the beautiful and in that of politics. He took pleasure in grandeur and magnificence, and conceived of these only in terms of what he himself represented, since he viewed them as conditioned by a well-observed order, a grand style which sprang from strict discipline. In tune with his era, he sought in his religion less an outpouring of the heart than a rule to which he might return when he had failed to follow it scrupulously. He had an imperturbable faith, if not an enlightened sense of charity. In the interest of the throne, he condemned sedition and trouble, and, more convinced than anyone else of the divine right of kings, he had neither to invent nor formu-

[20] Lacour-Gayet, op. cit., p. 303.—Ed.
[21] *Journal de Louise de Savoie,* Michaud et Poujoulat, eds. (Paris, 1838), p. 87. In her memoirs, Louise of Savoy repeatedly refers to Francis I, her son, as "Caesar." —Ed.

late it since it was proclaimed by everyone. Like his times, he was
concerned with the welfare of the state, and associated the interest
of the state with the strengthening of the crown. But quite unlike the
tyrants whom he would have been the first to condemn, he conceived
of his power only as the highest element in a state, a society, and a
land well ordered by good laws. Here too he was in tune with his
times. Like them, he lived, as Madame de Maintenon said, "with
symmetry." Within this "symmetry," he upheld the beautiful, the
good and the true. The seventeenth century has been called "the age
of Louis XIV." Rather, it was Louis XIV who was "the man of the
seventeenth century," a cultivated gentleman on the throne.

The first thing that one noticed was his beauty, and even this had
something of his century: it was regular and moderate, a well-
modeled head without the spiritual expression of a Henry IV or the
exuberant physiognomy of a Francis I, but a mixture of charm without expansiveness and of majesty without pride. In 1661, he was
charming in all ways. The portrait engraved by Nanteuil shows him
thus, with, however, a certain distrust in his glance and in the corners
of his mouth, a young man who did not give of himself and was on
guard against pitfalls and even the mere shortcomings of others.

This distrust he had acquired from the events of his childhood,
such as the Fronde that he would never forget, and it had been further strengthened by the lessons of Mazarin. In addition, he had
learned from his teachers the pride of his blood. He had lived without
companions, for it was thought that contact with adults would make
him "reasonable." "He rarely laughs," said an observer when Louis
was five years old. The root of his gravity was an overpowering
sense of his dignity as king. The blood of the Escorial, which he had
received from his mother, made this grandson of Henry IV a great-
grandson of Philip II, a man who did not take his royalty lightly and
who carried it as a permanent sacrament. After being restricted in
his youth, he was quickly surrounded with obeisances. Even his
education had been entirely molded so that he would acquire an
unqualified conviction of his grandeur.

From all this there resulted, together with his sense of sovereign
dignity, an ingenuous, self-fostered pride. This pride might have been
unbearable, but at the age of seventeen, the young prince, who retained a heavy sadness from his inheritance and his childhood, kept

company with "all the distinguished men and women" at the home of
the Countess of Soissons, and assumed "that air of urbanity and
politeness, which," adds Saint-Simon, "he preserved throughout his
life." This "air of politeness" veiled a gracious arrogance.

He was quite willing to be "gracious," and "when he was gracious,"
said the unpolished but charmed Princess Palatine, "one loved him
with all one's heart." From Madame de Sévigné to Saint-Simon who
knew him during the two extremities of his life and were not his tools,
the witnesses are unanimous.

Saint-Simon says that he was "born good and just." He was in
fact tolerably good in the sense that he did not possess a trace
of wickedness. But he did not, if I may so state it, glow from the heart,
since he may have held the opinion that Napoleon would later express,
to wit, "when it is said that the king is good, the reign is a failure."
On the other hand, one of his most recent historians seems to have
unduly discounted his intelligence. An "ordinary" intelligence, "almost entirely passive, without any initiative, not at all inquiring," and
one who, he adds later, "needed the ideas of others."[22] This estimate
is contradicted in the same volume by Ernest Lavisse himself, when,
in attempting to define the responsibilities of the king, he writes, "It
may be easily stated that he first followed Colbert and later Louvois.
The truth might well be that the method of Colbert suited him first,
and later that of Louvois."[23] The facts are uncertain; one must choose.
Perhaps he did not have such need of "the ideas of others," but knew
how to use them, which is an attribute of great men. How may we
accuse a man of having "ordinary intelligence" when he made use of
a Colbert and so many others like him? What may be said is that he
did not have a very quick or profound mind; he had neither the
genius of Richelieu nor of Bonaparte. Being reasonable, he never
climbed to the heights from which one surveys the world, but from
which one does not always see it clearly. His mind was entirely re-
flective. When someone spoke to him of a matter, said the Princess
Palatine, he answered, "I shall see."[24] All the witnesses of the reign
heard these famous words. This was not a way of dismissing the
matter, but of gaining the opportunity to deliberate with himself and

[22] E. Lavisse, *Histoire de France* (Paris, 1911), vol. 7[1], pp. 124, 157.—Ed.
[23] Ibid., vol. 7[2], p. 60.—Ed.
[24] Cf. Lacour-Gayet, op. cit., p. 119.—Ed.

several others. Mazarin had advised him to "reflect twice"; he decided to reflect thrice. He did not like "misguided decisions." And as for his "curiosity," it embraced all things at an early age, according to the testimony of Mazarin. But he was apt to be secretive and distrustful. He observed without speaking, and this distrust, when expressed in his *Memoirs,* occasioned remarks that indicate a tolerably shrewd and somewhat cruel psychology by virtue of which certain of Louis' maxims have an affinity with those of La Rochefoucauld or La Bruyère, and this does not make him a fool, I wager. Great genius, no, but a very discerning intelligence.

He subordinated his heart and intelligence entirely to reason. This was the dominant trait of his character, and it was this above all that linked him with his times. "A quiet nature and an enemy of cruelty and violence," he was reasonable and moderate. After reading his *Memoirs,* it is impossible not to have a strong impression of his calm reason. "Keep to the middle course," he wrote frequently. And elsewhere, "Let common sense prevail."[25] He understood reason through his sense of the real, the possible, and the expedient. "Conduct oneself according to the temper of the times."[26] he wrote. In this, he was perhaps not as Cartesian as his times; his mind felt repugnance to doctrinaire principles in politics, which Colbert would have willingly preached.

Many reflections in the *Memoirs* concerning his manner of conducting himself reveal a great love of his position, "of the profession of king" as he called it. "The profession of king is great, noble, delightful, when one feels worthy of everything that one undertakes."[27] He cherished his "profession of king." During his childhood, his tutor had said to him, "A king must find his delights in his duties." He labored and held strictly to constant, regular and methodical work, he who loved pleasure, festivals and travel. He was too industrious by disposition not to be naturally hardworking. It is certain that he forced himself to labor because this was the primary element of his "profession of king" which, although delightful, was not exempt from "distress, fatigue, and anxiety."[28] In tune with his century, reason

25 Louis XIV, *Mémoires,* vol. 2, p. 428.—Ed.
26 Ibid., vol. 2, p. 102.—Ed.
27 Ibid., vol. 2, p. 519.—Ed.
28 Ibid., vol. 2, p. 519.—Ed.

dictated his conduct, and his will bent him under his self-imposed yoke which he nevertheless loved.

However, pride remained. What shall I say? It was the center of everything. He knew, in 1661, that France awaited him. He was told that he would be a great ruler, and he did not intend to fall short of what was expected of him. "Virtue" to him was the search for glory, and he understood glory to be the constant augmentation of the grandeur of the state. He believed himself capable of increasing the grandeur of all its elements. This pride contained nothing base or narrow; he recognized the necessity of pride to a king. To reproach Louis XIV for having been proud is almost naive; one might as well reproach him for having been King of France during his century. This pride, always considered and in no way capricious, was never begrudged him by his age. His times, as we know, loved grandeur, and one of the major foundations of the state was the pride of the king.

"The state" was his first preoccupation. "The interest of the state should always take precedence,"[29] and besides, "when one works for the state, one works for oneself. The good of the one enhances the glory of the other."[30] If he was the state, the state was France. But in the mind of the king, such was the strict fusion of the three terms, throne, state, and nation, that his pride ended by becoming impersonal. The king had received a magnificent heritage, and he sought to strengthen it less because of personal vanity than because of a very real conviction concerning his obligation to the France of his ancestors, as well as to that of his grandnephews.

The king loved France. The proof is that he understood her strengths and her weaknesses, as certain features of his *Memoirs* testify. Although he had studied little national history, he was capable of summarizing it in a word: "France would be the mistress of the world, if the divisions among her children had not too often exposed her to the jealous furies of her enemies."[31]

In the future, who would save the France that he wished to render great from these divisions? The king. What was the king? The exclusive depositary of all authority. The French monarchy seemed quite naturally to him the only regime capable of assuring the greatness

[29] Ibid., vol. 2, p. 518.—Ed.
[30] Ibid., vol. 2, p. 520.—Ed.
[31] Ibid., vol. 2, p. 10.—Ed.

of France. The sovereign should be the master. The king was the lieutenant of God, and was, in addition, the head of the great family that was the nation. As each group of subjects had its role which it should not exceed, as well as its rights and duties, the "common father" was the arbiter between his "children," a fundamental role. But the "common father" was also "absolute lord": kings "hold naturally the complete and free possession of all property; they are born to possess all and to command all."[32] The will of God was that "whoever is born a subject obeys without question."[33] In order to preserve the superiority which everything attributed to him, the prince, "lieutenant of God," "common father," "supreme possessor of property," should be "so raised above the others that there is none who may be confounded or compared with him."[34] This was not a vain "matter of ceremonial," but a matter of "respect."

The king, master in his land, should also be master in his council. There must be no first minister, and here also Louis was in accord with the wishes of his subjects. The "ministry" had been odious; Richelieu and Mazarin had been tyrannical. The latter himself had often energetically urged the young prince not to name another. "A king who is incapable of ruling," he said, "is not worthy of governing."[35] A king who governs! All order would flow from him, and would be assured by the maintenance of every discipline. And thus France, reunited under the sceptre of a sage, would no longer be subject to those "divisions" without which she would long ago have been "mistress of the world."

Did the king invent the system? Not at all. If he had set forth his ideas in 1661 before France assembled, everything indicates that all would have applauded them. It was one of those moments when, sedition having wearied minds and ruined commerce, the mass of the citizens preferred order to any liberties whatsoever. It seemed to the nation that order might be assured only by a strong and respected power which, while reforming all elements of the state, would subject it more firmly than ever to monarchical government. Louis XIV was in tune with his times both because of his character

32 Ibid., vol. 1, p. 209; vol. 2, p. 303.—Ed.
33 Ibid., vol. 2, p. 285.—Ed.
34 Ibid., vol. 2, p. 15.—Ed.
35 Lacour-Gayet, op. cit., p. 132.—Ed.

and because of his principles. For this reason, the work of national restoration was coupled with a movement of political subjection. This double endeavor was to fill the first part of his reign.

Louis XIV was awaited and he arrived, taking at its word an age that longed to receive a law.

Roland Mousnier

LOUIS XIV, REVOLUTIONARY

Among the French historians who are currently investigating the early modern period, Roland Mousnier is undoubtedly the most outstanding scholar of his generation. Formerly at the University of Strasbourg and now Professor of Modern History at the Sorbonne, his original work lay in the field of institutional history. To this, however, he soon added a considerable number of studies in social, economic, and intellectual history. More recently, he has undertaken works of very broad synthesis, such as that excerpted here. The following selection summarizes a number of the most recent interpretations relative to the institutional and social evolution of France under the government of Louis XIV, whom Mousnier views as continually struggling against the "perpetual crisis" of the seventeenth century.

Absolutism was the wish of the multitudes that sought their salvation in the concentration of power in the hands of a single man, who should be the incarnation of the realm and the living symbol of the desired order and unity. Everyone endeavored to behold the image of God in the king: "You are God on earth. . . ." To this concept, many added the time-honored dream of the humanists: the king should be a hero, loving glory as the ancients, protecting letters as Augustus and the Church as Constantine, a legislator like Justinian, but with a "predilection for arms," for "the role of conqueror was deemed the noblest and highest of titles" by all contemporaries.

Lieutenant of God, the king was sovereign. "The sovereign prince makes the law, and is consequently absolved from law."[1] He acted ac-

From Roland Mousnier, *Les XVI*^{e}* et XVII*^{e}* siècles,* vol. 4, *Histoire générale des civilisations* (Paris, 1954), pp. 229–236. Reprinted by permission of Presses Universitaires de France. Editor's translation.

[1] Pierre de L'Hommeau, *Maximes générales du droit français* (Rouen, 1614), p. 5. —Ed.

cording to his good pleasure. From this it followed that kings "have by nature the full and free disposal of all goods, whether secular or ecclesiastical, to use them as wise stewards, that is, according to the needs of their states."[2] The public good took precedence over property rights. In consequence, the Church was subject to the sovereign, and owed him rentals for its possessions that had been given to it "for the general good of all the realm." From this it resulted that: "As the sovereign power of the prince is a ray and fragment of the omnipotence of God, likewise the power of officials is a fragment and manifestation of the absolute power of the prince. . . ."[3]

The comparison with the sun arose naturally, and Louis XIV's emblem with its motto, *Nec Pluribus Impar* (None His Equal), merely reemphasized an ancient monarchical symbol.

But, image of God, the king should be Providence on earth. He should cause justice to prevail, "the precious trust that God has placed in the hands of kings as a participation in His wisdom and power."[4] He should perfect each of the professions that together constitute society, for "each makes its contributions which the others may forego only with great difficulty. . . . This is why, far from despising any social status or raising one at the expense of the others, we should attempt to bring them all as far as possible to the perfection that is their due,"[5] an ideal of society in which social functions were directed and the professions pyramided according to the needs of mankind. Finally, the king should be the protector of the weak; he should "give the people who are subject to him the same marks of paternal benevolence that we receive daily from God," having "nothing more at heart than protecting the weak from oppression by the more powerful, and enabling the destitute to obtain relief in their misery."

Louis XIV lived his ideas, but Henry IV almost as much as he, and Louis XIII hardly less than his father; all desired to be the hero, the sovereign, Providence on earth.

The king's power was wielded in two different fashions according to the times. When the sovereign was incompetent, like Louis XIII,

[2] Louis XIV, *Mémoires,* edition cited, vol. 1, p. 209.—Ed.
[3] Charles Loyseau, *Cinq Livres du droit des offices,* Book I, chapter 6, no. 8, in Œuvres (Lyon, 1701), p. 34.—Ed.
[4] Louis XIV, *Mémoires,* vol. 2, p. 399.—Ed.
[5] Ibid., vol. 1, pp. 250–251.—Ed.

or too young, like Louis XIV from 1643 to 1661, there was established the rule of a ministry. A first minister such as Cardinal Richelieu or Cardinal Mazarin in France, or the Count-Duke Olivares in Spain, governed in the name of the king and was responsible to him. When the king was Louis XIII, this relationship was no mere formality. Richelieu said: "The few square feet of the council chamber of the king were more difficult for me to conquer than all the battlefields of Europe."

During the periods when the first minister exercised royal power, he went so far as to build a personal following that was bound to him by feudal ties of vassalage and protection, and to assume the demeanor of the Mayor of the Palace during the age of the last Merovingians. He surrounded the king with his men, placed his followers in all important offices, created his own dynasty, made his relatives Marshals of France, generals of the galleys, dukes and peers, married his nieces to the princes of the royal blood, had, as Richelieu, fortified places and ports such as Brouage and Le Havre which he willed to his heirs, and possessed troops and companies of infantry and noblemen. The king was gradually abandoned by his captains who entered into the service of the minister, and in time he found himself alone and powerless, confronted by his minister in command of the best swords, and unable to obtain the obedience of the realm except through the intervention of the minister and his men. Under these circumstances, the death of the minister was always a deliverance for the king.

Therefore, when Louis XIV constructed the system which Henry IV had instinctively sought, he resolved that he would be his own first minister, so that only he would understand the totality of affairs and become indispensable. The king was thus drawn into an existence that was more and more bureaucratic, regulated, and organized for maximum efficiency. "With an almanac and a watch, one might, 300 leagues from him, tell what he was doing."[6] He was obliged to isolate himself at Versailles, in a palace and a city constructed for the work of the king quite as much as for his renown and pleasure. Some have attempted to discover an imitation of Spain in this bureaucratic

---

[6] Saint-Simon, *Parallèle des trois premiers rois Bourbons*, p. 87, in *Ecrits inédits de Saint-Simon*, edited by M. P. Faugère (Paris, 1880).—Ed.

existence. In reality, it appeared in all places where absolutism developed. It sprang from necessity.

During the period of the ministry,[7] institutions were systematized. But institutional development bestowed rights on great and dangerous men as well as the first minister. Louis XIV originated a contrary movement which left the field open for the royal will. During the rule of the ministry, government was still a matter of family, birth, titles and offices. The members of the royal family, the princes of the blood, the dukes and peers, the Chancellor and the Superintendent of Finance all entered into the Supreme Council *(Conseil d'en Haut),* and thereby held the rank of minister. Aside from those who entered by hereditary right, these ministers held their offices by virtue of royal letters, and regarded them as "possessions" of which they might not be deprived without cause. Louis XIV created a revolution. He removed from the Supreme Council all persons who might claim political power by virtue of birth, title, or office. First his mother, his brother, and the princes of the blood were excluded; government ceased to be a family affair and became truly personal. Next came the turn of the Chancellor of France, the ecclesiastics and the great lords, and finally the high officials. During Louis' personal rule, not one of the secretaries of state was a minister. To be a minister ceased to denote office or status. There were no more letters or warrants. A minister was created on the day when the king caused him to be called to the council by the usher; he ceased to be a minister on the day when the usher no longer called him. The king at certain moments discussed his affairs with those persons who suited him. No one except the king had the slightest right in government. All was concentrated in the person of the king.

During the period of the ministry, there was a great effort to develop further that instrument of royal authority, the council. New subdivisions, the Council of Dispatches for internal affairs and the Council of Conscience,[8] had been created. The political division, the

---

[7] This phrase is used here and later in this selection to indicate the years during which the first minister exercised royal power, particularly the long period, 1624–1661, when Richelieu and Mazarin, in effect, governed France. This period is contrasted with that after 1661, when Louis XIV governed in person and abolished the office of first minister.—Ed.

[8] The Council of Conscience (called *le Conseil d'Eglise et de Conscience*) was organized under Richelieu and was the portion of the royal council that considered

Council of Affairs or the Supreme Council, and the administrative divisions, the Council of Finances, Council of State, and Privy Council had become more specialized with a new and better division of functions. Louis XIV, on the contrary, distrusted these councils. Not being able to get along without them, he sought to reduce them to mere routine. He worked alone, alternately with each of the secretaries of state and his controller general of finance. He decided all important questions, which no longer came before the councils except as a mere formality, or did not come before them at all. Thousands of decrees of the council were signed at the "command" of a mere secretary of state or the Chancellor, without ever having been seen by the Supreme Council, the Council of Dispatches or the Council of Finance.

The king likewise distrusted his ministers and his secretaries of state. He reverted to a division of labor, and made every attempt to subdivide consideration of interrelated affairs in such a way that no specialist might be in position to contravene his will. He set his officials against one another, provoked them, divided them, fanned their mutual jealousies, and regarded the hostility of the Colbert and Le Tellier families as a guarantee of his power.

In both periods, the king's problem was not only to secure the obedience of his subjects, but also to control his own officials who had become independent through venality of office, and to exercise full powers of legislation, adjudication, and administration.

For this purpose, the king made use of *lettres de cachet* by means of which he directly informed individuals and groups of his will. With a *lettre de cachet,* the king arrested, imprisoned, and exiled; at the request of families, he punished the misconduct of a son or a spouse; he forestalled resistance and arbitrarily punished sedition and plots with the enemy. When the king himself had spoken, there remained nothing but to submit to his authority, the legal source of justice.

More and more, the king made use of commissioners appointed by himself and removable at will. The councillors of state in the ad-

religious and ecclesiastical matters. At the beginning of the reign of Louis XIV, it consisted of the Grand Almoner, the Archbishop of Toulouse, Hardouin de Péréfixe, then Bishop of Rodez, and Father Annat, the royal confessor. Louis XIV gradually allowed this council to fall into disuse.—Ed.

ministrative councils were mere commissioners. During the period of the ministry, the king accorded these councils the position of highest body in the realm, with authority over the so-called sovereign courts, even in the absence of the king. After 1632, the councils were permitted to annul and set aside any decree, even of the Parlements, which had been issued contrary to the ordinances, the royal authority, the public utility or the rights of the crown. The councils evoked cases to themselves and judged them, thereby dispossessing the sovereign courts of their functions. Under Louis XIV, the authority of these councils was maintained largely as a useful fiction, since the decrees of the council often emanated in fact from the king and his immediate officers, the secretaries of state or the controller of finance.

In both periods, the authority of the king, theoretically acting in his council, was asserted over the sovereign courts. In 1641, the king solemnly reserved to himself all cognizance of affairs of state, reduced the Parlement's remonstrances before registration to two in matters of finance, and prohibited them entirely after registration in matters of state.[9] In his turn, Louis XIV reserved to himself all affairs of state, and, in 1673, he ordered the sovereign courts to register edicts immediately and without change; remonstrances might be presented only afterward, and but once. At best, the courts could merely express an opinion. In this way, the sovereign courts found themselves excluded from general policy and constitutional questions. The unlimited authority of the king in political matters, his legislative omnipotence, and, in consequence, his power to collect taxes at will and to utilize the proceeds without responsibility of any sort, were thus confirmed. The king caused commissions of his devoted assistants to draw up codes (Civil Ordinance of 1667, Criminal Ordinance of 1670, Commercial Ordinance of 1673) to which the king alone gave the force of law quite without registration, consultation of any office holders, or participation by constituted bodies, a step that repre-

[9] It was traditional that no royal edict or ordinance might acquire the force of law without "registration" in the rolls of the French Parlements, the most important of which was the Parlement of Paris. In case of serious disagreement between the administration and the Parlement concerning any new enactment, the latter body might send repeated remonstrances to the royal council or directly to the king. This procedure placed a severe check upon the royal power of legislation. In 1641, Richelieu and Louis XIII attempted to curb this authority of the Parlement, through the measure described above.—Ed.

sented a distinct tendency toward unity and equality, a revolutionary work.

The king appointed special commissions from the council to judge a case, to follow the execution of an edict, to perform special functions such as serving as a court of justice of the Arsenal in 1631 or judging the governors of La Capelle and the Châtelet after the Peace of Corbie, etc. These commissions were not mere investigating bodies; in fact, they rendered the verdict.

The king made use of intendants in the army and in the administration of justice, police, and finance. They were primarily inspectors, commissioned to keep the officers and subjects of the king under surveillance and to report to the council. The council might then settle the matter forthwith by a decree, or it might give the Intendant the necessary power to decide, judge, or regulate the question by an ordinance. For this purpose, the Intendant might be present in the council of the governor and give his advice; he might preside over courts of justice, regulate procedure according to the ordinances, determine whether officers were fulfilling their duties, suspend them if they were not, hear complaints of the king's subjects, and ensure that they were rendered justice by the judges. The Intendant presided over municipal assemblies, supervised elections, examined the debts of communities, and kept watch over the application of orders and rules; it was the beginning of administrative tutelage. The Intendant supervised the collection of taxes, directed the bureaus of finance, and ensured the observation of ordinances and regulations. Only in the following instances did he have general, discretionary power and the authority to make final judgment: malpractices and peculation by finance officers, and illicit assemblies, seditions, revolts, and the raising of men at arms.

The Intendant was a very supple instrument. In time of war or internal crisis, the council might extend his powers indefinitely, to the point where the Intendant filled all functions of the permanent officials and left them merely empty titles. In these periods, the intendants and their subdelegates erected an administration of commissioners in competition with that of the regular officials. But the royal government, Richelieu as well as Colbert, regarded these periods as exceptional and an unfortunate necessity. In time of peace, the king strove to limit the Intendant, who was always desirous of extending his powers, to the role of inspector. The king forbade him to take the place of the regular officials and ordered him merely to oversee them, and, if they functioned badly, to report this to the council and await authorization to remedy the situation.

The king made use of a political police. It was made operative by the intendants and by spies and agents scattered about everywhere, by the governor of the Bastille in Paris, the chief criminal officer, and, after 1667, the lieutenant general of police, La Reynie. At a badly construed word, master or servant found himself in the Bastille. On the slightest suspicion, the intendants or the council fabricated accusations of lese majesty, and judgment was rendered on mere presumption; for Richelieu, Louis XIII and Louis XIV all held that in the event of a conspiracy, it was almost impossible to have mathematical proofs, and that one should not await the outcome which might cause the loss of all. More often, however, the king dispensed with the trial altogether and had recourse to preventive imprisonment of undetermined length, through a *lettre de cachet.*

A permanent army of mercenaries, regularly paid and strictly disciplined, ensured the execution of royal orders.

In all important offices, such as those of minister, secretary of state, or controller general, Louis XIV desired only "devoted servants" who would combine domestic services with their public functions, and who, like Colbert, would convey notes to his lady friends and receive the adulterine children of the king at the childbirth of the royal mistresses. He utilized the concept of vassalage, but wished to be its sole beneficiary. He sought to consummate absolutism by his direct contact with all Frenchmen through a personal tie, as vassals were bound to their suzerain. He wished to be the unique and universal suzerain, or at the very least, the universal protector. "All eyes were fastened upon him alone; it was to him alone that all wishes were directed; he alone received all deference; he alone was the object of all expectation; one strove, one understood, and one achieved anything only through him. His good graces were regarded as the sole source of all possessions; one thought of raising oneself only to the extent that one might approach his person or rise in his esteem; all the rest was sterile."[10] All ties of emotion and interest

[10] Louis XIV, *Mémoires,* vol. 2, pp. 16–17.—Ed.

converged upon the king who consequently embodied the wishes and hopes of all his subjects. Through this, no less than the exercise of personal power, he concentrated the state in himself, realized in himself the unity of the state, and thus, by using very old sentiments, prepared his subjects to advance to the concept of the impersonal state. By utilizing medieval survivals, Louis XIV laid the foundations of the modern state.

The king also prepared the way for this by opposing class to class and raising the bourgeoisie in the social scale. More and more during the reign, the king chose his ministers, councillors, and intendants from among the bourgeois jurists. They were his men, "sprung from pure and perfect commonality," and "exalted above all grandeur." The king ennobled the Le Tellier and Colbert families, making them lords designated by the names of their lands, Louvois, Barbezieux, Croissy, and Torcy. He created dynasties of ministers, bourgeois family groups and collateral lines, and used their strength against the dynasties and family groups of the nobles. The roll of the capitation of 1695 assigned the ministers of state to the first class, and placed the Chancellor and the controller general of finance on a parity with the princes of the blood. In the administrative sections of the Council of State, the proportion of jurists increased. The regulation of 1673 fixed the number of titular councillors at 24 jurists, 3 clerics, and 3 nobles. Again, for the latter, there was no longer a minimum requirement of several degrees of nobility; the son of a jurist might qualify. Among the councillors who enjoyed traditional right of membership in the Privy Council, the dukes and peers gradually disappeared. The regulation of 1673 omits them. The councillors of state received titles of nobility transmissible from father to son. They were presented at court with their wives, and were admitted to do homage to the king. They were the holders of fiefs and great lords. Their sons often wore the sword and served in the regiments of the king, at least for a time, before holding office. In this manner, the king systematically raised the jurists who were dedicated to his service, and made them a nobility of the robe. More and more, it was the service of the sovereign, the embodiment of the state, that determined one's rank in society.

The nobles grumbled. They despised these "bourgeois." "It was the reign of vile bourgeois," muttered Saint-Simon. They suffered from the leveling brought about by a state that mowed down all resistance. The prisons were full of prisoners of distinction: the Count of Cramaing, Marshal de Bassompierre, and Baradas, one of the favorites of Louis XIII. The kings also sought to provide honors and means of livelihood for the nobility. They reserved the offices of governor for them, most of the ranks in the army, and the majority of ecclesiastical appointments went to their younger sons; they used them in their service, instilled the spirit of subordination into them, and little by little rendered them functionaries. Louis XIV completed this by organizing the court. He grouped around himself at Saint-Germain, Fontainebleau and Versailles, all who counted among the nobility. He consummated their ruin by alternating between the burdensome life of the camps and the ostentatious life of the court. He did not shrink from war as a means of finding them employment and opportunities for glory and reputation. He rendered them servile with pensions, dowries, and properties of the church. "It may happen that in paying court to him, we may find ourselves dependent upon what he tosses to us,"[11] like faithful dogs, said Madame de Sévigné. He even provided a psychological alibi for the nobility. In a series of marvelous, fairylike festivals, the king appeared attired as the Olympian god, with the courtiers as lesser divinities or heroes. In this way, they were able to transmute their vain dream of power and greatness in this imitation of the life of the immortals, exalted above common humanity, and, if they must obey, they would at least obey the Lord Jupiter, the king-god. Etiquette habituated them to seeing a superhuman being in the king. Men uncovered themselves before the king's bed, and women did a genuflection as in church before the high altar. The princes of the blood disputed over the honor of tendering him a shirt sleeve at the *lever.* A great ceremonial in which reverences abounded governed his rising, his retiring, his meals, his entire life. It was all summed up by a courtier who, at the death of Louis XIV, exclaimed, "After the death of the king, one may believe anything."

The court and its etiquette were not mere imitations of things Spanish, but were dictated by the state of society and the nature of things.

In this way, the king, by apportioning offices among the two classes but reserving the more important for the lesser class, the bourgeoisie,

---

[11] Madame de Sévigné, *Lettres,* January 12, 1680.—Ed.

systematically raised the latter while pitting it against the nobles, the more powerful. He brought the struggle of the classes to a position of equilibrium which assured his personal power, and maintained unity, order, and hierarchy in the government and the state. But also, crises and war may have constrained him to level and equalize more and more as a duty that he owed the state, without intentionally changing the social structure of the realm. When Louis XIV obtained total submission and obedience without limits, his power became both autocratic and revolutionary.

G. P. Gooch

THE LEGACY OF LOUIS XIV

During much of his long career, George Peabody Gooch (1873–1968) was well known in the English-speaking world as an outstanding historian in the liberal tradition. Although he never held an academic chair, he enjoyed a wide following as editor of the Contemporary Review *for forty-nine years and as the author of a steady stream of books, articles and reviews on historical and historiographical subjects. One of his best-known books is his* History and Historians in the Nineteenth Century. *His historical works were grounded not upon original research but on his vast reading, extensive insights and ability to synthesize. The present selection is one of the best summary treatments of the Sun King's legacy to the French nation.*

The principal legacy of Louis XIV was a powerful and centralized France. Though *Le Roi Soleil* was no superman in the sense that he would have fought his way to the front had he not been of royal descent, he gave his name to the greatest era in French history and his rays penetrated to every corner of Europe. He owed his success to the combination of his political heritage and his personal qualities. Frederick the Great saluted the French of the age of Louis XIV as the Romans of the modern world. The founder of dynastic autocracy was Richelieu, who broke the power of the feudal nobility and the Protes-

From G. P. Gooch, *Louis XV: The Monarchy in Decline* (London: Longmans, Green & Co., 1956), pp. 1–29. Reprinted by permission of Longman Group Ltd.

tants and by the creation of intendants asserted the authority of the Crown over the whole country. So decisive was his achievement that the Fronde was little more than a straw fire, and Condé was the last of the *Noblesse de l'Épée* to draw his sword against the throne. The most sordid episode in the history of seventeenth-century France left the monarchy stronger than it found it, for the angry disgust it aroused led to a national demand for the curbing of anarchy by a firm hand at the helm. The *Noblesse* and the Parlements had discredited themselves, and Mazarin steered the ship of state into calmer waters without shedding blood. *Le Grand Siècle* had begun.

If Richelieu's edifice was to outlive its architect it demanded rulers of ability and industry. Louis XIII, the most colorless of the Bourbon monarchs, preferred hunting to politics and left the management of the state to the mighty Cardinal. There was no need for Anne of Austria to anticipate the injunction of another royal widow a century later, "George, be a King." Though but a child during the hectic years of the Fronde, Louis XIV never forgot the humiliations of the royal family during the dark days of the Fronde, the early morning flight from the Palais Royal, and the thunder of Condé's cannon in the Faubourg St. Antoine. Even before the death of Mazarin he had resolved to be his own master, to allow no minister and no favorite, male or female, to shape his course, to make the nobility the ornament instead of the rival of the throne. His veto on the duel, which had taken heavy toll of the aristocracy during the reign of his father, embodied his desire to preserve the *Noblesse* while abolishing its power. Its chief function, as he saw it, was to contribute to the splendor of the court and the prestige of the Crown. Landowners of limited means who vegetated on their estates, called *Noblesse de Province,* were disapproved, and when their names came up in conversation he curtly remarked: "C'est un homme que je ne connais pas." "I intend to be my own First Minister," he announced, and he kept his word. Court posts naturally went to the *Noblesse de Cour,* but the business of state was largely transacted by lawyers and other capable *roturiers* who owed everything to the sovereign. The king demanded from his people obedience, not collaboration. Never for a moment did he question his capacity to fulfil the task allotted to him by Providence, and the incense by which he was surrounded confirmed his massive self-assurance. His ability was above the average, his industry unique in the annals of the Bourbon dynasty. Even under the shock of military disaster or domestic sorrow he remained calm and dignified, though at times when alone with Mme. de Maintenon tears came to his eyes. He was the first and last demigod to occupy the throne of France.

"There was nothing to be compared to him at reviews, fêtes, every occasion on which the presence of ladies created a tone of gallantry, a gallantry always majestic," testifies Saint-Simon, a rather unfriendly observer, saluted by Sainte-Beuve as the Tacitus of France. "Sometimes there was gaiety, but never anything misplaced or indiscreet. His slightest gesture, his walk, his bearing, his countenance, all was measured, appropriate, noble, majestic but quite natural. Thus in serious matters such as the audiences of ambassadors and other ceremonies no one was ever so imposing. One had to get used to him in order to avoid embarrassment when speaking to him. His replies on these occasions were always brief and to the point, rarely without some obliging or even flattering remark when the occasion demanded. In every company his presence imposed silence and even fear." Never was any human being more obviously born to be a king. Nothing suggests more vividly the awe he inspired than the suicide of the unhappy cook when the fish for dinner on a royal visit to Condé at Chantilly failed to arrive, and the confession of one of his generals on entering the royal presence: "I never trembled like this before Your Majesty's enemies." Like other autocrats he made costly mistakes, but his devotion to his tasks is beyond challenge. He believed in the system bequeathed by Richelieu as implicitly as he believed in himself. If Henry IV was the most popular of the Bourbon rulers, his grandson earned the maximum prestige. That the longest reign in French history was also the most illustrious is the conviction of Frenchmen who agree in little else. It was a glittering vision, the splendor and strength of which aroused the envious admiration of the world. With such a monarch there seemed no need for the States-General. The army was without a rival in Europe, and the navy, the most enduring of his creations, was double the size of the British fleet. Under the fostering hand of Colbert industry and commerce grew apace. The master of twenty million Frenchmen was the richest and most powerful prince in Europe and scarcely anything seemed beyond his grasp. Since Charles II of Spain was childless, he reflected, perhaps a Bourbon might soon replace a Hapsburg at Madrid. In the technique of kingship he was not only unrivaled but unapproached. "He was born, prudent, moderate, friendly, and just," testifies Saint-Simon; "God had given him enough to make him a good king and perhaps a fairly great king. All the evil came from elsewhere." The ceremonies of the *lever* and *coucher* recalled the solemnity of a religious cult.

The essence of Richelieu's system was the concentration of authority. It was said of the Hohenzollern Empire after the fall of Bismarck that in the most elaborately organized of European states there was anarchy at the top. The young Louis XIV was resolved that there should be no flicker of anarchy, no thought of challenge to his will, no division of power. The Cardinal's *Testament Politique,* published in 1687, uttered a solemn warning against nerveless rule: better too much severity than too much lenity, for weakness was the ruin of the state. The *Memoirs* of Louis XIV, first published in full in 1860, were at once a summary of the first decade of his personal rule and a manual of political instruction for his son. He portrays himself as the effective ruler of his kingdom and a jealous guardian of the prestige of the Crown, while fully realizing how much is expected from an absolute sovereign. Here are a few of his precepts.

It is essential for princes to master their resentments. In scheming to injure someone who has caused us trouble we may injure ourselves. Exercising as we do a divinely appointed function we must appear incapable of the agitations which might lower the standard. If it is true that our heart, knowing its frailty, is conscious of the emotions of the common herd, our reason ought to conceal them directly they threaten the public weal for which alone we are born. A King must hold the balance between the many people who strive to tilt it to their side. So many pay court to us for personal reasons under specious phrases. You cannot satisfy everyone. Do not assess the justice of a claim by the vigor with which it is pressed. The result of the decision is more important than the merits of the claimants: the greatest of rulers would soon be ruined if he granted everything to deserving cases. Since those of our rank are never forgiven we must weigh our words. Kings are absolute lords and have full authority over all people, secular and ecclesiastical; use it according to the needs of the state. Never hurry. Take long views. The King must know everything. Empires are only preserved by the same means by which they are created, namely vigor, vigilance, and hard work.

So far we seem to have been listening to the calm accents of the father of the gods on the summit of Olympus, but the young ruler goes on to admit the temptations of the flesh. Princes, he declares, can never live too prudent and innocent a life. To reign happily and gloriously it is not enough to issue orders if they do not regulate their own conduct. He felt it right to recognize his daughter by Mlle. la Vallière by granting a title to her mother.

> I could have passed over this attachment as a bad example, but after drawing lessons from the failings of others I could not deprive you of those you could learn from mine. The Prince should always be a perfect model of virtue, all the more since he lives in a glass house. If, however, we yield in spite of ourselves we must observe two precautions as I have always done. First, that the time allotted to a liaison should never prejudice our affairs, since our first object should always be the preservation of our glory and authority, which can only be achieved by steady toil. Secondly—and more difficult to practice—that in giving our heart we must remain absolute master of our mind, separating the endearments of the lover from the resolution of the sovereign, since the influence of a mistress is much more dangerous than that of a favorite.

Despite this frank admission of human frailty, the whole of this *Testament Politique* breathes the robust conviction that absolute monarchy is the best form of government and that the author is a blessing to his country and a pattern to the world.

Never for a moment after the death of Mazarin left him a free hand did Louis XIV allow a minister or a mistress to deprive him of a fraction of his authority. The Chancellor, who kept the royal seal, the Controller General of Finance, the Ministers of State without portfolio, and the departmental Secretaries of State, were merely executants of his will. The three successive *maîtresses en titre,* La Vallière, Montespan and Fontanges, possessed no political influence, and there is no ground for the belief that the course of events in the closing decades was deflected by the virtuous Mme. de Maintenon. The concentration of power which formed the core of his political faith involved unlimited responsibility before his subjects and posterity. When a minister apologized for referring decisions to the king on the ground that he was still new to his job, he was informed that he would never have to decide about anything and that his only duty would be to obey orders. Business was transacted by four principal

Councils, three of which he regularly attended. The small *Conseil d'État,* the nearest equivalent to a Cabinet, discussed and decided the great issues of national policy. The *Conseil des Dépêches* dealt with internal affairs, the *Conseil des Finances* with taxation. The *Conseil Privé,* consisting of lawyers and rarely attended by the king, was the highest judicial court in France. None of the Councils possessed any statutory rights, and they were regarded as purely advisory bodies. When Colbert and Louvois were gone the era of supermen was over, and during the closing phase he had no one on whose judgment he was inclined to lean. Never did he attempt to shield himself behind a subordinate when things went wrong; that would have been beneath his dignity. Like Mazarin, he imposed his authority without shedding blood. *L'État c'est moi* was his slogan, even if he never coined the phrase. Of all the princes in modern Europe Louis XIV and Frederick the Great came nearest to the ideal of father of the country, the first servant as well as the master of the state.

Every potential focus of opposition to the royal will was neutralized if not removed. The Parlement of Paris, which had roughly challenged the court during the turmoil of the Fronde, was paralyzed by a veto on its traditional privilege of recording remonstrances against the decisions of the crown, and no further trouble arose while Louis XIV was on the throne. It was a high-handed proceeding, for the magistrates regarded themselves—and were widely regarded—as guardians of the fundamental laws. The Parlement, an offshoot from the old Curia Regis, could boast of centuries of service as the Supreme Court of Justice, dealing especially with appeals from lower courts. At its foundation by Philippe le Bel the President and Councillors were appointed yearly, but they were usually reappointed. As business increased it was divided into the *Chambre des Enquêtes,* dealing with most of the appeals, the *Chambre des Requêtes,* with petitions on points of law, and a third chamber with criminal cases. The most important decisions were reserved for the *Grande Chambre.* Twelve provincial Parlements were instituted during the following centuries. In addition to its judicial functions the Parlement of Paris was required to register the royal edicts, but under Louis XI it claimed the power of remonstrance and delay, and the claim grew into a recognized right. The ruler, however, could override opposition by a *lit de justice,* and Louis XIV was determined to keep the magistrates strictly to their legal duties. The Estates still met occasionally in various provinces but were allowed little power, and the provincial governors, the French equivalent of the English Lords Lieutenant, were merely ornamental nominees of the king. The work of administration was carried on by the thirty Intendants, usually chosen from the bourgeoisie, who took orders from and reported to the King and his Councils at Versailles.

In 1692 Louis XIV abolished the right of the towns to elect their functionaries and further reduced their prestige by the sale of municipal offices in order to raise money for his wars. The local tribunals were no less dependent, for their decisions could be overruled by the king. The Intendants could prevent cases coming into court and could sentence to the galleys or imprisonment. What Richelieu had begun was completed by *Le Grand Monarque,* who had no scruples about using his power to the full. Blackstone bracketed France and Turkey as the countries where civil rights were most unreservedly at the mercy of the Crown, for in the absence of habeas corpus or trial by jury an innocent citizen had little chance of securing his rights.

With equal determination Louis XIV clipped the wings of the Church by reaffirming the principles of Gallicanism first formulated by Francis I, the essence of which was the supremacy of the Crown except in matters of belief. The celebrated Four Articles of 1682 drafted by Bossuet threw down a ringing challenge to the Pope and the Jesuits. "Kings and princes," declared the first article, "are not by the law of God subject to any ecclesiastical power nor to the keys of the Church with respect to their temporal government. Their subjects cannot be released from the duty of obeying them nor absolved from the oath of allegiance." Even in the field of doctrine the power of the Vatican is strictly circumscribed. "The Pope has the principal place in deciding questions of faith," runs the fourth article, "but his judgment is not irreversible until confirmed by the consent of the Church." The Declaration, signed by thirty-four bishops and thirty-four lesser clergy, was registered by the Parlement at the command of the king. An edict was issued prescribing that the Four Articles should be taught in all universities and accepted by all professors of theology, and the archbishops and bishops were summoned to enforce the decree. Though the angry pontiff considered the issue of a formal censure of the articles, no action was taken against Gallicanism, for the king, with the nation behind him, was too powerful to be coerced. Such influence as the Church retained could only become operative with the consent of the Crown.

His ideal was a homogeneous nation, looking up with pride, affection and gratitude to its head. This monolithic conception of the state left no place for religious minorities, and when he turned *dévot* under the influence of his Jesuit confessor and Mme. de Maintenon his zeal for uniformity became an obsession. The Revocation of the Edict of Nantes was as much an assertion of the principle of national unity as an affirmation of the Catholic faith. Richelieu had been content to destroy what little political influence the Huguenots retained after the Wars of Religion, and at the opening of his reign Louis XIV paid public tribute to their loyalty during the Fronde. That these orderly and industrious citizens asked only for a quiet life was recognized by all. The clergy had always detested the Edict, and their Quinquennial Assemblies demanded its abrogation or at any rate its drastic modification. Twenty years of mounting persecution, including the closing of churches and schools and the nightmare of the *dragonnades,* led thousands of Huguenots to seek shelter abroad and thousands more to avoid almost intolerable suffering by nominal conversion. Declaring that it was his duty to convert all his subjects and extirpate heresy, and encouraged to take the final plunge by his confessor Père La Chaise, Harlay Archbishop of Paris, and Louvois the ruthless Minister of War, he revoked in 1685 the Edict of his grandfather. In a frenzy of fanaticism he exclaimed that he would complete the conversion of the Huguenots even at the cost of his right hand, and the greatest of French ecclesiastics piled incense on his altar. "Let us make known the miracle of our times," exclaimed Bossuet; "let us make known what we feel about the piety of Louis; let us raise our acclamations to the skies; let us say to this new Theodosius, this new Charlemagne: Here is the supreme achievement of your reign. It is this which gives it its true character. By your deed heresy exists no longer. God alone has wrought this miracle." Huguenot ministers were ordered to leave France within ten days or go to the galleys, but laymen were forbidden to cross the frontier. Churches were demolished, services in private houses forbidden, meetings held in the mountains; children were to be baptized by Catholic priests and brought up as Catholics. Hundreds of thousands defied the fury of their persecutors till the Revolution established equality before the law. The greatest crime of the reign was also the gravest blunder, for the thousands of skilled artisans who streamed across the frontiers before and after the Revocation weakened France as much as they strengthened England, Holland, Prussia and other Protestant states in which they found a new and happy home. A few even sought refuge in South Africa. The ferocious onslaught transformed the bolder spirits into rebels, and during the War of the Spanish Succession the bloody guerrilla struggle in the Cevennes added to the anxieties of the Crown.

The king's detestation of the Jansenists was scarcely less vehement than that which he entertained for the Huguenots, though the repression was less severe. The precise nature of their doctrinal deviation was beyond him, for he was no theologian. What stirred his anger was the thought that so many of his subjects, including a section of the clergy, continued to hold Augustinian ideas on grace proclaimed by Jansen, Bishop of Ypres, and popularized in France by Saint-Cyran and Antoine Arnauld. Five propositions concerning predestination in Jansen's *Augustinus* were declared heretical by Innocent X in 1653; and the Jansenist hostility to the Jesuits, which inspired Pascal's flaming *Lettres Provinciales,* increased the determination of the king to enforce uniformity. It was no easy task since the Jansenists were widely respected for their piety and austerity. Their attitude was restated in Quesnel's *Réflexions Morales sur le Nouveau Testament* which enjoyed immense popularity and led to new measures of repression, culminating in the expulsion of the inmates of Port Royal des Champs, the demolition of the convent buildings, and the issue of the Bull *Unigenitus* in 1713. It was not the end of the struggle, but the old king died in the belief that another focus of opposition had been removed.

Compared to the fierce battles against Huguenots and Jansenists the Quietist controversy was a storm in a teacup. An extravagant variety of mysticism taught by Molinos, a Spanish priest, and commonly described as Molinism, was embraced with fervor by Mme. Guyon and with greater circumspection by Fénelon. The aim of Quietism was to rise above ceremonies, sacraments and dogmas into a rapturous vision of the Divine Essence by the *via negationis,* self-annihilation, an emptying of the soul from all thought, feeling and will. That such a rejection of external authority and direct moral responsibility might degenerate into antinomianism was obvious, but Fénelon believed that much could be learned from this gospel of renunciation. His attitude was defined in his *Maxims of the Saints,* a devotional treatise saturated with mystical theology. Like all the great mystics from St. Theresa and St. John of the Cross to Molinos, his goal was complete surrender of self: all that mattered was to love God. At this stage Bossuet, the national champion of orthodoxy and authority, entered the lists and fulminated against the new heretics. When Fénelon appealed to Rome the Pope condemned his book and the author submitted. Regarding himself as the guardian of orthodoxy, the king deprived him of his post as Preceptor to the Duc de Bourgogne and excluded him from the court. Mme. de Maintenon, who counted him and Mme. Guyon among her intimate friends, bowed as usual to the royal will. In one of his temperamental outbursts Saint-Simon complained that the Court vomited hypocrisy. In his later years the king was a gloomy fanatic, but hypocrisy could no longer be laid to his charge. The last of his Jesuit confessors, Le Tellier, incarnated the spirit of intolerance which contributed to the growth of anticlericalism at least as much as the shafts of Bayle and Voltaire. Even during the later years of the *Grand Monarque* there was a good deal of unbelief in high circles. In 1699 the Duchess of Orleans reported to her German relatives that faith was extinct and that every youngster wanted to be an atheist. Doubtless she was thinking of her son, the future Regent, who made no pretence of sharing the beliefs of the Royal Family. Regarding the Church as a pillar of the throne, Louis XIV never worried about anything except an open challenge to its authority which he regarded as an indirect challenge to his own.

The political ideology of Louis XIV was formulated by the most eloquent preacher of the age. In his massive treatise *La Politique tirée de l'Écriture Sainte* Bossuet spoke for France with the same authority as Locke and Halifax interpreted the England of 1688. As in his better known *Discours sur l'Histoire Universelle,* compiled for his pupil the Dauphin, the Bishop of Meaux draws his arguments from scripture, history and reason in support of the system of dynastic autocracy. The Bible, he argues, is the touchstone of truth in the political no less than in the religious sphere. Sharing the conviction of Hobbes that by nature men are wolves to one another, he reaches the same conclusion that absolute power, preferably exercised by hereditary monarchy, is needed to keep them in order. He rejects the Aristotelian maxim that man is a political animal, and attributes the creation of society to the instinctive physical need for self-preservation. To fulfil his duty of securing the public welfare the sovereign must possess unfettered authority; his right once established, all other rights fade away. *"O rois, vous êtes des dieux."* Private rights are valid only if recognized by the law which the ruler decrees. Having entrusted all their power to a single person, the people can do nothing against him: even their lives are in his hands and in case of disobedience he may take them. Bad princes, even tyrants, possess the same right to obedience as good ones, and the early Christians performed their duty in praying for Nero. If opposition is permitted for any purpose, the state is in peril for public order is threatened. The ruler is no less under an obligation to maintain his authority unimpaired than his subjects to obey his commands, for its diminution would paralyze his capacity to keep the peace: the best government is that which is furthest removed from anarchy. All benefits should derive from him alone. It is right that he should be loved but he should also be feared. Caring nothing for political or religious liberty, Bossuet denies both the need and the value of constitutional guarantees, for it is as easy to sign a scrap of paper as to tear it up. Hereditary monarchy has proved the best system, for in working for his state the monarch is working for his own children.

So far Bossuet's premises and conclusions are pure Hobbes, but as the argument develops vital differences emerge. While the free-thinking publicist is an incurable pessimist about human nature, the pious bishop sees the stars shining in the heavens since Christian ethics point the way to a better life. Though subject to no terrestrial authority the ruler is under the moral law, and is in duty bound to maintain ancient institutions, fundamental laws and inherited privileges. Tradition, which meant as little to Hobbes as it was later to weigh with Bentham, possessed for Bossuet an authority which he dared not and had no wish to ignore. He believed in the wisdom of

our ancestors, and in his eyes the passage of time gradually legiti-
mized conquest. If, however, the ruler neglects his duties – even if
he openly flouts the laws of God and orders his subjects to do the
same – he could be neither punished nor resisted: like the early
Christians they must if necessary suffer and die. While the system of
Hobbes rested on the fear of punishment, the political edifice of
Bossuet was theoretically cemented by love. He was too fine a spirit
to flatter, and his paean to the ruler breathes genuine devotion.

> *A good subject loves his prince as the embodiment of the public weal and*
> *the safety of the state, as the air he breathes, as the light of his eyes, as*
> *his life and more than his life. He is more than the head of the state*
> *and the fatherland incarnate. Next to the love of God comes love for the*
> *prince, and how greatly must he love his people in order to retain their*
> *love! All men are brothers and should love each other like brothers. If*
> *he fears the people, all is lost. If he fears the great nobles, the state is*
> *weak. He must fear God alone, The more exalted the office, the greater the*
> *severity of the divine judge: mercy is for the little man, torments for the*
> *mighty. Without the divine judgment-seat absolute authority degenerates*
> *into arbitrary despotism.*

Both as a believer in an all-powerful executive and as a pillar of
the Catholic Church, Bossuet rejects liberty of conscience as a challenge to the true faith and a threat to the spiritual solidarity of the
state. As an embodiment of the mystique of absolute monarchy on a
Christian basis in seventeenth-century France Bossuet's treatise ranks
with the writings of James I and the Divine Right teachings of High
Church theologians in the reign of Charles I. Its purpose was to
convince the heir to the throne that a Christian prince was the representative of God on earth with all the powers, privileges and obligations appertaining to the post. Written when *Le Roi Soleil* was at the
height of his glory, it breathed boundless confidence in the strength
and stability of the Bourbon monarchy. As, however, the reign moved
towards its close an atmospheric change, arising from the almost
unceasing wars and the ever-increasing frustration and resentment,
stimulated a search for alternatives.

The critical spirit of a younger generation found its most eloquent
expression in Fénelon who, like Bossuet, was appointed to train an
heir to the throne, though he was allotted a more promising pupil.
No preceptor could have struck sparks from the indolent and mind-

less Dauphin, but the qualities of his son, the Duc de Bourgogne, seemed to authorize the highest hopes. Saint-Simon's portrait of Fénelon is one of the gems in his gallery. "This prelate was tall and thin, well proportioned, with a big nose, eyes from which fire and intelligence poured like a torrent, and a face unlike any I ever saw and which, once seen, could never be forgotten. It was full of contradictions, yet they always harmonized. There were gallantry and gravity, earnestness and gaiety; there were in equal proportions the teacher, the bishop, and the Grand Seigneur. His whole personality breathed thought, intelligence, grace, measure, above all nobility. It was difficult to turn one's eyes away." For Saint-Simon the Archbishop of Cambrai was the most dazzling ornament of the court. No French ecclesiastic except Richelieu has left such a legend of personal distinction; no Frenchman of his time looked so far ahead and gave his contemporaries such sound advice. In Acton's words he was the first who saw through the majestic hypocrisy of the court and knew that France was on the road to ruin. A century before the Revolution he proclaimed that the pyramid must rest not on its apex but on its base, and two centuries before the League of Nations he pleaded for an interdependent world. It was characteristic of this practical idealist that his earliest publication was a plea for the higher education of women.

Télémaque, like *Gulliver's Travels,* is a *roman à thèse,* a political tract in fictional form: everyone realized that it was a broadside against autocracy in general and Versailles in particular. Translated into many languages, it was read with delight by the king's enemies, including the persecuted Huguenots at home and abroad. Mentor is the oracle, Télémaque, the son of Ulysses the eager pupil. Every incident contains a moral or implies a criticism. "Love your people, Telemachus," declares Mentor, "as if they were your own children. A good king is all-powerful over his people, but the laws are all-powerful over him. His power to do good is absolute, but his hands are tied when he would do ill. The laws give him the people in trust as the most precious thing they can bestow on condition that he looks on himself as their father. He should live more soberly, less luxuriously and with less outward magnificence and pride than others." Mentor's sharpest arrows are aimed at the craving for fame and the wars of conquest to which it led. Though he scarcely ranks with his contemporaries William Penn and the Abbé Saint-Pierre among the pioneers of a league of nations, he denounced the slogans of arrogant nationalism with equal vigor. "The whole race is one family. All men are brothers. Say not, O ye Kings, that war is the path to glory. Whoever puts his own glory before the dictates of humanity is a monster of pride, not a man." A meeting of kings should be held every three years to renew their alliance by a fresh oath and take counsel together. Not merely wars but the trade barriers of Colbert's mercantilist system were an offense against the unity of mankind. War was the costliest of royal follies, but the building mania was not far behind. Believing that all people and all nations are brothers, he paints a picture of the Elysian fields, a Christian Utopia, a land of peace and joy. "Peu sérieux," commented Bossuet, "et peu digne d'un prêtre." Though the Eagle of Meaux had powerful wings he lacked originality and never soared into the upper regions of the sky. He was the greatest of conservatives before Joseph de Maistre, Fénelon the greatest liberal of his age.

The attack on the principle and practice of autocracy was developed in an unpublished *Lettre à Louis XIV* so vehement in tone that its authenticity might be challenged but for the survival of the autograph manuscript, doubtless a first draft. "All your Ministers," begins Fénelon, "have abandoned all the old maxims in order to glorify your authority. People no longer speak of the state, only of the king and his good pleasure. They have raised you to the skies; but absolute power is only a sham, for real power resides with the ministers, who have been harsh, arrogant, unjust, violent, false." The king's worst fault was his passion for war, and the Dutch War had unleashed all the misfortunes of France. "Your Majesty was driven into it to enhance your glory, but such a motive can never justify a war." A terrible and obviously exaggerated picture is drawn of the plight of France in 1691.

> *Your peoples are dying of hunger. Agriculture is almost at a standstill, all the industries languish, all commerce is destroyed. France is a vast hospital. The magistrates are degraded and worn out. It is you who have caused all these troubles. The whole kingdom having been ruined, everything is concentrated in you and everyone must feed out of your hand. The people which loved you so much is beginning to withdraw its affection, its confidence and even its respect. Your victories no longer arouse*

delight. There is only bitterness and despair. Sedition is boiling up. You do not love God; you only fear Him with a slavish fear. It is hell you are afraid of. Your religion consists of superstition and ceremonies. You relate everything to yourself as if you were God on earth.

That the letter was read by the proud monarch is inconceivable.

The death of the Dauphin in 1711 turned all eyes to the Duc de Bourgogne who might be expected to succeed his septuagenarian grandfather at any moment; and then, it seemed, was the chance of the ardent reformer at Cambrai. "Our trouble," he wrote to the Duc de Chevreuse, "is that this war has been the personal enterprise of the king, who is ruined and discredited. It should be made the concern of the whole nation which must save itself." Since he might perhaps be called to power, he felt bound to draft a new policy for the new reign. After prolonged discussions with his old pupil's closest friends, the Duc de Beauvilliers, his ex-governor, and the Duc de Chevreuse, he formulated maxims in which he approached closer to practical issues than ever before. The first tasks were to overcome the active or passive resistance of the court, abolish sinecures, curb the building craze, introduce simpler furniture and cheaper apparel. Such austerity could only become effective if the people joined in the reforming campaign. For this purpose it would be necessary not only to summon the States-General which had not met for a century, but to integrate it into the life of the nation, meeting every three years and sitting as long as circumstances required. Since the members would doubtless be as moderate and loyal as the Estates of Languedoc and Brittany, they could discuss every aspect of policy at home and abroad. In his anxiety to limit the power of the ruler he argued that Gallicanism was no longer necessary since the authority of Rome had so sharply declined. Give the Church a little more freedom and let the parishes have curés of their own choice. The most conspicuous omission in this generous program of reform is the absence of any reference to liberty of conscience, for Fénelon approved the Revocation of the Edict of Nantes and had no use for the Jansenists.

A few other points are made in a little essay, *Examen de conscience des devoirs de la royauté,* which urges the sovereign to inform himself in detail of the state of the various classes and the working of central and local institutions. Above all he must have no favorites and must strive to avoid war, the mother of misery; if forced to fight, he should observe the laws of war. "He is the cleverest and the most fantastical head in the kingdom," grumbled the old king. Had he peered more closely into that scintillating brain he would have recoiled in anger at the audacity of its schemes. That the Duc de Bourgogne never came to the throne was the tragedy of Fénelon's life and was a major misfortune for France, for the first seeds of revolution were sown in the closing years of Louis XIV.

A scarcely less formidable critic of the *régime,* though he attacked on a narrower front, emerged from a different camp. Among the Marshals whose triumphs built up the renown of Louis XIV none occupied a loftier place in the regard of his countrymen and the court than Vauban. Though Condé and Turenne were his superiors on the battlefield, he was the prince of military engineers whose fortresses on the eastern frontiers remained the admiration of Europe long after his death. He was also a man of noble character whose interests embraced the problems of peace no less than war. Staggered by the Revocation of the Edict of Nantes, he deplored in a letter to Louvois the blow struck at industry and commerce and the revival of religious strife. He forwarded a copy to Mme. de Maintenon, but the appeal fell on deaf ears. The decision, he argued, weakened France by the loss of industrious citizens and strengthened her enemies. Kings were masters of the life and property of their subjects but not of their opinions, and they should not press their prerogative too far.

His next venture was more ambitious and might appear to have more chance of success, for the financial plight of war-worn France was notorious. The Peace of Ryswick in 1697 was merely a truce after a generation of continuous struggle which emptied the treasury and almost beggared the people. The Intendants were instructed to investigate and report on the condition and needs of their districts. It was the wrong method of approach, for they were likely to minimize the evils and in some cases to conceal the causes which brought them gain. Far weightier was the counsel of Vauban who had studied conditions on the many journeys and marches of his long life. No one since Sully had displayed such deep and unflagging interest in the peasantry which he regarded as the backbone of the state. When the return of peace afforded him ampler leisure Vauban summarized his conclusions in *Le Dîme Royale.* Since France, he estimated, could support 24 millions but contained only 19, there was no overpopulation; the climate was temperate, the soil good, the peasantry thrifty and industrious. Why then was there such misery? Taxation was heavy but not unbearable if the burden were fairly distributed. The fundamental cause was that many contributed too much while the nobility and the clergy were exempt. The privilege of the former was an inheritance from feudal times, when the landed proprietors were expected to aid the Crown from their own resources in time of war. The exemption of the clergy was equally a survival from the ages when the Church was a law to itself. These financial entrenchments Richelieu himself had not attempted to storm. The gross injustice was resented by the *Tiers État,* but there were no channels through which it could express discontent. Every year the King's Council fixed the sum required from the several districts, and the local collectors required police protection. It the taxpayer could not meet the demand, his animals, agricultural implements, and even his furniture might be seized. The knowledge that a substantial portion of the yield never reached the coffers of the state increased the smart.

Minor changes, argued Vauban, were useless and a new deal was required. A tax should be levied on all citizens, ranging from 5 to 10 percent according to the needs of the state, in place of the existing *taille,* local *douane* and *aides.* The idea of a tenth was familiar to the Jews, the Greeks, the Romans, and the early French kings. The Church tithe aroused little complaint and involved no corruption. The hated *taille* was not adjusted to the capacity to pay, since the value of properties changed and gross favoritism was rife. To avoid the *taille* peasants often concealed their resources and went about in rags. Comparing the yield of tithe and *taille* in some fifty parishes, he discovered that the former yielded the larger sum. The *Dîme Royale* would be assessed on land, houses, mills, fisheries, salaries, pensions, and every other source of income, concealment of assets being punishable by confiscation and doubling the demand. Manual workers should only pay a thirtieth, since they were frequently unemployed and their standard of life was low. Passing to changes in indirect taxation, the author proposed the reduction of the salt tax which many were too poor to pay, and an extra charge on wine supplied in cabarets, a measure which might help to keep peasants at home and not waste their money on drink. The new system should be introduced gradually so that the whole country could witness its benefits. It was not intended to increase the total yield of taxation but to diminish the burden on those least able to bear it. Vauban expected opposition from the "leeches and harpies." He accepted autocracy but declared war on the swarm of parasites up to the highest levels.

The old soldier wrote, not to inflame the public, for his book was not on sale, but to convert the king and his council, expecting that his record of service would ensure attention if not gratitude. A manuscript copy was sent to the king who, if made aware of its contents, cannot have resented it, for the author was promoted a Marshal two years later. When, however, it was printed anonymously in 1707 without seeking the usual permission of the police, which he feared would be refused, a storm blew up. Though the book was presented only to a few influential friends the authorship was no secret, and it was denounced by the tax farmers and other vested interests. A demand was raised that the audacious reformer should be sent to the Bastille and his book destroyed. The shock was too much for the old warrior, who died of a broken heart. When the king heard the news he exclaimed: "I lose a man greatly attached to my person and the state." Perhaps he may have felt a momentary twinge of conscience that he had not held his shield over a faithful servant who was saluted by Saint-Simon as the best of Frenchmen. Three years later he was vindicated when the king imposed a special war levy of a tenth for three successive years.

On the same day, March 14, 1707, which witnessed the condemnation of the *Dîme Royale*, another formidable indictment of government action and inaction was suppressed by decree. Speaking with inside knowledge of provincial administration Boisguillebert, a respected official in Normandy, described the sufferings of the people without sparing his superiors. While his *Détail de la France*, published in 1697, had been mainly statistical, his *Factum de la France*, published ten years later when the sky had become even darker, clamored for the reform of taxation and the liberation of agriculture, the dominant industry of the country, from the stifling restrictions on purchase and sale. His appeal, like that of Vauban, fell on deaf ears, and the courageous critic was disgraced and transferred to the center of France. The *ancien régime* had scarcely reached its zenith than it began its slow decline. Unfettered absolutism leads to the abuse of power, and the abuse of power to resistance, at first in thought and later in deed. Yet the pace was very slow and nothing could be done till the middle class, steadily increasing in numbers, wealth and self-confidence, took matters into their own hands. During the reign of Louis XIV far more *roturiers* dreamed, like Molière's *Bourgeois Gentilhomme,* of buying their way into the privileged classes than of attempting to alter the social stratification which reserved the highest prizes for the chosen few.

Louis XIV lived too long for his reputation, and during the last two decades of his reign he forfeited much of the respect he had enjoyed in his prime. The Augustan Age of French history had been as brief as it was brilliant. The change from the major to the minor key was recorded by many witnesses, with Saint-Simon and Madame, Duchess of Orleans, at their head. He himself was growing old and weary, though he put a brave face on his misfortunes. The distress which had inspired the composition of Vauban's *Dîme Royale* rapidly increased as the latest, longest, and fiercest of his many conflicts, the War of the Spanish Succession, dragged on year after year, with the scales turning steadily against France under the hammer blows of Marlborough and Prince Eugene. National bankruptcy was in sight. Critical pamphlets and verses began to appear for the first time since the *Mazarinades* in the days of his youth. The fruits of absolutism proved as bitter as those of feudal anarchy. In 1709 nature conspired to swell the mounting tide of misery with the cruelest and most prolonged winter in the history of France. The young Apollo who had trampled the serpent of faction under his feet and gathered the laurels of victory in a series of campaigns had withered into a disillusioned old man fighting for his life against a coalition provoked by placing his grandson on the throne of Spain.

He had always been industrious, and when Colbert and Louvois were gone he worked harder than ever. For eight or nine hours daily he presided over the Council of Ministers, studied reports from his generals, gave audiences to ambassadors, dictated replies and instructions, and occasionally, as in the correspondence with his grandson the King of Spain, wrote letters in his own hand. It was an exacting profession. The scandals of the early years were now a distant memory, and Mme. de Maintenon had little reason to complain. The secret marriage left her official status unchanged. *La veuve Scarron,* ex-governess of the royal bastards, continued to be styled the Marquise de Maintenon, second *dame d'atours* of the Dauphine, but the royal ménage told its own tale. From 1685 onwards they were inseparable, and her apartments at the various places were connected with his own. His free moments were spent with her, and every evening he worked with one or other of his ministers in her room. Though she took no part in the discussions she knew everything that was going on, and he discussed his many problems with a cool-headed and sympathetic woman who cared as little for money as for intrigue. "She is a saint," declared the King. "She has all the perfections and plenty of intelligence, and I have none." One day he remarked: "Madame, a King is called Your Majesty, the Pope Your Holiness, and you should be Your Solidity."

Döllinger's well-known description of Mme. de Maintenon as the most influential woman in French history is unjust to Joan of Arc, Catherine de Medicis and Mme. de Pompadour. That she took a lively interest in ecclesiastical affairs was known to everyone, but here too the king's will was her law. If he was ever influenced by any human being it was by his Jesuit confessors. Knowing the limits of her power she never dreamed of crossing the boundary, for unquestioning subordination was the condition of her hold on that wayward heart. She was fortified by the conviction that her sacrifice – she often felt it to be her martyrdom – was the will of God; she had rescued the proudest of European monarchs from a life of sin and enhanced the dignity of the Crown. She was also sustained by her love for the Duc du Maine, the Duchesse de Bourgogne, and her little girls in the École de Saint-Cyr. Romantic love she had never known, for her marriage to the semi-paralyzed Scarron was a legal ceremony and nothing more, and her second venture was a *mariage de raison.* To understand her character and her trials we must turn from the caricature of Saint-Simon and the malice of Madame to her letters and to the affectionate record of her beloved secretary, Mlle. d'Aumale. Saint-Simon's unscrupulous schemer was a woman of unblemished repute, unfailing tact, culture and refinement. The mud hurled at "the old Sultana" and Mme. Ordure by Liselotte does not stick. A fairer verdict was recorded at her death in the journal of Dangeau who had studied her at close range for many years: "a woman of such great merit who had done so much good and prevented so much harm that one cannot overpraise her." That this tribute was denounced by Saint-Simon as "a stinking lie" reflects discredit on the spiteful little duke, not on the morganatic wife.

"Do you not see that I am dying of grief," she wrote, "and am only saved from collapse by the grace of God? Once I was young and pretty, enjoyed pleasures and was a general favorite. A little later I spent years in an intellectual circle. Then I came to favor, and I confess it all leaves a terrible void, a disquiet, a weariness, a desire for change." The atmosphere of the court filled her with disgust, and Mlle. d'Aumale often saw her in tears. "I witness every kind of passion, treacheries, meannesses, insensate ambitions, disgusting envy, people with hearts full of rage, struggling to ruin each other, a thousand intrigues, often about trifles. The women of today are insupportable, with their immodest garb, their snuff, their wine, their gluttony, their coarseness, their idleness. I dislike it all so much that I cannot bear it." Yet bear it she did for thirty years. Too reserved to radiate very much warmth, she was respected by those who knew her well and loved by those who knew her best. The notion that she wished or the king wished her to be queen is fantastic. She possessed too much good sense, he too much pride.

Next to Mme. de Maintenon the old monarch found his chief happiness in Marie Adelaide, "the Rose of Savoy," grandchild of Monsieur and his first wife Henrietta of England, the child-wife of the Duc de Bourgogne, who brought a gleam of sunshine into the gloomy halls of Versailles and in the words of Madame, Duchess of Orleans, made everyone feel young again, for she was only eleven. "She is a treasure," reported Mme. de Maintenon to her mother, the Duchess of Savoy.

She is the delight of the King, amusing him with her gaiety and pranks, though she never goes too far. One can talk seriously to her without being bored. She dislikes flattery and is grateful for advice. She gets prettier every day. She is growing a little and her figure is perfect. She dances well and no one ever possessed such grace. I never exaggerate. No one dreams of spoiling her. Perhaps it will not always be so. Traps are set for princes as for ordinary folk. I hope God will protect her. She fears and loves Him, and has a great respect for religion. Her education has been excellent and her range of knowledge is surprising.

Her only failing was a passion for the card table, which the king unwisely encouraged by paying her debts. In her combination of youthful levity, natural charm, and warmth of heart she reminds us of Marie Antoinette. During the first phase she appealed more to the king and Mme. de Maintenon than to her austere husband, who disliked society and loved to shut himself up with his books; but as motherhood ripened her character she learned to appreciate his noble qualities, and it grew into the first happy marriage in the Bourbon family.

When the shadowy figure of the Dauphin, his father's only legitimate child, passed away at Meudon, few tears were shed. The most colorless of the Bourbons had sought relief from his lifelong inferiority complex in the pleasures of the table and the chase; "sans vice ni vertu" comments Saint-Simon disdainfully. He had lost his Bavarian wife, and his three sons meant as little to him as he to them. His death at the age of fifty in 1711 was welcomed, not only because it removed the threat of a ruler totally unfitted for his task, but because it opened the way for a successor of exceptional promise. In dynastic autocracies the abilities, virtues and vices of the Royal Family make history. Twice in the course of the eighteenth century there seemed to be a chance of the monarchy renewing itself, and twice the cup was snatched away by a cruel fate. When the full measure of the unworthiness of Louis XV came to be realized, the nation looked back nostalgically to the Duc de Bourgogne, the pupil of Fénelon. The king was very fond of him, testifies Mlle. d'Aumale, and the whole court adored him. He was born a terror, records Saint-Simon, and during his youth he made his entourage tremble by paroxysms of fury, for he could not bear the slightest opposition. Often there were storms so violent that his body seemed ready to burst. He was obstinate to a degree, with a passion for all kinds of pleasures – good cheer, the chase, music. He radiated intelligence. His repartees were astonishing, his answers pointed and profound, the most abstract subjects his delight. From this blend of dross and precious metal his admirable governor the Duc de Beauvilliers, and his preceptor

Fénelon, we are told, fashioned a casket of shining gold. "The marvel was that in a very short time their devotion made him another man, changing his faults into corresponding virtues. Out of this abyss we have witnessed the emergence of a prince affable, gentle, human, generous, patient, modest, humble and – for himself – austere. His only thought is to fulfill his duties as a son and a subject as well as those to which he is summoned by destiny." His youthful passion for the card table had been overcome, and Mme. de Maintenon, an exacting critic, described him as a saint.

Among the papers found in his desk after his death was a meditation on the call awaiting him which confirms Saint-Simon's portrait.

Of all the people who compose a nation the one who deserves most pity and receives least is the sovereign. He has all the disadvantages of grandeur without its delights. Of all his subjects he has the least liberty, the least tranquillity, the fewest moments for himself. Soldiers go into winter quarters, magistrates have vacations, everyone has periods of rest: for the King there are none and never will be. If he changes his residence, his work follows him. A day of inaction involves a crushing task next day or else everything stagnates. His whole life is spent in a whirlpool of business—a round of ceremonies, anxieties, disagreeable tasks, solicitations without end. His plans go wrong. The people, conscious of their evils, ignore his efforts to help. In appointments he seeks for merit but is deceived. He tries to make someone happy, but he reaps discontent and ingratitude. He has palaces which he has not seen and riches which he does not enjoy. He fulfills St. Paul's ideal of a Christian: he has everything and possesses nothing. Strictly speaking he is the poorest of his subjects, for all the needs of the state are his needs and they always exceed his fortune. A father is never rich when his income does not suffice for the sustenance of his children.

The Duc de Bourgogne was fortified by the counsel and affection of friends who composed what Saint-Simon calls *le petit troupeau*, which stood for piety, austerity, and reform. He needed moral support, for the disastrous campaign of 1708, in which he held a high command, had depreciated his stock. The leader of "the little flock" was the Duc de Beauvilliers, one of the few stainless figures, *sans peur et sans reproche,* on the crowded stage at Versailles. At his side stood his brother-in-law, the Duc de Chevreuse, who shared his devotion to the heir to the throne. Both of them looked up to Fénelon, who, though banished from the court, remained in close touch by cor-

respondence. The youngest member of the group was Saint-Simon
who in long private talks urged him to restore the political influence
of the *noblesse* when he was called to the helm.

His testing time came sooner than he expected, for his father died
of smallpox. During the five days of his illness the duke and his wife
held open court and were equally gracious to all comers. In Saint-
Simon's glowing phrase it was like the coming of spring. Not only
was the whole court there but *tout Paris et tout Meudon* flocked to
worship the rising sun. When the news of the Dauphin's death reached
Versailles late at night Saint-Simon rushed out of his apartments and
found *tout Versailles* assembled or assembling, the ladies emerging
from their beds or bedrooms just as they were. The new Dauphin—
"tout simple, tout saint, tout plein de ses devoirs"—embodied the
hopes of all that was best in France. He had discussed financial reform with Vauban and was prepared for still more fundamental measures: the machinery of government must be transformed and a
popular element introduced. Looking beyond the walls of the palace
he longed to aid the common man and the common soldier who had
never had their chance. It was a false dawn, for within a year the
Dauphin, his wife, and their eldest son died within ten days. For once
Saint-Simon, who could love as well as hate, gave way to passionate
grief. The duke, he declares, was born for the happiness of France
and all Europe. "We were not worthy of him. I wished to withdraw
from the Court and the world, and it needed all the wisdom and influence of my wife to prevent it, for I was in despair." To the Duc de
Beauvilliers he exclaimed after the last scene at St. Denis: "We have
been burying France," and Beauvilliers agreed. Their grief was
shared by Mme. de Maintenon, who wrote to the Princess des Ursins:
"Everything is gone, everything seems empty, there is no more joy.
The king does his best to keep up his spirits, but he cannot shake off
his sorrow." Never in the history of France has there been such
universal regret at the death of a reigning monarch or heir. In the
words of Duclos it would have been an era of justice, order, and
morals.

The Duke of Orleans, now marked out as the future Regent for
the little boy of two who was to become Louis XV, shared some of
the views of the Duc de Bourgogne, but he never inspired the devotion and respect which had been so widely entertained for the pupil

of Fénelon. The three remaining years of the most memorable reign in the history of France were a gloomy time. The routine of Court life, the music, the gambling, continued, but the sparkle had disappeared. The weary old monarch, like Francis Joseph at a later date, plodded joylessly through his papers. The fairest flower of the Court, the only member of the Royal Family whom he had taken to his heart, was sorely missed, and Mme. de Maintenon, always a restful rather than an exhilarating influence, was nearing eighty. The victory of Villars at Denain saved the French cause on the brink of catastrophe, and procured an honorable settlement in the Treaty of Utrecht, for the king's grandson retained the Spanish throne. Yet the country was exhausted by half a century of warfare, poverty-stricken and depressed, and the ruler felt that he was no longer beloved. It was time to go, and he died with the dignity which had never deserted him in good and evil times. The sun went down in a bank of dark clouds, for the heir was a delicate lad of five. The second grandson was far away in Madrid and had resigned his claim to the throne. The third grandson, the Duc de Berry, had passed away in 1714. On his deathbed the king sent for his great-grandson and addressed the little boy in words which deeply moved all who were present. "My child, you will one day be a great king. Do not imitate me in my taste for war. Always relate your actions to God, and make your subjects honor Him. It breaks my heart to leave them in such a state. Always follow good advice; love your peoples; I give you Père Le Tellier as your confessor; never forget the gratitude you owe the Duchess de Ventadour." He embraced the child, gave him his blessing, lifted his hands and uttered a little prayer as he watched him leave the room. "Not a day passed," testifies Villars, "without some mark of strength, goodness, and above all, piety. His instructions for the funeral were given with such clarity and self-control that he seemed to be making arrangements for someone else."

Shortly before his last illness the king drafted instructions for his great-grandson which he requested Marshal Villeroi to hand to him on reaching the age of seventeen.

My son, if Providence allows you to shape your own life, receive this letter from the hands of the faithful subject who has promised me to deliver it. You will find therein the last wishes of your father and your King who, in quitting this world, feels such tenderness for you in your childhood that the troubles he apprehends during your minority cause him more anxiety than the terrors of approaching death. If anything can soften my pain it is the promise of good subjects who have sworn to me to watch over you and shed their blood for your preservation. Reward them and never forget them, nor the services of my son the Duc du Maine whom I find worthy to be placed at your side. This distinction will doubtless be assailed by those whose desire to rule it frustrates. If anything happens to him, or if my dispositions in his favor are set aside, I desire you to restore everything to the position existing at my death, both as regards religion and the Duc du Maine. Have confidence in him. Follow his advice. He is quite able to guide you. If death deprives you of such a good subject, preserve for his children the rank I have bestowed on them, and show them all the friendship you owe to their father who has sworn to me only to abandon you at death. Let the ties of blood and friendship ever unite you to the King of Spain and allow no reason or misunderstood political interest to separate you. That is the only way to preserve peace and the European equilibrium. Maintain an inviolable attachment to the common father of the faithful, and never for any reason separate yourself from the bosom of the Church. Place all your confidence in God, live rather as a Christian than a King, and never incur His displeasure by moral irregularities. Thank Divine Providence which so visibly protects this kingdom. Set your subjects the same example as a Christian father to his family. Make them happy if you desire happiness. Relieve them as soon as possible of all the heavy burdens necessitated by a long war which they bore with fidelity and patience. Grant them the long periods of peace which alone can restore your kingdom. Always prefer peace to the hazards of war, and remember that the most brilliant victory is too dearly bought at the expense of your subjects' blood, which should only be shed for the glory of God. This conduct will earn the blessing of heaven during your reign. Receive my blessing in this last embrace.

The future of France was constantly in his thoughts. Addressing the courtiers and officials from his bed he commended his successor to their care. "He is only five. He will greatly need your zeal and fidelity. I request for him the same sentiments you have often shown for myself. I advise him to avoid wars. I have made too many, and they compelled me to lay heavy burdens on my people. This I deeply regret and I ask the pardon of God."

A briefer and somewhat similar declaration of faith was embodied in the maxims for his grandson on leaving to assume the crown of Spain in 1700.

Love your wife, and ask God for one to suit you—not an Austrian. Beware of flatterers. Esteem those who risk your displeasure, for they are your real friends. Only wage war if you are compelled, and then take command yourself. Never have a favorite or a mistress. Be the master. Consult your Council but decide yourself. God, who has made you King, will provide all the wisdom you require so long as your intentions are good.

Having by this time dispensed with mistresses the royal moralist no longer claimed indulgence for the weakness of young rulers which he had regretfully recognized thirty or more years earlier.

The closing scene was most vividly described by his sister-in-law the Duchess of Orleans in a letter written four days before the end.

Today we have witnessed the saddest and most touching scene imaginable. Our dear King, after preparing himself for death and receiving the last sacraments, sent for the little Dauphin, and gave him his blessing. Then he summoned the Duchesse de Berry, myself, and all the other girls and grandchildren. He bade me farewell with such tenderness that I wonder I did not faint. He said he had always loved me, more than I knew; that he regretted to have hurt me at times; begged me to think of him sometimes, which he believed I should do as I had always felt affection for him. He gave me his blessing and wished me happiness. I fell at his knees and kissed his hand, and he embraced me. Then he spoke to the others and exhorted them to unity. I thought he was speaking to me, and said I would obey him in that as in everything. He smiled and said: I was not speaking to you, for I know you are too sensible; I was speaking to the other princesses. The King's self-control is indescribable. He issues his orders as if he were merely going on a journey.

Louis XIV had raised France to the highest pinnacle in the first half of his reign, but he lived long enough to destroy much of his handiwork. "I noticed in my youth," wrote Duclos many years later, "that those who lived longest under his reign were the least favorable to him." The colossal national debt resulting from many years of war hung like a millstone round the neck of his descendants, and the system of government could only be operated by a ruler of equal capacity. The population had fallen by one-fifth in half a century owing to war casualties, the expulsion of the Huguenots, and widespread starvation. Agricultural production had declined in an even more alarming ratio. Considerable areas went out of cultivation, the country swarmed with robbers, and bread riots were frequent. Direct and indirect taxes, tithes and feudal burdens were a nightmare at a time of bad harvests and dear bread. Old taxes had been increased and new ones – the *capitation* and the *dixième* – imposed. Every possible source of revenue was exploited, including forced loans, lotteries, the issue of paper money, the sale of titles and official posts, and the depreciation of the currency. France, still almost entirely an agricultural country, was sucked nearly dry. Huge annual deficits added to the national debt, and the revenues of the coming years were mortgaged to meet immediate needs. The glitter of a lavish court offered a grim contrast to the spectre of hunger which stalked through the land. The sufferings of the people were far more grievous in 1715 than on the eve of the Revolution in 1789. Such was the price his subjects had to pay for the greater glory of the *Roi Soleil*.

Pierre Goubert

LOUIS XIV AND THE FORCES IN FRENCH SOCIETY

Pierre Goubert is professor of modern history at the University of Paris at Nanterre and is one of the most influential directors of research at the VIe Section of the Ecole Pratique des Hautes Etudes in Paris, where a large group of historians are investigating French economic and social history with highly sophisticated statistical methods. His success with this technique he demonstrated with his Beauvais et le Beauvaisis de 1600 à 1730, 2 vols. *(Paris, 1960). Among scholars who have published general studies of the reign of Louis XIV, Professor Goubert is unique in that only his book incorporates many of the findings of the school of research of which he is one of the leaders. In the excerpt given here, he places Louis XIV in the context of his time, attempts to give an objective judgment of the king, and suggests major qualifications of the traditional interpretation of his reign.*

Lucien Febvre, one of the guiding lights of French historical studies, once wrote that the historian had no business "to pronounce judgment . . . to set himself up as acting judge of the valley of Jehosaphat."

He said many times that the historian's besetting sin was the sin of anachronism, although he stated also that history was "a child of her time" and that none of her practitioners could detach themselves from the preoccupations, currents of thought and general "climate" of their own times. One might also maintain that a degree of passion is necessary to the historian, that it is those works which are most vibrant with personality which remain the most vivid and fertile, even if only because they provoke contradiction and are bound to produce the more important work of analysis and painstaking research inseparable from any serious study.

So let us leave to the sovereign judges, of Jehosaphat or anywhere else, the honor or ridicule of passing judgment on Mazarin's godson. In any case, whoever judges Louis-Dieudonné, judges chiefly himself. But for the would-be impartial historian, there is one question which cannot be avoided and which does seem to belong genuinely to the historian's province. That is the question of what were the precise extent and limits of King Louis' own personal acts in the course of fifty-five long years which were no more than so many seconds in the whole history of the world.

The King's Acts: His Personal Sphere

As early as 1661, as he declared in his *Mémoires,* Louis meant to have sole command in every sphere and claimed full responsibility, before the world and all posterity, for everything that should happen in his reign. In spite of constant hard work, he soon found he had to entrust the actual running of certain departments, such as finance or commerce, to a few colleagues, although he still reserved the right to take major decisions himself. There were, however, some aspects of his *métier de roi* to which he clung absolutely and persistently, although his persistence was not invariably absolute. Consequently, it is permissible to single out a kind of personal sphere which the king reserved to himself throughout his reign, although this sphere might vary, while the rest still remained, as it were, under his eye.

As a young man, Louis had promised himself that his own time and posterity should ring with his exploits. If this had been no more than a simple wish, and not an inner certainty, it might be said to have been largely granted.

As a hot-headed young gallant, he flouted kings by his extravagant gestures and amazed them by the brilliance of his court, his entertainments, his tournaments and his mistresses. As a new Augustus he could claim, for a time, to have been his own Maecenas. Up to the year 1672, all Europe seems to have fallen under the spell of his various exploits and his youthful fame spread even as far as the "barbarians" of Asia. For seven or eight years after that, the armies of Le Tellier and Turenne seemed almost invincible while Colbert's youthful navy and its great admirals won glory off the coast of Sicily. Then, when Europe had pulled itself together, Louis still showed amazing powers of resistance and adaptability. Even when he seemed to be aging, slipping into pious isolation amid his courtiers, he retained the power to astonish with the splendors of his palace at Versailles, his opposition to the Pope and the will to make himself into a "new Constantine," and later by allying himself with Rome to "purify" the Catholic religion. When practically on his death bed, he could still impress the English ambassador who came to protest at the building of a new French port next door to the ruins of Dunkirk.

Dead, he became a kind of symbolic puppet for everyone to take over and dress up in his chosen finery. Voltaire used him, in the name of "his" age, as ammunition against Louis XV. On the other side, he long stood as the type of bloodthirsty warlike and intolerant despot. Even the nineteenth-century Bourbons preferred to celebrate their descent from "good king Henry" with his white cockade, or from the "martyr" of 21 January. The great school of historians which flourished from 1850 until 1915 did not spare him, but studied his entourage and his reign most carefully. In the twentieth century, the royalist academicians Bertrand, with superb naïvety, and Gaxotte, with more talent and disingenuousness, have made him a symbol of order and greatness, of patriotism and even of virtue. At the same time, the teaching of Lavisse which, although hostile, also shows great subtlety and unrivaled scholarship, still dominates the field in the scholarly academic tradition. Finally, there are the young historians, strongly influenced by philosophers, sociologists and certain economists, who pass over the king's personality and entourage – to be left to the purveyors of historical gossip and romance – in favor of concentrating on those problems of institutions, attitudes of mind, religious observances, social strata and the great movements of fun-

damental economic forces which, in their view, transcend mere individuals and events. While all this is going on, the general public is
subjected to diatribes on "classicism," which is an illusion, on
Versailles and its "significance," the Man in the Iron Mask, the Affair
of the Poisons, on the king's mistresses, successive or contemporane-
ous, and on the "policy of greatness."

For precisely three centuries, Louis XIV has continued to dominate,
fascinate and haunt men's minds. "The universe and all time" have
certainly remembered him, although not always in the way he would
have wished. From this point of view, Louis' personal deeds have
been a great success. Unfortunately, his memory has attracted a
cloud of hatred and contempt as enduring as that which rises from
the incense of his worshippers or the pious imitations of a later age.

In his personal desire to enlarge his kingdom, the king was successful. The lands in the north, Strasbourg, Franche- Comté and the
"iron belt" are clear evidence of success. In this way Paris was
better protected from invasion. But all these gains had been made
by 1681 and later events served only to confirm, rescue or reduce
them. It has even been maintained that considering his strong position in 1661, surrounded by so many kings who were young, unsure
of their thrones or simply incompetent, Louis might have hoped for
greater things. He might have aimed at the annexation of the Spanish
Netherlands, although Holland and England would always have
managed to prevent him. Lorraine was vulnerable and Louis was
less powerful there in 1715 than in 1661, while with a little shrewd-
ness or cunning, there were Savoy and Nice to be had, to say nothing
of the colonies which he tended to disregard, leaving them to traders,
adventurers, priests and a few of his colleagues. He was satisfied
with losing one West Indian island and the gateway to Canada while
a handful of brave men were striving to win him an empire in America
and another in India.

As absolute head of his diplomatic service and his armies, from
beginning to end, he was well served while he relied on men who
had been singled out by Mazarin or Richelieu but he often made a
fool of himself by selecting unworthy successors. He was no great
warrior. His father and his grandfather had reveled in the reek of
the camp and the heady excitement of battle. His preference was
always for impressive maneuvers, parades and good safe sieges

rather than the smoke of battle, and as age grew on him he retreated to desk strategy. Patient, secretive and subtle in constructing alliances, weaving intrigues and undoing coalitions, he marred all these gifts by ill-timed displays of arrogance, brutality and unprovoked aggression. In the last analysis, this born aggressor showed his greatness less in triumph than in adversity but there was never any doubt about his effect on his contemporaries whose feelings towards him were invariably violent and uncompromising. He was admired, feared, hated and secretly envied.

If, as a good libertine and a poor theologian, he began by taking little interest in the matter of religion, this became, from his fortieth year onwards, one of his favorite "personal spheres." But here he met with total lack of success. In his conflict with the great authoritarian and pro-Jansenist pope, Innocent XI, he was forced to give way and, from a passionate Gallican became ultramontane to the point of embarrassing later popes. Against the Jansenists as a matter of policy rather than of doctrine, he only succeeded, despite repeated acts of violence, in strengthening the sect and uniting it with Gallicans in the Parlement and the Sorbonne and with the *richériste* priests suppressed by the edict of 1695. Whatever may be claimed, the extirpation of the "Calvinist heresy" resulted in the weakening of the kingdom, the strengthening of her neighbors and a formidable amount of hatred, national and European, whether real or assumed. In the end, not many *religionnaires* were converted. They recanted, resisted, revolted or appealed to the enemy, and calmly rebuilt their churches in the Midi, while in Paris, the great Huguenot businessmen were generally tolerated because they were indispensable. The Catholic Counter-reformation undoubtedly made great strides during the reign owing to the missions, the seminaries which were finally established, and the admirable Jansenist parish priests, but the basic foundations had in fact been laid long before 1661.

For some fifteen or twenty years, it was Louis' ambition to gather around his person the cream of artists and writers. In this field Colbert, who had learned his trade from Mazarin, was able to help him considerably while he had the power and the money. After 1673, money grew short and from 1689 downright scarce, while in the ill-fated year of 1694 even such a magnificent undertaking as the Gobelins very nearly failed. On the other hand, Louis very early began concentrating his efforts on his works at Versailles and later at Marly, and neglecting the rest. After 1680, patronage as a whole slipped away from the monarchy. Ideas became freer and more diversified and the main themes of the eighteenth century began to appear while the critical and scientific spirit progressed rapidly, shaking the old dogmatic ideas, and by that time Louis had largely lost interest in intellectual matters unless it was a case of checking some dangerous "innovation." But for fifteen years, there was a happy meeting of talents which shed, as it were, a luster on the finest period of the reign. The young king had given proof of taste and even of daring. There was in him a very great *"honnête homme,"* in the sense of the period, capable of appreciating, singling out and making others appreciate (even Molière), and sometimes showing great tolerance. As time went on and he was burdened with other cares, less ably supported and in any case he was growing set in his ways, turning his back on changes in manners and ideas, he became obstinate or frankly gave up. The so-called *"grand siècle,"* with the "Great King" as its patron was a brilliant firework display which lasted no more than fifteen years.

Louis was a child of the Fronde and although its detailed execution was left to the small fry among his servants, the humbling of all the great "Corps and Estates" of the realm remained his constant concern. The officers' companies were debased, humiliated and taxed out of existence, the Parlements, estates, communes and consulates annihilated, the arrogant nobility reduced to begging for his favors where they had once been conspirators and instigators of provincial revolts. Most of the clergy were turned into courtiers, and all the ancient nobility tamed and barred from his councils, while the new were treated with contempt for all the cheapness of their titles. Last of all the Béarnais, Catalans, Cévenols, Bordelais, Poitevins and, above all the Bretons, with any others who persisted in untimely uprisings were massacred outright. Such repressive measures were bound, by their very violence, to lead to passionate reactions. The new regency and the new century were certain to give striking occasion for them.

As the head of a dynasty which he could trace back to Charlemagne and which was, it went without saying, the first in the world, Louis maintained the interests and dignity of his whole family with great arrogance. It was, in the last resort, for his grandson's sake that he embarked on and pursued the War of the Spanish Succession. Once Philip V's future was assured, he turned his attention to his own survival through his remaining legitimate and illegitimate descendants by means of the will of 1714 which he altered in 1715, only to have it broken as soon as he was dead, a will of which we may well ask ourselves whether it was the work of a stubborn, a benighted or a desperate man.

Everlasting glory, te ritorial aggrandizement, and dominion abroad; at home mastery of all political and administrative life, of religion, society and thought, and the protection of the dynasty and the succession: these were the vast spheres which, for all or part of the time, Louis dared to reserve for his own sole jurisdiction. The results of his actions varied from dazzling success, through partial or temporary success to semi-failure and absolute disaster.

For all his bravery and diligence, his frequent opportunism and his sense of greatness, he was after all, no more than a man with a varied and honorable mixture of virtues and weaknesses. His ministers, also, varied in quality, his executives often lacked means of persuasion and he was surrounded on all sides by forces which opposed his will and his glory. It remains to take a look at the actions of the men who served him and at the forces with which he had to contend.

The King's Responsibilities: The Spheres of His Agents

More often than not, and permanently in some cases, administrative details and the complete running of certain sectors of the administration were left to agents appointed by the king and responsible to him. Louis rarely resorted to the cowardly expedient of laying the blame for failure on his subordinates. Not until the end of his life, and notably in the case of the bishops, did he indulge in such pettiness. Everything that was done during his reign was done in his name and Louis' indirect responsibility in matters he had delegated was the same as his direct responsibility in his own personal spheres. Moreover, the two sectors could not help but be closely connected.

A policy of greatness and prestige demanded an efficient and effective administration as well as adequate resources, both military and financial. We have followed the various endeavors undertaken in this field down the years. Now it is time to add up the reckoning.

In order to disseminate the king's commands over great distances and combat the complex host of local authorities, a network of thirty Intendants had been established over the country. These were the king's men, dispatched by the king's councils and assisted by correspondents, agents and *subdélégués* who by 1715 were numerous and well organized. By this time the system was well-established and more or less accepted (even in Brittany). It met with reasonable respect and sometimes obedience. Sometimes, not always, since we only have to read the Intendants' correspondence to be disabused swiftly of any illusions fostered by old-fashioned textbooks or history notes. The difficulties of communications, the traditions of provincial independence, inalienable rights and privileges and the sheer force of inertia, all died hard. Lavisse used to say this was a period of absolutism tempered by disobedience. In the depths of the country and the remote provinces, the formula might almost be reversed. Nevertheless, there is no denying that a step forward had been made and that the germ of the splendid administrative systems of Louis XV and of Napoleon was already present in the progress made between 1661 and 1715. Some of the great administrative bodies which subsequently set the tone and example for others, such as the registry office, the postal service, the highway department were even then in existence, although it must be admitted that the first of these was introduced as a purely fiscal measure, the second farmed out and the third in an embryonic state.

In one adjacent but vital field, ministers and jurists labored valiantly to reach a unified code of French law, giving the king's laws priority over local custom and simplifying the enormous tangled mass of statute law. Colbert's codes and two or three great collections of law and practice, such as those of Ricard, Domat and Savary, will serve as examples. But how did all these excellent works fit in with the spirit of the time and with the daily march of justice? Every tiny province still persisted in judging cases according to its own local custom, fixed and written down in the sixteenth century with a mass of later glosses added. The king's law was only one law among many. It had to be ratified by the sovereign courts which, since they could

not reject it, had become most skillful in the arts of delay and pre-
varication. Moreover, royal decrees, even the Revocation of the Edict
of Nantes, seldom applied to the whole kingdom. Ordinances regu-
lating the maximum rate of interest (the *denier*), for example, varied
from one province to the next and were easily circumvented. As for
the monetary ordinances, every man turned them to his own advantage: the merchants had their own rates and *équivalences* and the
time was not far off when ordinary farm contracts would be coolly
inscribed "actions of the prince notwithstanding" in stipulating means
of payment. As for the notorious regulations put out by Colbert and
his successors, we have already seen, in passing, the extent to
which they could be ignored and flouted daily in one city, Beauvais,
which was less than eighty kilometers from Paris. Too much interest,
routine, privilege and sheer habit stood in the way for royal legislation to be properly applied. The great efforts towards centralization
and unification which were made were only partially successful but
they did pave the way for the great legislators and unifiers of the
eighteenth century and still more for those of the Revolution and the
Empire.

Of the means to the achievement of power and glory, one, diplomacy, was in the hands of individuals rather than institutions. Long
before the "great reign" a great tradition had existed which is called
to mind in the mere mention of such names as Servien, de Lionne,
d'Avaux, not to mention the two formidable cardinal-diplomats. They,
their colleagues, their successors and their children continued the
tradition. In their different ways, Louis XIV's diplomats were among
the best in Europe but they were up against brilliant adversaries in
the Dutch, the British and the Romans. Two novelties, perhaps, were
a degree of "institutionalizing" and a "career in diplomacy" and, more
important, the emergence of a much higher level of negotiation of
men like Mesnager of Rouen, the great merchants of the realm, whose
activities had previously been cloaked in a certain obscurity.

The navy, rescued from virtual oblivion by Colbert who gave it
arsenals, shipwrights, gunners, talented designers, its finest captains
and fresh personnel obtained by means of seaboard conscription,
distinguished itself particularly from 1672 to 1690. After that, it declined for lack of resources and any real interest on the part of a
king who was a landsman at heart and private enterprise took the

lead once more. Even then, Louis and the excellent staff on his navy office did not fail to encourage and make use of the fleets belonging to the shipowners and merchants of the great ports, the capitalists who backed them and the bold captains who brought them both glory and profit.

. The greatest of all the king's great servants were those who helped him to build up an army, which in size and striking force was for the most part equal to all the other armies of Europe put together. They were first Le Tellier and Turenne and later, Louvois and Vauban. Many others of less fame, such as Chamlay, Martinet, Fourilles and Clerville would also deserve a place in this unusually lengthy roll of honor if the historian's job were the awarding of laurels, especially military ones. The fighting strength was increased at least fourfold, discipline was improved, among generals as well as officers and men, and a civil administration superimposed, not without a struggle, on the quarrelsome, short-sighted and in many cases incompetent and dishonest military one. New ranks and new corps were introduced; among them the artillery and the engineers, as well as such new weapons as the flintlock and the fixed bayonet, and a new military architect, Vauban, all helped to make the army more efficient. Most important of all, the army at last possessed a real *Intendance* with its own arsenals, magazines, and regular staging posts. Uniforms became more or less general, providing employment for thousands of workers. The first barracks were an attempt to put an end to the notorious custom of billeting troops on civilian households. The Hôtel des Invalides was built, on a grand scale. The instrument which these invaluable servants placed at their master's disposal was almost without parallel in their time, a genuine royal army, growing ever larger and more diversified, modern and disciplined.

Naturally, the people of the realm were not always bursting with pride in it. The army was very expensive. It still went in for billeting and foraging, even within the borders of the kingdom, and still, like the navy with its "press gang" in the ports, claimed far too many young men who would have preferred to stay at home in their own villages. Too much conscription and to an even greater extent the militia were the cause of much of the king's unpopularity in his old age.

To please his trusted servant Colbert, the king, while a young man, did try for a time to study his finances and to keep simple accounts of his private income and expenditure, but he always believed in his heart of hearts that such occupations were beneath his royal dignity. This book has already shown in some detail how Colbert's work was endangered by the first coalition (1673) and ruined by the two which followed. Quite obviously, it was not the king's building program, his court, his "favors" or his petty cash which wrecked the kingdom's finances once they had been put in order by a good finance minister. The one and only reason was the length of the wars and the ever-broadening fronts on which they were fought.

Louis' finance ministers, remarkable both for honesty and inge-nuity, did what they could to provide for the constantly renewed wars. They acquiesced in or invented measures which, with more courage and determination, might have been real and radical re-forms: the capitation tax, the *dixième,* the *Caisse des Emprunts* and even the introduction of paper money. But all in all, they could not do more than scrape the utmost from a financial, social and admin-istrative system so petrified that it rejected even the slightest at-tempt at reform. The richest went on paying ludicrously little, or nothing at all. The state failed to maintain its credit or to set up a national bank, while England was managing to do so in spite of all her difficulties. The Ancien Régime under Louis XIV was an accumula-tion of old forms, old habits and old ideas, the more deeply respected the older they were, which proved incapable of reshaping or even of reforming its financial system. To do so would have meant denying its very nature, tearing down the antiquated edifice which had been shored up a score of times although it still presented a glittering façade to the world, and daring to face up to the march of time and the nature of things. The old house stood for another seventy-five years. No one in 1715 could have foreseen how comparatively immi-nent was its collapse.

For all this, successes, good intentions, failures, inadequacies and refusals, Louis XIV remains, through his ministers, ultimately re-sponsible.

Responsible, that is, if it can be truly said that any man, even a king and a great king, has the power to act effectively against the great political, demographic, economic and intellectual forces which may, after all, finally command the overall development of a kingdom which is not alone in the world. Among these forces were some which, whether the king knew it or not, were acting directly against him. Others, working more slowly and obscurely and almost invariably unknown to the king, had nonetheless a powerful long-term effect which some historians have regarded as crucial.

The Opposing Forces

An ambition to astonish the world with magnificence and great armies is all very well so long as the world is prepared to be astonished.

At the beginning of his reign, when Louis surveyed the rest of Europe, he saw nothing but weakness and decline. Some of his observations, as regards Spain and Italy, were perfectly correct. In others, he was mistaken. He stupidly underestimated the United Provinces, as though a small, bourgeois and Calvinist population were an inevitable sign of weakness. Yet another observation was swiftly belied by the changes which occurred in two highly dissimilar entities, England and the Empire.

Louis XIV found himself balked at every turn by the diplomacy and dogged courage, as well as by the seapower and the immense wealth of the United Provinces. It is no longer fashionable to believe that the "Golden Age" of the Dutch was over in 1661. For a long time after that, their Bank, their Stock Exchange, their India Company, their fleets and their florins remained as powerful as ever. The invasion of 1672 weakened them only temporarily and even in 1715, whatever may be said to the contrary, the Dutch sent as many or even more ships than before to the Baltic, to Japan (where they were the only nation to trade), to Batavia, to Asia and all over the high seas. Their wealth, currency and bankers remained powerful and respected and often decisive. Their policy was not yet tied directly to England's. It was simply that they no longer enjoyed undivided supremacy: another nation's economy had reached the same level and was about to overtake them.

Louis XIV always did his best to ignore economic factors but they would not be denied and they took their revenge. In addition, Louis' aggression in 1672 had a miraculous effect upon the patriotic feelings of the Dutch and brought about the revolution which carried William of Orange to the leadership of the Republic. The last quarter of the seventeenth century belongs, in fact, as much to William as to Louis. Stubborn, clever, with the whole wealth of the Republic behind him, William was a determined enemy, in spite of his bad luck in the field, and he was the soul and the financier of all the coalitions. No sooner was he dead than his place was taken by a Dutchman of no less greatness who had already seconded him on the Continent, Heinsius.

With masterly ineptitude, the King of France, having made William master of the United Provinces, went on to help make him King of England. For a long time, Louis XIV believed he had England at his mercy because he thought himself sure of both Charles II, who was in his pay, and the papist James II, and also because he was convinced that the island kingdom must have been greatly weakened by a revolution and by Cromwell. This was to reckon without the English constitutional traditions, without the deeply anti-Catholic religious feelings of most Englishmen and without the fleet, the London merchants and the pound sterling. Louis XIV's English policy from 1685 to 1712 was one long series of mistakes and almost continual provocations. During that time, the power of Parliament, of trade, of seapower and of the Bank of England were growing and reaching out across the seas to lay the firm foundations of a strong empire, which would ultimately devour the French empire and was, indeed, already nibbling at it. The final quarter of the seventeenth century was marked by the rise of Britain, spectacularly endorsed by the treaties of 1713, much more than by the dominance of France.

Even the Empire, for which Louis had nothing but contempt, though impotent and enfeebled by the treaties of Westphalia, was ruled by a monarch who, despite his initial youth, nervousness and timidity, succeeded gradually in making an unexpected recovery and emerging as the leader of a crusade against the Turks. He had goods advisers and with the support of the Pope, the majority of the German princes and kings like Sobieski, more Catholic than politic, he succeeded in halting the infidel advance for the first time in three hundred years and then in driving them back to their Balkan fastnesses. By liberating Vienna, Hungary and Transylvania, he enlarged his domains much more than Louis had extended his and relieved Europe of the Ottoman pressure once and for all. As a result he became, in his own lands, the great Emperor who had succeeded where all others had failed. Artists and writers sang his praises and for all good Germans this end of the century was the time, not of Louis the Devastator but of Leopold the Victorious.

Louis XIV, for his part, put off such German sympathizers as he possessed in 1661, offending them by his ravages and his measures against the Protestants and no longer able to attract them with his impoverished treasury which was powerless in competition with the florins and the sterling which could now purchase new allegiances across the Rhine. It may be that the absence of any French contingent from the great Catholic victory of Kahlenberg in 1683 was considered shameful. It was undoubtedly a mistake, which was more serious. Violent propaganda began to issue from certain quarters in the Empire, lambasting the errors of the King of France and the sanguinary excesses of his troops. In this way, Louis XIV made his own contribution to the birth of German national feeling. Not even Leopold's death in 1705 released him for he had earned the undying hatred of his successors. By an additional irony, Prince Eugène, who had at first asked nothing better than to be allowed to serve France, outlived Leopold as Heinsius and Marlborough had outlived William.

What of the suggestion that, as a kind of compensation, French language, art and letters were making a peaceful conquest of the Europe of the coalition? It is true that every ruler and every petty princeling was, or soon would be longing to have his own Versailles and his own Maintenon and set about reproducing them with varying success, but even so, we incorrigibly patriotic Frenchmen should not be in too great a hurry to proclaim a triumph of the French spirit. To do so would be, firstly, to ignore the real character of baroque art, with its strong Austrian and Spanish elements. And then, what of Locke and Leibnitz, to mention only two, whose influence was by no means negligible? And were the prodigious advances in the scientific field a purely French affair? And finally, if it did become fashionable in certain foreign circles to adopt French airs and graces, how many eminent Frenchmen from Descartes onward also went abroad, to Holland and still more to England, to find a breath of freedom?

Louis found other forces of opposition within the borders of his kingdom. We have seen how he dealt with the most obvious and persistent and there is no need for a repetition. We have also seen that they, or others like them, appeared again at the end of his reign, while some waited until the despot was dead before bursting into the full light of day. And we have seen, lastly, those which would not be put down: the small, determined flock of Christians who did not follow Rome, the proud, intelligent and tenacious little group of Jansenists and the Gallicans with whom they ultimately joined.

But is there, in fact, no more to be said? There is one thing: to try to convey some idea of the ancient, traditional and heavily calculated weight of inertia possessed by that collection of "nations," *pays, seigneuries,* fiefs and parishes which together made up the kingdom of France. Each of these entities was accustomed to living independently, with its own customs, privileges and even language, snug in its own fields and within sound of its own bells. The king consecrated at Rheims was a priest-king to be revered and almost worshipped, but from afar. When someone sent by him turned up in the village accompanied by an escort of armed or black-clad men, or merely bearing an order in writing, he was met, on principle, with suspicion or even open hostility. What "newfangled idea" had he brought with him? A blow struck at local custom? Or a levy of money, horses or men? There is no end to the amount which might be written about this sequestered existence with its local patriotism, its deep-rooted horror of all novelty, its fears and terrors which made up the very texture of life in France under the Ancien Régime. Making the king's voice heard in the depths of the countryside was easier said than done when the curé, who was the only means of spreading it, garbled, scamped or merely forgot a task which was clearly no part of his duties; when courts of law were far off, costly, unreliable and even less respected, the forces of law and order never there, the Intendant a mystery and his assistants powerless. We have only to look at poor Colbert, trying to establish his manufactures, his tentative regulations and his companies. No one wanted them because all had their own traditions, habits and interests and clung fiercely to their own independence. We have only to look at every administrator, religious or secular, striving to apply contradictory instructions regarding the "so-called reformed church" to his own particular province. We have only to look at the books of the forestry department and the papers concerned with the *gabelle,* to see the incredible number and variety of infringements which appeared whenever the well-armed dared to set foot in a region to put them down. We have only to stress, in addition, the rash of desertion prevalent in the regular army and still more in the militia (where it may have been as high as 50 percent) at a time when parishes and even whole provinces were ready to condone, hide and feed the deserters.

If, dazzled by the splendors of Versailles, we let ourselves forget the constant presence of these seething undercurrents, we will have understood nothing of the France of Louis XIV and of the impossible task which the king and his ministers had set themselves, or of the massive inertia which made it so difficult. Moreover, we have said nothing of the inertia of the clergy and of the nobility and their refusal to make any contribution to progress in the kingdom beyond a few prayers and rapier thrusts and some small, grudging alms, when they might have placed all their power, wealth and talent at the service of these grand designs. But was it even asked of them? They remained the first and second orders, and the only service which they owed was by prayer and the sword. This was yet another instance of the inertia, the rejection of all change and progress towards efficiency, in a regime whose end no one could as yet foresee.

The Forgotten Forces

The inherent inertia of that great, tradition-ridden body which was the monarchy of the Ancien Régime, the growing antagonism of the major European states, the forces, vague or precise, foreseen or unforeseen, of which Louis XIV was more or less consciously aware, were all ultimately and undeniably in strong opposition to his designs. But were there no other forces at work, more mysterious and perhaps more powerful but for which no allowance was made in state affairs and which may not even have occurred to the minds of those who ruled it? These, surely, were the forces which ultimately controlled the very life of the kingdom, reducing the activities of one small king of one small country to nothing more than the meaningless gesticulations of insects in relation to the universe.

For some years now, younger historians of a certain school have tended to ignore the bustle of individuals and events in favor of what they call revealing, measuring, defining and illustrating the great, dominant rhythms which move world history as a whole. These rhythms emerge as largely economic. The method may have a certain rashness and temerity but it bears fruit. Suppose we give way to it for a moment.

Setting aside the gesticulations of the human insects, the economic, social and political life of France and half the world may well have been dictated by the pace of extracting, transporting and circulating the "fabulous metal." The discovery of the "Indies," and the mines of Mexico and Peru, which poured ever-increasing amounts of precious metals into Europe, goes a long way to explain the prosperity, brilliance, ostentation and sheer wealth of the seventeenth century, just as, later on, Brazilian gold was behind the mounting prosperity of the eighteenth century and Californian gold gave rise to the *belle époque* of Badinguet. But from 1600 onwards, the quantities of silver reaching Spain from America grew less and less until by 1650 the imports were only a fifth of what they had been in 1600. A probable revival of the mines of central Europe was insufficient to make up the deficit. First gold, and then silver, grew scarce, giving rise to hoarding. Copper from Sweden or Japan (via Holland) tended to take their place but it was a poor substitute. The whole age of Louis XIV was an age that Marc Bloch has called "monetary famine." The king had difficulty in paying the English for Dunkirk. Ministers and private citizens complained of "shortage of cash" and "hoarding" and everyone paid their debts in *rentes* which meant pledges on the future. We have laid some stress on the way in which this situation might explain some aspects of Colbert's work and their lack of success as well as some continuous problems of government and also a certain style of opposition. But money was not the only thing.

Historians and economists have long been aware that the seventeenth century as a whole and the period from 1650–1690 in particular, or even 1650–1730, was marked by a noticeable drop in the cost of basic foodstuffs as well as of a great many other things – a drop quite separate from annual "accidents." Landed incomes, offices and possibly moneylending, all seem to have been affected by the same general reduction. François Simiand and later Ernest Labrousse, collating and studying these observations in the 1930s, came to the conclusion that in between the great phases of economic expansion which occurred during the sixteenth and eighteenth centuries, the seventeenth, and particularly the time of Louis XIV, was a period bearing all the signs of, at best, stagnation and at worst economic recession and depression. They were followed by other historians who carried the idea further, sometimes to the point of crude exaggeration. Huguette and Pierre Chaunu, following the same general lines and supported by a remarkable statistical analysis of relations between Spain and America, drew a sweeping cross through the whole of the seventeenth century from a maritime angle from 1600 onwards, although still recognizing that elsewhere, in the north and on the Continent, the natural rhythm of growth persisted longer, an observation confirmed by others. The same authors, again supported by impressive documentary evidence, go on to describe a new linking up of circumstances favorable to maritime development round about 1700, a move towards a new expansion which spread slowly inland from the great ports. Similar observations have been made for Provence, Dauphiné and the region of Beauvais.

René Baehrel, on the other hand, argues fiercely against this cross which seems to stand by the name of the "sad seventeenth century," although admittedly he argues only on behalf of the rural south of Provence, where he sees economic growth continuing, while at the same time agreeing that the rate of this growth slowed down considerably between 1655 and 1690. But rural southern Provence is not representative either of France or of western Europe. It is a corner of the Mediterranean, and the man who studies it a born controversialist.

Setting aside these scholarly arguments, what was the real overall bearing of the great movements of the economic conjuncture, movements rarely perceived at the time unless in some vague way by one or two exceptional minds? Do they, to echo Chaunu, reveal the "deep breathing of history"?

There remains a strong impression that the period of Louis' reign was one of economic difficulties, suffering both from sudden, violent crises and from phases of stagnation and of deep depression. It is not easy to govern under such conditions especially when, like the king and most of his councillors, one is unaware of them. But what they tried to do and sometimes, despite such obstacles, achieved, remains nonetheless worthy of interest and even of admiration.

It is possible, therefore, that France under Louis XIV may have been unconsciously subject to powerful economic forces which are still much disputed and not fully understood. Social, demographic, mental and other factors, wholly or partly incomprehensible to the rulers, may have played their part also. How and within what limits would they have affected the nation's course?

In a century which possessed no mass media of communication, Louis and his champions of scholasticism fought a pale rearguard action against the irresistible advances of science and of the spirit of criticism. But Descartes, Harvey, Newton and Bayle were not to be gainsaid, and neither was the swing which was to follow the apogee of the Roman Catholic faith with a compensating downward trend. If the seventeenth century was "the age of saints" (and the Church certainly needed such champions), its last decades, as we have seen, looked forward to the Age of Enlightenment, when Voltaire was king. Bossuet died defeated, like Louis XIV, by his confessors and his dragoons. There is no going against nature.

About the great mass of French society and its slow, ponderous development we know almost nothing, only a few glimmers here and there. How did it happen? Louis XIV seems to have thought the existing social structures all very well so long as he was in control, and he was ruthless in his determination to remain so. But apart from such superficial movement, the society of the Ancien Régime seems to have petrified more than it evolved. The nobility, in its anxiety to remain pure and predominant, may have made some efforts to confirm its position but continued to live in the same spendthrift fashion, drawing wealthy bourgeois into its ranks, hunting their fortunes and their daughters. At the end of the reign, social life seemed dominated by the great businessmen, bankers, merchants, tax-farmers, ship-owners and tradesmen of Paris, Lyons and the other great ports with their great fortunes, often made almost over night, their credit and their patronage, but had things been so very different at the end of the preceding reign, in the time of Mazarin, with the triumph of Fouquet and the Italian or German banks?

And yet, in the manufacturing towns, the small, independent tradesmen seemed to be disappearing, social distinctions becoming more clear cut and relations between bosses and workers hardening. A tendency to concentration? The growth of a proletariat? Perhaps, but all we know at present concerns Beauvais and Amiens. In the heart of the country, around Paris and still much further north, but also in Languedoc, some elements of a similar process seem to have been found: the small, independent peasant-farmers grew fewer and less influential, there was a vast number of impoverished day laborers and a sudden increase of powerful middlemen, a kind of rural bourgeoisie in close touch with the great landowners, whether noble or otherwise, clerical or secular. In the same regions, it has been possible to distinguish the early signs (1600–1670) of some kind of seigneurial (or feudal) reaction, characterized by a renewed interest in landed property, more scrupulous collection of tithes and dues, revival of old rights and fresh encroachments on to common lands. But here too, René Baehrel has stated, and perhaps proved conclusively, that nothing had changed in southern Provence and there remain any number of provinces in the southwest, the center and the west still unexplored. All that can be said for certain is that the acts of the king and his administration, wherever we find them, tended to preserve and maintain the rights of the most powerful section of this mixed and largely landed aristocracy which always came off best in the courts whenever its vassals and dependents dared to plead against it.

Apart from one small, passing effort of Colbert's, the state of Louis XIV seems to have taken little thought for any kind of demographic policy. The general feeling was that fertility in France was more than adequate to cope with the ravages of plague and "mortality" and people were convinced that the population of the kingdom, the densest in Europe, was in no danger of diminution. For the most part, they did not think at all, or thought about other things, and nature took its course. Apart from Vauban and a few others now forgotten, no one took much interest in "the people" except in terms of taxation. The chief demographic victory of the regime, the control of the plague, is largely to the credit of the local authorities. But this did not stop the unknown masses from suffering, all through the reign, from the individual and collective miseries of shortages and epidemics. Except among the very small ruling class, the demographic characteristics of the kingdom changed very little, or if they did, these changes have not yet emerged. The numbers in each age group varied wildly, but the population as a whole (within fixed limits) may have grown from time to time, in Brittany and one or two other places. More often than not, it certainly decreased or possibly remained static. Within this population, the cycles of poverty and ease, the many christenings and hasty interments went on, very much as they had done in biblical times. There was no apparent sign of change and hardly anyone expected it.

The court, the kingdom and the collection of princes which, for Louis, constituted the chief of the old Continent, these were the accustomed limits of his royal horizon. Far, far beyond them, Muscovy, Asia, the Americas and the whole world continued to exist for all that, and to develop. A new Caesar arose in Russia but his peculiarities were of interest only to the court and to the city. Only a few missionaries and traders concerned themselves with China, at the other end of the world, or had any inkling of her incomparable civilization. Only the Dutch had access to one small hostile Japanese island, and they reaped huge profits from it. War was soon to break out in India but Louis took little notice of such pagan empires. Africa provided Negro slaves and some other merchandise but two or three poorly protected trading posts were his only interest there. The English, while making thrifty investments in the Spanish Main, were moving further north and beginning to win a decisive battle which did not interest the Great King who cared little for Canada or Louisiana. Brought up by Mazarin in a world of court intrigues, dynastic squabbles and problems of successions and of frontiers, Louis rarely looked beyond his own lands and almost never to the world at large. Twenty nuns at Port-Royal-des-Champs, a few buildings at Marly and two or three strongholds seemed to him worthier objects of glory.

It is true that Louis XIV, like most men who grew up between 1640 and 1660, was incapable of rising beyond the limits of his education, let alone of taking in, at one glance, the whole of the planet on which he lived, to say nothing of infinite space. A king to the depths of his being, and a dedicated king, he had a concept of greatness which was that of his generation: military greatness, dynastic greatness, territorial greatness and political greatness which expressed itself in unity of faith, the illusion of obedience and magnificent surroundings. He left behind him an image of the monarchy, admirable in its way, but already cracking if not outworn at the time of his death. Like most men, and many kings, he had grown stiff and sclerotic with old age.

By inclination a man of taste, and a politician by nature, education and desire, he always despised those material accidents called economy and finance. Such commonplace things were merely appendages to his great plans. It never occurred to him that they could one day topple the throne of the next king but one. For him, all social upheavals and ideals were lumped together as "uprisings" and "cabals" to be forcibly suppressed.

Isolated at Versailles at an early stage by his own pride, the machinations of a woman and a few priests and courtiers, he neither knew nor cared that his age was becoming the Age of Reason, of Science and of Liberty. From first to last, he refused to recognize the power of Holland, the nature of England or the birth of an embryo German nation. He gave Colbert little support in his courageous maritime and colonial policies and failed to pursue them seriously. He was always more excited by one fortress in Flanders or the Palatinate than by all of India, Canada and Louisiana put together.

And yet he and his colleagues left behind them a France that was territorially larger, militarily better defended, with a more effective administration and to a large extent pacified. And although he neglected it and often fought against it, there was a time when he built up and maintained what was to be, for a long time to come, the real greatness and glory of France. The Age of Enlightenment was dominated, at least in part, by the language and the culture of France.

Like many another King of France, he went to his grave amid general dislike and the particular execration of Parisians. His dead body had already become a symbol. Louis was turning into the stuffed mummy singled out for future deification by the nostalgic and for supreme contempt by his passionate enemies.

All we have tried to do is to understand Louis XIV against the background of his own time without attempting to idolize him.

Suggestions for Additional Reading

The following suggestions for further reading are not intended to cover all aspects of the enormously complex reign of Louis XIV. Instead they are designed to increase the student's knowledge of those elements of the reign that are directly related to the problem of Louis' greatness. Because the literature concerning the reign of Louis XIV is very extensive and diversified, any effort toward further investigation of his historical significance will require reading in a wide variety of works, a large majority of which are not available in English translation.

The standard guide to the printed sources of the reign, with occasional references to modern works, is E. Bourgeois and L. André, *Les Sources de l'histoire de France: XVIIᵉ siècle,* 8 vols. (Paris, 1913–1935). The most comprehensive listing of the enormous monographic literature of the reign is contained in E. Préclin and V. L. Tapié, *Le XVIIᵉ siècle: 1610–1715 ("Clio")* (Paris, 1949). This has been extensively supplemented by R. Mandrou, *La France aux XVIIᵉ et XVIIIᵉ siècles ("Nouvelle Clio")* (Paris, 1967). Lengthy general bibliographies are available in the volumes in the Langer Series: F. L. Nussbaum, *The Triumph of Science and Reason, 1660–1685* (New York, 1953), and J. B. Wolf, *The Emergence of the Great Powers, 1685–1715* (New York, 1951). Professor Wolf's article, "The Reign of Louis XIV: A Selected Bibliography of Writings Since the War of 1914–1918," *Journal of Modern History* 36 (1964): 127–144, is likewise worthwhile. By far the most comprehensive recent bibliography relative to all aspects of the reign is in J. C. Rule, ed., *Louis XIV and the Craft of Kingship* (Ohio State University Press, 1969).

Of the more influential nineteenth-century interpretations of Louis XIV that are not included in this book of selections, those of Chateaubriand, Martin, Michelet and Acton should be mentioned. F. A. de Chateaubriand, *De Buonaparte et des Bourbons* (Paris, 1814), and *Analyse raisonnée de l'histoire de France,* in vol. 7 of the *œuvres complètes* (Paris, 1836) (completed by Chateaubriand in 1831). While not the best of Chateaubriand, these historical works, especially the latter, contain significant insights into the nature of Bourbon monarchy and exercised considerable influence on its study. Henri Martin, *Histoire de France,* 4th edition (Paris, 1861–1865). Part VII, on Louis

XIV, was published separately as *The Age of Louis XIV,* translated by Mary L. Booth 2 vols. (Boston, 1865). This work was based upon extensive examination of the sources and was repeatedly mined by later historians. Regarding his view of the reign of Louis XIV, Martin states in his preface to the American edition that while he "professes principles quite opposed to those of the Ancient Régime and the old French Monarchy, [he] has set forth, with all the impartiality in his power, the luster and greatness of this monarchy, and the brilliant society of which it was for some time the nucleus; but, the more resplendent were men and things, the more decisive is the conclusion, since all this glory ended only in one vast ruin."

Jules Michelet, *Histoire de France,* vols. 13 and 14 (Paris, 1860–1862), is a great work of inspired scholarship and presents a vivid and thoroughly critical picture of the reign. The first volume carries the narrative to 1688 and places great emphasis on the Revocation of the Edict of Nantes and attendant barbarities. Michelet called the Revocation the mutilation of France. The second volume, 1688–1715, covers the period which he regarded as the dissolution of old French society, in the sense that royalty, clergy and nobility all sank into ruin. He also found that in the final phase of the reign the personal dictatorship of Louis XIV resulted in the collapse of the administrative system. Thus royalty finally stood alone, triumphant but unsupported and tottering on the brink of destruction with nothing to save it. These views were reiterated in many later works by other writers.

On the other hand, Lord Acton, in his *Lectures on Modern History* which he delivered at Cambridge University in 1899–1901, devoted two lectures to Louis XIV and presented a very different view of the reign of the Sun King. Essentially, Acton regarded human history as slow, painful progress toward greater freedom and liberty. During the intermediate phase of Western development, which he generally equated with the early modern period, Acton found the leadership of rulers to be indispensable to human advancement, since the peoples of Europe lacked the capacity for self-government. This was Acton's explanation of the historical necessity of absolutism, and his investigations convinced him that Louis XIV was its most outstanding exemplar in recent centuries. The place of Louis XIV in Western history was therefore to fulfill, through a thoroughgoing and successful absolutism, the functions of government as determined by his age, thereby leading his subjects toward an era when they would enjoy greater liberty under new and different institutions. For this reason Acton regarded Louis XIV as one of the greatest rulers of the early modern era.

The following general histories of the reign include interpretations of Louis XIV's contributions and significance. Ernest Lavisse, *Histoire de France,* vols. 7¹ to 8¹ (Paris, 1911). In spite of much additional publication, this remains the best general treatment of the reign. J. Boulenger, *The Seventeenth Century,* (English translation) (New York, 1920), presents a detailed, sympathetic picture of French history during the century. Many recently developed views are ably summarized in H. Méthivier, *Le Siècle de Louis XIV* (Paris, 1962). The book edited by J. C. Rule, cited above, contains a variety of views on important elements of Louis XIV's policies. Volumes V and VI of *The New Cambridge Modern History* (Cambridge, 1961, 1970), include valuable chapters on France during the period.

By far the best biography of the Sun King is J. B. Wolf, *Louis XIV* (New York, 1968). Although Wolf's emphasis is upon foreign affairs and wars, he adequately examines other elements of Louis XIV's rule. The earlier book of D. Ogg, *Louis XIV* (London, 1933), is largely political and retains its value, but the other biographies of Louis XIV are now largely superseded.

For the study of Louis XIV as a person and his understanding of the responsibilities of government, the basic instrument is his *Mémoires.* The original critical edition was edited by Charles Dreyss in two volumes (Paris, 1860). For English-speaking readers, the best and most convenient edition is that of P. Sonnino, *Louis XIV: Mémoires for the Instruction of the Dauphin* (New York, 1970). The most extensive work on Louis XIV's education is G. Lacour-Gayet, *L'Education politique de Louis XIV* 2nd ed. (Paris, 1923). G. Mongrédien, *Louis XIV* (Paris, 1963), contains many revealing opinions and estimates of the king by his contemporaries.

The concept of divine right of kings, so fundamental to Louis XIV's reign on the ideological level, may be investigated by reading Bossuet, *Politique tirée de l'Ecriture sainte,* the classic statement of the position. A convenient critical edition of this work, edited by J. Le Brun, was published in Geneva in 1967. J. Truchet, *Politique de Bossuet* (Paris, 1966), is a comprehensive guide to the famous bishop's political views. The *Mémoires* of Louis XIV also set forth implicitly, and sometimes explicitly, important elements of the divine right of kings. The best available treatment of contemporaries' understanding of divine right absolutism during the first generation of the reign is Book II of Lacour-Gayet, cited above. H. Sée, *Les Idées politiques en France au XVIIe siècle,* is useful only as an introduction to the subject. G. Lanson, *Bossuet* (Paris, 1891), contains a valuable section on Bossuet's political ideas. An important analysis of certain elements of seventeenth-century absolutism is R. Mousnier and F. Hartung, "Quelques problèmes concernant la monarchie absolue," *Relazioni del X Congresso Internazionale di Scienze Storiche* (Florence, 1955), vol. 4, pp. 1–55.

The study of Louis XIV's foreign policy may best be initially approached by reading Wolf's biography, cited above. The essentials are given in G. Zeller, *Les Temps modernes,* vols. 2 and 3, *Histoire des relations internationales* (Paris, 1953, 1955), which is somewhat more hostile to Louis XIV than Wolf is. L. André, *Louis XIV et l'Europe* (Paris, 1950), is a straightforward, objective treatment of the subject. Important studies of Louis' foreign policy are included in "Problèmes de politique étrangère sous Louis XIV," *XVIIe siècle,* Nos. 46–47 (1960), and in R. M. Hatton and J. S. Bromley, eds., *William III and Louis XIV: Essays 1680–1720 by and for Mark A. Thompson* (Liverpool, 1968). The methods whereby the king conducted his relations with foreign powers are analyzed in C. G. Picavet, *La Diplomatie française au temps de Louis XIV* (Paris, 1939).

The more significant institutional developments which both reflect and made possible Louis XIV's rule over his subjects may be studied in the following. G. Pagès, *La Monarchie d'ancien régime (De Henri IV à Louis XIV)* (Paris, 1928), is the best brief treatment of the evolution of the central institutions of government. It was written partially in the tradition of Lemontey. J. E. King, *Science and Rationalism in the Government of Louis XIV, 1661–1683* (Baltimore, 1949), is an elaborately documented but not entirely successful attempt to demonstrate the "rationalization" of the royal administration during the period of Colbert. Solid studies of the upper reaches of the administrative system are to be found in P. Viollet, *Le Roi et ses ministres* (Paris, 1912), and A. de Boislisle, "Les Conseils sous Louis XIV," in the appendixes to vols. 4–7 of his edition of the *Mémoires* of Saint-Simon (Paris, 1884–1890). R. Mousnier et al., *Le Conseil du roi de Louis XII* à la Révolution, analyzes the composition of the royal council from the social and statistical standpoints. E. Glasson, *Le Parlement de Paris, son rôle politique,* vol. I (Paris, 1901), examines the relations between the Parlement and the crown. An excellent study of the all-important Intendants is G. Livet, *L'Intendance d'Alsace sous Louis XIV, 1648–1715* (Paris, 1956).

The economic policies of Louis XIV's government may be examined in P. Boisonnade, *Colbert, le triomph de l'étatisme. . . , 1661–1683* (Paris, 1932), which presents an extensive, detailed and systematic analysis of state control over all phases of the French economy that were susceptible to governmental regulation. C. W. Cole, *Colbert and a Century of French Mercantilism,* 2 vols. (New York, 1939), and *French Mercantilism, 1683–1700* (New York, 1943), are solid, reliable compilations of much detailed information. G. Martin, *La Grande Industrie sous le règne de Louis XIV,* studies the relations between the central government and the large-scale industry that it fostered. The best analysis of royal taxation in the period is E. Esmonin, *La Taille en Normandie au temps de Colbert (1661–1683)* (Paris, 1913). Contemporary criticism of royal fiscal policies may be studied in E. Coornaert, ed., *Projet d'une dixme royal . . . par Vauban* (Paris, 1933), and H. V. Roberts, *Boisguillebert: Economist of the Reign of Louis XIV* (New York, 1935).

The impact of Louis XIV's policies upon French society and its consequent evolution are analyzed in general terms in the first volume of P. Sagnac, *La Formation de la société française moderne, 1661–1788* (Paris, 1945). Much more reliable although of limited geographical scope is the very important statistical study by P. Goubert, *Beauvais et le Beauvaisis de 1600 à 1730: Contribution à l'histoire sociale de la France du XVIIe siècle,* 2 vols. (Paris, 1960) (published in reduced form under the title, *Cent Mille Provinciaux au XVIIe siècle: Beauvais et le Beauvaisis de 1600 à 1730* [Paris, 1968]). A revealing analysis of Louis XIV's policies relative to the nobility is R. B. Grassby, "Social Status and Commercial Enterprise under Louis XIV," *Economic History Review* 13 (1960): 19–38. Trouble with the lower classes is examined in L. Bernard, "French Society and Popular Uprisings under Louis XIV," *French Historical Studies* 3 (1963–1964): 454–474. The condition of the peasantry in an important province may be examined in the monumental work of E. Le Roy Ladurie, *Les*

Paysans de Languedoc, 2 vols. (Paris, 1966) (published in reduced form under the same title [Paris, 1969]).

The following are the best works on the vast military establishment that was created to serve Louis XIV. C. Rousset, *Histoire de Louvois et de son administration politique et militaire,* 4 vols. (Paris, 1862–1863). Although partially superseded, this pioneer study remains a mine of information. The best later works are those of L. André, *Michel Le Tellier et l'organization de l'armée monarchique* (Paris, 1906), and *Michel Le Tellier et Louvois* (Paris, 1942). Equally expert is A. Corvisier, *L'Armée française de la fin du XVIIᵉ siècle au ministère de Choiseul,* 2 vols. (Paris, 1964). The methods of Vauban, the famous military engineer, may be studied in G. A. Rothrock, ed., *A Manual of Siegecraft and Fortification, by Sebastien Le-Prestre de Vauban* (Ann Arbor, 1968). By far the best general treatment of French naval history in the period is C. de La Roncière, *Histoire de la marine française,* vols. 5 and 6 (Paris, 1919, 1932). The difficulties that Louis XIV's ministers experienced in staffing the army and the navy are described in G. A. M. Girard, *Le Service militaire en France à la fin du règne de Louis XIV: racolage et milice (1701–1715)* (Paris, 1921), and E. L. Asher, *The Resistance to the Maritime Classes: The Survival of Feudalism in the France of Colbert* (Berkeley, 1960).

Louis XIV's complex policies toward religious problems may be approached initially through E. Préclin and E. Jarry, *Les Luttes politiques et doctrinales aux XVIIᵉ et XVIIIᵉ siècles, vol. 19¹, Histoire de l'Eglise* (Paris, 1955). Although a general study of the Roman Church, the work is strongly oriented toward France. On royal Gallicanism, which climaxed during Louis XIV's reign, consult V. Martin, *Le Gallicanisme et le clergé de France* (Paris, 1929), and A. G. Martimort, *Le Gallicanisme de Bossuet* (Paris, 1953). J. Orcibal, *Louis XIV contre Innocent XI* (Paris, 1949), is an important study of the relations between Louis and the papacy during the period of greatest tensions. On Jansenism, C. A. Sainte-Beuve, *Port-Royal* (many editions) is still the fundamental work. The best later general study is A. Gazier, *Histoire générale du mouvement janséniste depuis ses origines jusqu'à nos jours,* 2 vols. (Paris, 1922). See also J. F. Thomas, *La Querelle de l'Unigenitus* (Paris, 1950).

Regarding Louis XIV's fateful policy toward the French Huguenots, the best comprehensive treatment is E. G. Léonard, *Histoire générale du protestantisme,* vol. 2 (Paris, 1961). H. M. Baird, *The Huguenots and the Revocation of the Edict of Nantes,* 2 vols. (New York, 1895), remains the most extensive treatment but is very biased in favor of the persecuted. The ablest recent study of royal policy is J. Orcibal, *Louis XIV et les protestants* (Paris, 1951). W. C. Scoville, *The Persecution of the Huguenots and French Economic Development, 1680–1720* (Berkeley, 1960), is a very important piece of historical revisionism and shows that the economic impact of the Revocation of the Edict of Nantes was not as extensive as earlier historians believed. W. J. Stankiewicz, *Politics and Religion in Seventeenth Century France* (Berkeley, 1960), examines the main lines of royal policy.

The importance of Louis XIV as a patron of the arts and learning, chiefly through the system of government-sponsored academies, is given brief, general treatment in the books by Lavisse, Boulenger and Ogg, cited above. The influence of official policies on literary effort is outlined in F. Masson, *L'Académie française, 1629–1793* (Paris, 1912), and in the initial pages of A. Adam, *Histoire de la littérature française au XVIIe siècle,* vol. 3 (Paris, 1952). H. D. MacPherson, *Censorship under Louis XIV, 1661–1715* (New York, 1929), sketches the effects of governmental interference in various areas of literary activity. H. Lemonnier, *L'Art français au temps de Louis XIV* (Paris, 1911), is a valuable analysis of the influence of the academies of art and architecture on the development of official canons of style. R. Schneider, *L'Art français: XVIIe siècle, 1610–1690* (Paris, 1925), and *L'Art français: XVIIIe siècle, 1690–1789* (Paris, 1926), are good, general treatments of the various arts, with special attention to Versailles. By far the most extensive and authoritative treatment of French architecture during the period is L. Hautecoeur, *Histoire de L'architecture classique en France,* vol. 2, *Le Règne de Louis XIV* (Paris, 1948). For the great significance of Versailles as a center of artistic endeavor and concentration of talent, consult the works of P. de Nolhac, *Les Jardins de Versailles* (Paris, 1913), *Versailles et la cour de France: Versailles résidence de Louis XIV* (Paris, 1925), and *Versailles et la cour de France: L'Art de Versailles* (Paris, 1930). The relations between the royal government and the Academy of Sciences are outlined in M. Ornstein, *The Role of Scientific Societies in the Seventeenth Century* (Chicago, 1928), and Harcourt Brown,

Scientific Organizations in Seventeenth Century France (Baltimore, 1934).

Students who wish to investigate further the new interpretations of Louis XIV's reign that are tentatively suggested in Pierre Goubert's selection, given above, will find a list of relevant works (chiefly studies of local history) in the English and French versions of his *Louis XIV and Twenty Million Frenchmen.*